PREFACE

—·⟨◦⟩◦⟨◦⟩·—

> "By medicine life may be prolonged,
> yet death will seize the doctor too."

WILLIAM SHAKESPEARE

WHEN WE SPOKE TO THE DEAD

HOW GHOSTS GAVE AMERICAN WOMEN THEIR VOICE

—◦◦⟨○⟩◦◦—

ILISE S. CARTER

sourcebooks

For my Uncle Dan,
Daniel Hymtan, PhD.
He was a mensch.

D on't embarrass me in front of David Bowie, Dad."

It's not like we spent much time hanging out with rock legends, but one thing and another, I had said similar things to him over the years in the presence of famous people: At the table reading of a friend's musical, "Don't embarrass me in front of John Waters,"* and another time after celebrity editor Tina Brown left him in the dust to network with fancy people at a cocktail party for one of his patients, I snarked, "Dad, if she wanted to hear long, boring stories, she would've stayed at *The New Yorker*!"† What made this conversation unique was that it was entirely in my head. At the moment, both David Bowie and Maurice C. Carter, ME, MD, were dead. The song "Heroes" was playing in the car on the way to my father's funeral, and in my mind, the afterlife—which I hadn't really had much use for up to that point—was a place where my dad (who had never had any use for rock 'n' roll) might run into Ziggy Stardust's creator and talk about me. I had just been plunged into the deep end of a bottomless pool of grief, and I had no real idea of how to deal it.

In that moment, I was handling it by talking to the dead.

COVID-19 had claimed my beloved father a couple days

---

* Not even sure how one would go about that. He's literally seen some shit, but I'm a fan girl. I want him to think I'm cool.

† Just kidding! I actually love *The New Yorker*; please hire me to write long, looping profiles of weird things.

before, and I was bereft. I loved my dad. At eighty-nine years old, he was still working, fixing things around the house, holding hands with my mom, and pretty much as sharp as ever. Until the last month, when he was tired and coughing up blood, and the intellectual verve and humor that had always defined him started slowly disappearing. Eventually, we had to drive him to the hospital and pray he'd come back home at a time when so many did not.

He didn't.

I heard the doctor call my mother on her cell phone and deliver the grim news. The one thought in my head was "no." I wasn't being offered options; this was simply the new state of things and one of many similar calls that poor beleaguered doctor probably had to make on that day alone. That's a weird thing about loss—it makes you feel alone, even if you're one of many.

I feel like I already kind of knew this as an adult who'd experienced the deaths of friends and loved ones, but I had to relearn it in a whole new way with the death of my dad. We are what my mother calls "cardiac Jews." We practice imperfectly: the closest we ever kept to kosher was a separate pan my Grandma Rose kept for bacon, we don't know the Hebrew,* but our connection comes from the heart, and we declare ourselves to be part of the tribe. So the loss of my father, who was both an atheist and a Jew, to COVID in the spring of 2020 left us—me, really—casting about for the proper way to mourn. I decided ritualization might make

---

* Well, my brother Adam does. He actually did the Hebrew school homework, so just recognizing that here. He's also a doctor like our father, grandfather, and great-grandfather. In other words, a real mensch.

me feel better, so I opted to wear *kriah*,* the traditional torn black ribbon, for the first thirty days. This act, which represents the grief and anger of loss, presented its own set of contemporary problems. I was on lockdown with the rest of America, so I had to set some rules:

1. No pinning it to the pajamas (you have to get dressed each day).
2. No putting it on the punk band T-shirts my dad hated, which put my favorite black concert tees out of circulation.
3. Leave it on the nightstand when you sleep.

I kept this up "religiously" for about three weeks until I mislaid the ribbon somewhere. (I've still never found it.) I took that as a sign that either dybbuks† had moved it or my dad was signaling from beyond that enough was enough. I'm not a superstitious person, but the former seems more likely given what a skeptic my dad was in life. I can't imagine that he would take up being a ghost from the next plane (which probably didn't exist anyway) or that would be the way he expressed himself. I had a lot of time to think about this sort of thing in those days and all the unfinished conversations there were to be had.

In a weird way, my dad's life was bracketed by pandemics. His parents both lost partners in the 1918 influenza pandemic, which would eventually lead them to finding each other and the 1931

---

* It literally means "tearing the cloth," and you're supposed to do it to your mourning clothes, but modern interpretation says the symbolically torn ribbon will suffice.

† In Jewish mythology, dybbuks are lost souls that can temporarily occupy a body, but in our house, they're little gremlins that move your keys, phone, and the like.

birth of their son Maurice Carl Carter, who was called Marty by everyone who know him more than a minute. His father, Abraham Kotliarsky,* was a Jewish-Ukrainian émigré with Bolshevik tendencies. Abraham had been ill most of his life with diabetes (this was before injectable insulin) and died when my dad was fourteen. They weren't particularly close; my dad always referred to his father as "the old man." This left his mother, Florence (known to the family as Florrie), the only one of my grandparents born in America, alone to raise a boy who wanted to see the world and was already exploring the northeast by bicycle. She supported them (before and after Abe) as a math teacher in the New York City public school system. My dad always thought Florrie (he called her that instead of Mom or Mother) was too "Victorian," and he developed a slight rebellious streak that inverted her sense of propriety.

He would grow up to be a man who was intellectual but outgoing, ambitious but kind, funny but prone to anger, and any number of other contradictions that make up a person. He was a good dude. He had served in the army to pay for his mechanical engineering degree and treated his post in Japan as study abroad. He returned home and got a job designing the springs that intercontinental missiles rested on and soon burned out on the profession. He recalled to me once that he was looking at a maquette in his shop and decided "it was a beautiful piece of machinery, and

---

* Just to note, having more than one name is kind of a family thing. My grandfather was also known as Arnold Kotliarsky for a spell when he lived in France. My dad changed his last name in college from Kotliarsky to Carter. It came from a cousin by marriage who had gone from the Ellis Island Cohen to the *Mayflower* Carter. I have a stage name, The Lady Aye.

they were just going to blow it up." He recalculated his life and decided, after rebelling against his natural instinct, that his future lay in medicine like his father and grandfather. He would spend more than fifty years as an orthopedist, a career that suited him well since it involved tools, physics, and talking to people. His office was forever running late because he would get to talking to patients and run into the next appointment and so on. As he aged, some people said he reminded them of Albert Einstein, some saw Groucho Marx; both worked. He was a Jewish guy with a mustache who drew from both of them.

He met my mother, the then Thelma Hyman, at City College in New York when she was a sixteen-year-old freshman and he was a senior. In those days, you didn't take a freshman out on a Saturday, but she insisted and he gave in, then choosing to spend the rest of his life's Saturday nights with her. They discovered they shared a love of musicals, art, books, and science. They married about two years later and would spend almost seven decades as a love story, a comedy team, and some weird, domestic form of the Supreme Court that we as children really had to prove our cases to. They bickered regularly about little things, but he was ultimately the original wife guy. They had been married about fifteen years before children, during which time they traveled extensively, saw a lot of theater, and earned their doctorates. When we arrived on the scene, we were kind of newcomers to their organization. Which is not to say we were unwelcome or outsiders—they loved their kids to a fault—but they had long been conjoined at the head and the heart before the pitter-patter of little feet joined in their dance. He and I were especially close because we shared a sense of humor and a love of spicy food. As a striver, his suit-and-tie sensibility didn't get my punk-rock choices, but he abided (eventually; often there'd be a door-slamming fight first). Whether nature and/or nurture, we were probably more alike than different. Whatever his dimensions in this life, and they are very hard to capture in a few paragraphs, he was my daddy, and I loved him.

My general sense of zeitgeist was that the world felt like a rickety roller coaster housed in a sewer. Mainly I napped, cried, snacked, and doomscrolled. By my calculations, our reaction to COVID, save for some initial applauding for nurses and other hard workers, brought out the absolute worst in us, a feeling that was cemented by George Floyd being murdered by a cop in broad daylight. That injustice and the fact that people would defend it just added to my sense that we were submerged in some sort of moral death spiral. Around this time, I spied an article titled "The Channeling of George Floyd and Spiritualism's Racist History,"[1] which took up residency in the back of my head where I keep my other grand unifying theories of American history and where it would have to remain for a while. During this period, I also sold my proposal for a book on lipstick as a lens for talking about women's experience in America to a publisher and subsequently would have to figure out how to write a whole book—specifically, how to write a whole book without the counsel of my biggest cheerleader and critic, my dad. Somehow, I managed. It also helped that there was nowhere to go and nothing to do, since my world was on hold thanks to the pandemic. I stayed with my mother, who was forced to adjust to life alone after sixty-seven years of marriage, and we left the news on in the background with its constant background hum of death tolls and political scandal as we went about our days.

With that as a kind of background radiation, I grieved, and I wrote my first book. I had Zoom calls with friends. I binge-watched *The Sopranos*. Eventually, I was double-vaccinated, released my first book, began to emerge a bit, and went on with the business of being alive in the world. Even still, grief hangs on. People on TV talk about "closure," but that's nonsense. Grief is entropic: you can only change its form; you can never really conquer it. You live with it. And I can't be the only one living with it. In that couple of years, the body count on the news went flying through hundreds of thousands of American souls, in addition to the very public deaths of Breonna Taylor, Ahmaud Arbery, and other victims of "law and order." Where was the crepe bunting? Where were drawn curtains? Where was the rending of clothes and the keening? They were nowhere to be seen in the public discourse of vaccine skepticism and cottage-core fashions. How do Americans grieve now? Do we just ignore it? These questions stayed with me.

Even with all its weird elements, it seemed to me like a good time for a revival of Spiritualism, since the initial movement grew out of the soil of huge losses of life and the need for radical social change. So I started looking around for it. I didn't see it, or rather, I didn't see it *literally* any more than I saw the cage bustle making a comeback in the era of athleisure. Not on the surface anyway. But after some deeper reflection, I concluded that it had left its mark on America. We are less involved in literal "table turning," but we still wind ourselves in the threads of wellness and girl bosses and the acknowledgment that Black Lives Matter.

In our past, massive, public quantities of grief have acted as an invasive species that changes the landscape and strangles the old growth. This was the form that Spiritualism took. It was a movement that spurred tens of thousands of Americans to view the loss of a loved one less as the end of a chapter and more as a conversation starter. Spiritualism, which arose in the mid-nineteenth century when more than 20 percent[2] of infants did not live to see their first birthday, would give mourners, particularly women who'd loved and lost, their voice by giving those who had passed away a chance to speak their piece. While it's remembered as something of a novel footnote today, often in the form of Mary Todd Lincoln's sad quest to be reunited with her assassinated husband, Spiritualism was no mere fad. It was tied to a wave of sweeping societal change and a legitimate course of study for both adherents and public intellectuals of all kinds. It stood as a colossus of a society at the crossroads of miracles and science, of progress and prejudice, and of mortality itself and life everlasting. It would be offered up as a slap in the face to the propriety that had long smothered women's voices, a tonic to society's ills, and a belt of patent medicine for the vulnerable looking for a quick fix. It would spend nearly seven decades as a serious, powerful, central part of the public discourse and then fade away like a ghost in the daylight in the years after the First World War.

At its base, Spiritualism was the belief that the human spirit did not end when the physical body died. Rather, it continued on to the Summerland, a plane that was neither heaven nor hell. From there, it could continue to communicate to the living through mediums, who could channel their words to the living. The space where the living and the dead meet is called the Borderlands. Spiritualism was ostensibly Protestant and Christian but not attached to any particular sect. A belief in God was (and is) required, but the other day-to-day details of how best to practice varied from practitioner to practitioner. It arose in earnest just before the middle of the nineteenth century and soon attached itself to such progressive causes as abolition, women's suffrage, and temperance. It would also be a serious part of the public conversations around science, literature, the arts, and politics. In some part, it would give us the Ouija board, some elements of goth fashion, votes for women, and chiropractors. It didn't exactly disappear; a more accurate description is that it was subsumed into the everyday.

This shift allowed Spiritualism and its trappings to change form and purpose, influencing the way we talk about health, death, faith, and politics. Like countless other histories that center on women, it was buried, partially alive, under the obfuscating dust of history whipped up by more "serious" men and their noteworthy accomplishments in science, business, and government. Given the concerns of our own era—high mortality, challenges to women's agency, the fight for and against religion as the center of public life—now is probably a good time for an excavation of Spiritualism and its continuing impact on our modern America.

Returning to my historian's perch after my first book, I decided that Spiritualism was a movement, it was a moment, and it remains a way of looking at America and her priorities and ambitions and thus deserves a book of its very own. I will endeavor to put aside my own skepticism or need for explanation and just observe the patterns of history. For myself, I will try and take no part as to whether we can talk to the dead; my hunt is for something less spiritual and more historical. Furthermore, confirming or dismissing the reality of ghosts and spirits is not in my self-created job description. I also have spent nearly twenty years as a sideshow* performer working with magicians, mentalists, and other people who make fooling you with occult powers their business, so I know how some of the conjuring is done and why people love to be taken in.

If you must know, I have described myself as "a skeptic but not an asshole." So I'm not here to prove or disprove the work of mediums. Raised by Jewish people who considered science to be its own sort of divinity (Dad was a mechanical engineer turned orthopedist, Mom is a PhD in immunology/microbiology), I view the miraculous as largely allegorical. That said, I basically keep my own questions about the paranormal in three baskets:

1. The Big Bad Basket: People who know they're scammers and are actively exploiting people with their so-called powers or waste their own time on the hunt for "closure" or claim to be able to cure cancer with essential oils or homeopathy. These people are bad.

2. The Condolence Fruit Basket: This one is for practitioners and seekers who believe sincerely and don't realize they're using things like cold reading or coincidence, because it brings them

---

* I am The Lady Aye, Sweetheart of the Sideshow. I eat fire, escape from a straitjacket, and swallow swords. I've worked with celebrities, appeared on a couple TV shows, and run for the title of Miss Coney Island. I have poor hand-eye coordination, so pretty much no magic from me, but my skills are cousins to those skills.

or their clients a sense of peace or control. We all end up in this basket now and again. We read our horoscopes before a job interview, we went through a tarot card phase in high school, we look for shooting stars. It's the junk food of divination; a little once in a while can't hurt, and why suck the small joys out of people's lives?

3. The Little Mystery Basket: This is my teacup-size one. I'm Gen X, so I'm salty but also raised on *In Search of…*, *That's Incredible!*, and *Unsolved Mysteries*. There's just unexplainable stuff out there. I can't know everything, so why not leave a little room for something awesome (in the original "inspires awe" sense).

Not to mention that being a devout cynic seems like a drag and the intellectual equivalent of smacking candy out of a baby's hands. Should we gorge ourselves on the bonbons of blind faith? Of course not, but my assignment in this life is also not to tell everyone every little thing they enjoy is wrong. Unless you're using it to deny someone else their rights, I'm with Thomas Jefferson on this: "It does me no injury for my neighbor to say there are 20 gods or no God. It neither picks my pocket nor breaks my leg." No, I'm not here to debunk; I am here to objectively assess the impact of a social movement and will try to describe it as accurately as I can. No promises though, because some of this stuff is objectively weird, and I have inserted myself into the narrative as framing device. So for now anyway, I am your medium channeling the past lives of the Spiritualist movement into creative nonfiction.

Along the way, mediums will tell me both that I am a powerful natural intuitive and that I have "a unique perspective." The latter would come from a reading I received recently from the legendary Boston medium Mina "Margery" Crandon, which was made all the more remarkable because I happen to know the real Mrs. Crandon died in 1941. Obviously, it wasn't really Mrs. Crandon; it was mentalist Krystyn Lambert playing her in an interactive cocktail experience in a speakeasy-themed bar in Manhattan that revolves around the real-life rivalry between "Margery" and Houdini. The producer was kind enough to comp me tickets in the VIP section since I'd interviewed her as part of researching this book and maybe tipped her off that I was there that night (and I specifically asked the spirits about my chances at success as an author as part of a "billet reading" demonstration).

I'm flattered and amused,* but these are not signs or omens; this is simply another information-gathering trip for me, albeit one with an eighteen-dollar old fashioned. So when the actor playing author and Spiritualist Sir Arthur Conan Doyle asks me what brings me here this evening, I don't even know where to start. Luckily my mom, who's my plus-one that night, chimes in with "the bus."† I am observing the crowd, the characters, the magic skills, and the costumes. The whole affair makes me slightly nervous since it brings back memories of years of being a strolling sideshow performer at bar mitzvahs, anniversaries, and nightclubs. It's my least favorite format, because people feel

---

* Incidentally, the spirits are not able to pronounce my first name either, and "Margery" refers to me as just "I." My legal first name is pronounced "eye-lease," and my stage name is The Lady Aye, but I've been introduced as the Lady A, so this is an ongoing issue with me.

† Ba-dum-bump!

entitled to touch you, smart-ass drunks always want to know how it's done (very carefully, sir), and trust me, it isn't easy to impress a generation of kids raised post–MTV's *Jackass* and TikTok. Just the thought of doing a show like this is making me sweaty. My feelings aside, the audience is digging it, and some have come dressed up in feathered headbands and bow ties as though they've stumbled into an actual Volstead Act–era gin mill rather than another pricey artisanal cocktail bar in the East Village.

And so the evening goes. The characters romp through the VIP section, performing sleight of hand, singing a song, chewing the scenery a little, chatting with the audience, and disappearing again until it all culminates in one last trance. Krystyn/Margery makes her prognostications on everything from romance to real estate and then fixes the room with a faraway gaze, intoning, "Some years ask questions and some years answer them." This line seems portentous, since the last few years have been a roller coaster of questions and answers.

What does 2025 ask that 1848 can answer? To learn that, we must pull back the curtain between the two worlds and see what those who have left this world have to say.

IT'S MOURNING IN AMERICA

THE ROOTS AND BRANCHES OF SPIRITUALISM

Mourning miniature in the Brooklyn Museum Collection.

UNSIGNED, BEQUEST OF SAMUEL E. HASLETT, MOURNING MINIATURE FOR "JB", BETWEEN 1795 AND 1799, BROOKLYN MUSEUM/PUBLIC DOMAIN.

"I want to believe so badly; in a truth beyond our own hidden and obscured from all but the most sensitive eyes. In the endless procession of souls, in what cannot and will not be destroyed."

FOX MULDER, *THE X-FILES*

rief is a chronic illness. It flares, it subsides, it mutates and metastasizes; it remains in the blood long after the initial infection, waiting for its moment to return regardless of its host's wishes and plans and treatments. There is no known cure. Which is not to say humankind hasn't tried any number of fixes: keening, drinking, singing, therapy, wakes, pyres, and parties. It's just that grief is stronger because it will always have the last word, because it has no words for us at all. Its power is in its silent finality.

Grief is that feeling of loss we get when someone we have feelings for dies. It lasts forever in some entropic form that changes shape and intensity as we go forward. Mourning, the public actions of going through those feelings, is more of a short-term process these days. It has a few initial rituals—we have a funeral/memorial/Zoom meeting; people send cards, flowers, food to prop us up; and shortly thereafter, we are expected to enter what we wrongly assume to be a linear path of healing. It's all very difficult and unsatisfying, and we have a lot of stupid myths about it like "closure" and that it works across a straight timeline. For most people, it's probably more like a roller coaster with heights and drops and a few loops that you just didn't see coming.

For a while, I was locked into this process of mourning my dead with very little means of escape. Stuck indoors at my mom's house, I was trying to keep the pandemic from prying into my life any further, churning out research and prose, earning money by writing for beauty companies that were flogging antibacterial skin care designed to fight the terrifying ravages of time and germs. I had a lot of time to be sad and would often excuse myself to cry alone—as if my mom didn't know. Eventually fear and sadness would loosen their grip and I would rebuild something of a life: releasing a book, going out to public places with friends, performing a little bit, trying to find something else to write about after having my say on lipstick, and even going on vacation once in a while. So believe me when I say mourning and the study of American history are a wild ride.

In fact, it's a Disneyland ride. Literally a ride. If you're willing to wait in line for an hour or so in the California sunshine, you will be ushered into a fine Victorian home by a "maid" or "butler" in a polyester uniform and plastic name tag. Located in an imaginary antebellum land between a miniature Mississippi River, a generic jungle (could be Africa, could be the Amazon or Asia, anywhere singing robot birds and Indiana Jones might intersect), and a pirate-themed gift shop, the Haunted Mansion is a Disney staple. It's supposed to be scary, but it's also air-conditioned with well-marked emergency exits and has been open for family fun since 1969. On a recent Los Angeles trip with a group of friends, we decided it was also a natural stop for a group of aging East Coast goths hopped up on caffeine, nostalgia, and happy vacation vibes.

Surrounded by bubbly, bright families with children, I muse as to whether our group looks like a tattooed black hole. I also assure my friend Meirav—who loves horror but hates jump scares— that she'll be fine or at least no worse off than the toddlers also waiting their turn. After a period of winding our way past the novelty gravestones,* the horseless hearse carriage, and the lush gardens, we finally make it inside. I am, as mentioned before, a dark-hearted punk raised on the lamentations of Siouxsie Sioux and Anne Rice, but I'm also a dork for American history, and it seems like this experience is going to be the Venn diagram of my interests, so I'm practically giddy by the time we get in line for our "Doom Buggies." Unfortunately, there's a bottleneck at this point and we're faced with another wait. As the "cast members"† clear up whatever it was that caused the traffic jam, I have a chance to take in the decor and start to wonder if they periodically clean around the cobwebs or polish the chandeliers and replace the carefully placed signs of decay.

Disney parks are known for their fastidious dedication to cleanliness. So much so that Walt himself rejected an early design for the Haunted Mansion as a typical, dilapidated haunt. Nothing in his worlds could seem broken or abandoned, so instead they turned to the plantations of Louisiana and the Winchester Mystery House for inspiration. Located to the north in San Jose, California, the Mystery House was the private residence of Sarah Lockwood Pardee Winchester. Poor Sarah lost her only child to disease in infancy

---

* There are thirteen of them, and they're mostly inside jokes about the Imagineers who designed the attraction and puns (e.g., Wee G. Board), except for the gravestone of Mme. Leota, who is the medium character in the ride.

† No matter their job or pay grade, Disney employees are all designated as "cast members," including my friend who works in the executive offices in New York and comped us the tickets. As such, they're all tasked with maintaining the bubble of illusion that is their universe. When my cast member friend is greeted warmly after he whips out his ID for a discount on our lunch is sincerely asked, "Where do you make magic?" we, as non–cast members, giggle and instantly make it scandalous.

and was the widow of William Wirt Winchester, whose family had made its fortune in the sort of firearms that "won the West" or simply massacred a lot of Indigenous people, depending on your view of history. It was under these circumstances—an empty house and a full bank account—that Sarah began expanding the house in 1886…and expand she did. Between 1886 and her death in 1922, her home grew to include twenty-four thousand square feet, comprising ten thousand windows, two thousand doors, forty-seven stairways and fireplaces, and seventeen chimneys, which is a lot for a lone soul and a small staff.

Why did she do it? Therein lies the mystery part of the Winchester Mystery House. Modern scholars have argued that the scant remaining archives of her own writing point to the work of an amateur architect using her house as a lab, but that narrative doesn't exactly sell tickets. Since it opened to the public in 1923, it's been linked with Spiritualism. The story suggests that mediums told Sarah that the souls of the Native people killed by Winchester guns would haunt her if she ever stopped building, which is both much sexier and fits in neatly with our collective impression of the Victorian widow and guilt about the whole westward expansion thing. Additionally, as a major American attraction, Sarah's house is meticulously maintained and open to ticketed visitors looking for her ghosts. The house even has licensing agreements with a retro clothing brand, the Oblong Box Shop, and themed eyeshadow palettes from the Vampyre Cosmetics company, so Mrs. Winchester's spooky girl influencer bona fides endure.

Speaking of gift-shop history, back in the kingdom of the mouse, the blockage has been cleared, and we begin to glide through the darkened rooms of the mansion to the tune of "Grim Grinning Ghosts." The house's "parlor" is instantly familiar to me and not from a childhood trip; this room is relatively new, having opened in 2004, and I haven't set foot in a Disney theme park since I was a child in the eighties. No, this is familiar in the sense that I can read the visual cues that make up the environment: a lady medium in a high-collared dress, a crystal ball, a tilting table, untouched instruments playing themselves. These are the trappings of Spiritualism. I factor in the notion that I'm currently researching the subject and "when you have a hammer, the whole world looks like a nail" and dismiss it. Well, not dismiss it—diminish it. This ride is not for me specifically; this ride is for the tens of thousands of visitors who walk through the gates every day. They are expected to take it in the same easy way they understand and accept country bears that play banjos as a stand-in for Appalachians or a powerless United Nations made up of singing animatronic children.

If you want to get fancy about it, this phenomenon of squeezing big stories or concepts into tiny dioramas is what semiotician Claude Lévi-Strauss referred to as "bricolage" in his screeds about the meaning of symbols. That is, these displays of history, whether the Hall of Presidents or Main Street USA, are constructions made of previously available things that audiences can easily recognize and process. It's the sort of cultural recycling that we love "making magic" from. Lévi-Strauss wasn't exactly referring to Cinderella's castle when he explained that bricolage "builds ideological castles out of the debris of what was once a social discourse,"[1] but he may as well have been. In the last segment of the ride, guests are winkingly warned to be on the lookout for hitchhiking ghosts, and by a trick of mirrors—voilà!—you see you've got one tagging along with you as you glide toward the exits. This is both an adorable immersive experience and a great metaphor for Spiritualism. The relics and principles of Spiritualism have tagged along with us even if we don't take them that seriously these days.

The old chestnut is "history doesn't repeat itself, but it often rhymes," so maybe I'm just searching for the lyric. That said, the current state of America seems similar: women seeking agency, mass death, and volatile political division all seem to point toward a similar setup. On the other hand, everything has changed, not the least of which are several constitutional amendments, people living longer, and just our general attachment to established religion, which is shrinking year over year. On the latter, according to a recent Gallup poll, "nearly half of Americans (47%) describe themselves as religious, another 33% say they are spiritual but not religious, and 2% volunteer they are 'both.' Although the vast majority of U.S. adults have one of these orientations toward the nonphysical world, the 18% who say they are neither religious nor spiritual is twice the proportion Gallup measured when it first asked this question in 1999."[2] However, as The *New York Times* points out, while fewer of us are in the pews in recent years, more of us believe in some sort of soul, saying that "In 1978, about 70 percent of those surveyed believed in the afterlife, and about 74 percent reported the same in 2018."[3] So how can this be? Part of it, the *Times* posits—and I tend to agree—is due to the fact that we live in a world that we genuinely fear. Which brings us back to our need for comfort.

As quantified by the Chapman University Survey of American

Fears Wave 7 (2020/2021), the list of things Americans are scared of is lengthy and far-ranging. Suffice it to say that number 2 on the list is "People I Love Dying" (58.5 percent of us), which is up from number 5 in 2019.[4] And what do we fear more than losing people to death? "Corrupt Government Officials" by a lot: 79.6 percent.[5] So probably not far off the everyday worries of our mid-eighteenth-century counterparts but with the added threats of clowns (5.6 percent),* zombies (9.3 percent), murder hornets (20.1 percent), and high medical bills (42.8 percent).[6] Wherever it lands on our Billboard Top 100 of phobias, our fear of death follows a pattern that's near a law of physics in its inability to ever be destroyed. It merely changes form. It is built into the system of being human, even if the twenty-four-hour news cycle makes it feel like we're in a particularly entropic phase and we need "new" ways to deal with it.

That's our present reality, but to understand Spiritualism's rise and impact, you also have to understand its place in the past. Specifically, a little bit about America's colonial origins, its laws as a fledgling nation, and its policies (or lack thereof) for women. If you've ever been in a Thanksgiving pageant, you know they're built on construction paper hats and the notion that America was founded by people seeking religious freedom, which is partially true. The bigger picture is that this freedom was sort of "for me but not for thee," since these were little theocracies formed under the protection of the British or Dutch crowns. You could still catch a

---

* As a longtime professional sideshow performer, let me say this: clowns, sure, but also sleep with one eye open around some magicians.

heresy charge for expressing yourself a little too freely. Moreover, can you name an outspoken woman of this era without the aid of Google? I suppose you could say the plaintiffs in the Salem Witch Trials, but really, how did that work out for them? Not a lot of opportunity for self-expression here.

Skipping ahead to the founding of these United States as a sovereign nation, women did not fare much better in the new republic. For all their fancy-pants Enlightenment notions of *Liberté, Egalité, Fraternité*, the Founding Fathers did not co-parent with the mothers of their fledgling nation. The ruckus around Spiritualism would arise both from what the Founding Fathers chose to say and what they decided to ignore. Our constitution is both a masterpiece of our highest aspirations as humans and just crap we don't want to talk about. Three points specifically would allow Spiritualism to flourish: the Establishment Clause of the First Amendment, which ensured there would be no more heresy charges (good); the Three-Fifths Compromise, which ensured enslavement would continue even if we didn't shout the actual word *slavery* out loud; and finally, women who made up about 50 percent of the population and were mentioned exactly zero times in its description of the rights and privileges of the law. As Spiritualism would try to demonstrate, it's often what goes unsaid that haunts us.

We were left out by design, which brings us to the rallying cry that still rings throughout every corner of society from Comic-Con to the White House—where are the women? Sure, some women would make their way by luck and pluck (and some by family connection or wealth), but the vast majority of women had few options outside of wife and mother. Through the mid-nineteenth century, we were still pretty much at home since every door was closed to us. Spiritualism would help change that, not on its own and not overnight, but it would do a huge amount to put women center stage and help them find their outside voices.

By the time we start to move into the nineteenth century, America is growing with an increasing population and expanding into new territories. During this time, while we have no official state religion or deity, we are also on record as having declared ourselves God's favorite nation. Just a couple years before 1848 when the Spiritualist movement kicks off in earnest, the nation's pundit class had deemed our annexation of Texas and our expansion to the shores of the Pacific "Manifest Destiny." This policy was dictated by financial possibility and wrapped in Romans 8:31: "If God is for us, who can be against us?" That is to say, the good Lord himself had deemed it right and necessary for these United States to expand her borders. If He was upset that doing so meant displacing His Indigenous children, who were already living there, or increasing the number of people held in chattel slavery to other areas, that went unsaid in His decree of expansion and prosperity. Additionally, within these widening borders, tension was starting to come to the boiling point over the issues of who exactly got to be free and who had the final say on what made a person worthy of citizenship.

Into this mix, add a boom era of scientific, industrial, and financial innovation. The planet was changing at an unprecedented pace with new technologies like the telegraph and photography both knitting the world together and unraveling the mysteries of the past. We were hardly done with our old gods, but many struggled with how to fit them into the new worlds of robber barons, plantation owners, and media impresarios. As Mary Shelley, the godmother of goth, wrote going into the nineteenth century, the superstitions of the past were banished, and we had to fend for ourselves in this age of science.

> *What has become of enchantresses with their palaces of crystal and dungeons of palpable darkness? What of fairies and their wands? What of witches and their familiars? and, last, what of ghosts, with beckoning hands and fleeting shapes, which quelled the soldier's brave heart, and made the murderer disclose to the astonished noon the veiled work of midnight? These which were realities to our fore-fathers, in our wiser age—Yet is it true that we do not believe in ghosts? There used to be several tradition-ary tales repeated, with their authorities, enough to stagger us when we consigned them to that place where that is which "is as though it had never been." But these are gone out of fashion.*[7]

Of course, her work would also create a new breed of monster that we would summon along with our own advancements, but suffice it to say the simple answers of an unelectrified world were slipping away. While not yet ready to swap science for faith by the midpoint of the nineteenth century, America had already gone through two revivalist "Great Awakenings"* and still had a growing appetite for creating its own novel religions and philosophies.

All of the above is a lot of words to say that the old-time

---

* The beginnings of evangelism, these revivalist movements mark America's break with Calvinist theology and the origins of very public declarations of religious fervor.

America we think of as so simple and quaint was actually a huge roller coaster of social, political, scientific, religious, and cultural factors. If Spiritualism isn't remembered well today, that's okay, and there are reasons for that that will be made clear as its story is laid out. You just have to take it on faith that the ghosts of its past still exist and can be contacted if you have the right tools. What's important now is to understand the past and be mindful of the present. Now that we have a general sense of the world that Spiritualism was born into, let's stop this haunted ride in 1848 and listen to the origin story of a movement that would become everything from women's suffrage to fairycore.

Smells Like Teen Spirits

MEET THE FOX SISTERS

The Fox Sisters, Maggie and Kate, with
their sister, Mrs. Leah Fox Fish (center).

> "Fear and guilt
> are sisters."

SHIRLEY JACKSON

In all fairness, if it's hard to look at it sincerely now, it's important to remember that the origins of Spiritualism itself as an American public phenomenon are also something of a joke. Literally speaking, a practical joke or, perhaps more accurately, an excuse meant to cover for the initial prank. In 1848, the two youngest Fox Sisters, Margaretta (known as Maggie) and Catherine (called Kate), regaled a neighbor with a tale of the mysterious "rapping" sounds that would emerge as they settled down for bed. Determined to hear the sounds for herself, the neighbor popped by one night (March 31, 1848, the eve of April Fool's, to be precise) and sat in the dark with the Fox family as they nestled into their beds. Indeed, the dark room was soon rocked by noises that seemed to have no discernible point of origin. Moreover, the sounds seemed both sentient and deliberate, answering yes or no questions and tapping out some basic numbers.

It may not sound like much now, but in the inky black stillness of a rural Western New York night, this mystery was a revelation. In the nights that followed, there would be more neighbors and more mysterious knocks and more questions for the spirit who dwelled in their home, who was alternately named "Mr. Splitfoot" and thought to be an itinerant peddler who had met with foul play over a financial dispute with a previous tenant. As with any "true crime" yarn, the neighbors became obsessed and began to show up in droves as amateur detectives. Accusations were tossed around, the basement would eventually be dug up to see if there were any remains, and while some bone fragments were found,* it was hardly a slam dunk case for the serious accusation of murder. Still, camps of fans and skeptics were being made. The former had even more questions for their loved ones on the other side, while the latter was already trying to figure out how they pulled it off.

The Fox Sisters' powers, whatever they were or were going to be, were about to go way beyond local curiosity. This peculiar moment was about to become a seed dropped on fertile ground that would grow and flower and spread its glory to the world. Before the Civil War would tear North and South apart or the Golden Spike would bring East and West together, a holy fire had been sparked that would soon consume theology, politics, and science. At this moment, within and without the family's quiet farming community, America itself was also young and ascendant as a power in the world, and the possibilities of science and democracy's promise seemed boundless to some. Everyday people were discovering gold in California, rejoicing in new technological breakthroughs that wrangled unseen forces, such as the telegraph and the camera, and declaring the rights of women at the nearby Seneca Convention. The time and place were fraught with possibilities. So if a veil had been ripped away and the possibility of life after death now lay tantalizingly within reach for the humble, god-fearing citizens of Hydesville, why shouldn't that revelation come courtesy of two otherwise unremarkable teenage girls?

In examining the arc of their careers, it can and has been argued

---

* Accounts vary, but these were most likely animal bones from another resident who had buried their trash in the dirt floor of the cellar at some point in the house's history.

that the girls were naturally gifted, that through practice, they would become attuned to mediumship, or that they were merely trying to stay out of trouble for duping their parents and their neighbors. Whatever the source of their abilities was or wasn't would soon become almost immaterial. While looking for a child-ish laugh, they had inadvertently struck gold and were about to be trampled in the otherworldly rush that followed.

After the small-town notoriety and stress that followed, their parents, John and Margaret, decided it might be best if the girls decamped for a while and stayed with their brother, David, at his house in a nearby town. Upon learning about the family crisis, the girls' older sister, Leah Fox Fish, suggested to their parents that the girls might fare better in the somewhat more cosmopolitan enclave of Rochester, New York. Later the birthplace of Cab Calloway, the Eastman Kodak company, and the world's first mail chute, by the mid-nineteenth century, Rochester was a boom town that was able to call itself both "Flour City," since it boasted America's most productive water-powered mills (thanks to the mighty Genesee River) and, slightly later, "Flower City," due to the prosperous lilac farms in area. In addition to being a business hub, the city was also a hotbed of progressive thought with residents like Frederick Douglass and Susan B. Anthony developing their dangerous and controversial national platforms from the relative safety of their Western New York homes. While an upstate industrial center might seem like a less likely place for radical ideas than the usual revolutionary towns of Boston, New York, or Philadelphia, it should be noted that this part of the state already had a long and storied history of religious innovation. As with lilac varietals, if one wanted to put a new spin on Christianity and/or human rights, the area way north of Manhattan and just south of Canada would prove to be fertile ground.

The area was so full of fire and brimstone (and the ensuing burnout that can follow the euphoria of rebirth) that Presbyterian minister Charles Grandison Finney would label it in 1876 in his posthumously published memoirs with "the western phrase…'a burnt district,'" which would become the "Burned-Over District" with popular use. Finney explained that "there had been, a few years previously, a wild excitement passing through that region, which they called a revival of religion, but which turned out to be spurious. I can give no account of it except what I heard from Christian people and others. It was reported as having been a very extravagant excitement; and resulted in a reaction so extensive and profound, as to leave the impression on many minds that religion was a mere delusion."[1] Like all entrepreneurial endeavors in America, creating a new faith was a hit-and-miss proposition. Not every revival or revelation launched out of the region was enduring as the Latter-Day Saints, who started out in Palmyra, New York, before their westward migration, or the Seventh-Day Adventists, who began as the Millerites in the Glenn Falls area. Sects sprang up quickly, introduced their new ideas, flourished briefly, and faded away just as rapidly due to infighting or lack of followers. Whether it was a function of the makeup of the population, some quirk of geography, or an unknowable alignment of the stars, by the time the Fox Sisters emerged from Hydesville some thirty years later, they (and the belief system that grew up around them) would be yet another theological sensation to come rocketing out of the Burned-Over District.

Prior to their arrival in Rochester, elder sister Leah Fox Fish had her own set of problems. Abandoned by her ne'er-do-well husband, she was a young single mother struggling to keep herself and her son afloat by offering piano lessons; the additional burden of caring for two teenage sisters was probably the last thing she needed. Unless, of course, her sisters could find a way to contribute to the household in some way. In dire financial straits, Leah may have considered the possibilities of the girls' abilities and discovered an opportunity inside her family obligation. While it's impossible to say with any accuracy what her level of belief was at the time, Leah was about to begin to make things happen for herself and her sisters.

She started off small by selectively introducing them to some friends of hers, Amy and Isaac Post, who might be open to Kate and Maggie's newfound powers. The Posts were a local power couple but modestly so, since as members of one of the more radical and progressive branches of the Quaker movements, they were required to keep outward appearances plain. Passionate abolitionists, Mr. and Mrs. Post were organizers, activists, and rabble-rousers who were involved in everything from hosting lectures from prominent speakers, such as Sojourner Truth, to hiding enslaved people making their way through the Underground Railroad to freedom. They were at first skeptical but soon came to believe that the sisters had managed to tap into something. What else could explain the self-playing piano and rappings that seemed to answer very intimate inquiries about their lost loved ones?

The Posts were soon convinced they were witnessing something truly spectacular and began to bring their friends along to witness these minor miracles for themselves. The resulting presentation was what would come to be known to Spiritualists as "circles." A central tenet and practice of Spiritualism, circles can range in experience from psychic development to prayer service; they can be a family practice or performed as a congregation. They can also resemble the séance format that people are familiar with from pop culture (sans opening portals to hell, Patrick Swayze, and the other tropes of cinema, of course), where participants sit around a table and attempt to contact the spirit world. The Fox Sisters were moving beyond their usual bedtime antics and into a more serious, more audience-friendly format that would ratchet up emotion and intimacy—particularly for the Victorian era, when the rules of social propriety were stringent and abundant. Sitting in a dimly lit room, hands clasped around the table, may have held the charge of possibilities that participants had not entertained in even the private confines of their own thoughts or had not been able to articulate without even the words to express them.

The younger Fox Sisters, Kate and Maggie, would spend the next few months in those rooms honing those skills under the watchful eyes of the eldest, Leah. Every day, they'd see visitors around their table and answer the questions posed to the spirit realm…for the reasonable fee of one dollar,* of course. This both provided for the Fox Sisters' general upkeep and allowed them to grow their following. The Posts and their connections were helpful, but ultimately the sisters would need to figure out how to stand on their own. Committing to full-time mediumship was a gamble that needed

---

* About forty dollars in today's money.

to pay off. For Leah, it meant a steady income as a number of her piano students had slipped away, likely due to their parents' religious objections or a general aversion to the sort of attention her family was now getting. For Maggie and Kate, returning to Hydesville was probably an unappetizing option thanks to the piercing judgment of the locals, who were still very much divided on whether their newfound skills were heaven sent or tools of the devil. For now, the three were in limbo, which functionally meant they had to find a mutually agreed upon course that would move them up and out.

Luckily for them, outside forces were spreading their fame and creating a demand for the new gospel they were establishing. Chief among their new fans was New York City newspaper editor and publisher Horace Greeley, who had both a taste for progressive causes and a sizable national megaphone for making his views known in the form of his widely syndicated columns from his daily *New York Tribune*. In the summer of 1850, after meeting with the sisters, he editorialized not only that he believed but also that Maggie and Kate were onto something entirely new and possibly world changing. Greeley wrote: "The ladies say that they are informed that this is just the beginning of a new era of economy, in which spirits clothed in flesh are to be more closely and palpably with those that have put on immortality—that the manifestations have already appeared in other families, and are destined to be diffused and rendered clearer, until all who will may communicate freely with their friends who have 'shuffled off this mortal coil.'" Greeley was also quick to dismiss any accusations of opportunism against the young women in the most patronizingly

Victorian way possible, by portraying them as both honest and helpless. "We believe it is the intention of the ladies to shun henceforth all publicity or notoriety, so far as that is possible. They do not wish make gain of the 'rappings...they hoped to be permitted hereafter to live in seclusion which befits their sex, their station, and their wishes."[2]

Whatever the sisters' plans to live quietly might have been before the media hubbub, soon the spirits themselves would provide a map to open up their circles even further, rapping out the missive to "Hire Corinthian Hall" during one of their regular meetings with the Posts. Darkened cottages and parlors were working well for them so far, but it seemed to all involved (or most; Maggie often expressed her dissatisfaction with being made to perform) that now was the time to level up the girls' visibility and to bring Spiritualism to new audiences. Thus, it was decided that the girls would make their public debut at Corinthian Hall on November 14, 1849, at 7:00 p.m. The spirits and their emissaries proved to be right about that booking, and the evenings that followed would prove fortuitous. But not all at once, since the sisters' theatrical debut was hardly a runaway hit, and their efforts received some mixed reviews and attracted some very tough critics. Over the course of that first shaky evening, raps were manifested and questions were answered, but not everyone in the audience was blown away. Instead, the presence of the spirits was met with both awe and applause and jeers and crude remarks. For everyone in the hall who was genuinely curious and ready to be wowed, there was a skeptical contingent that ranged from rowdy to downright bloodthirsty.

To slake that thirst, the next day, a panel of five well-respected men was assembled to interrogate the sisters in the hopes they could discern the source of their trickery. The Fox Sisters were then brought to a social hall where they were interrogated, inspected, and asked to perform ad hoc demonstrations such as standing with their feet on pillows and ankles tied together with handkerchiefs. Even so, the knocks and raps still arrived when prompted. Having failed to debunk them, the committee had to face the next night's audience and explain that they had yet to find an explanation for the mysterious sounds. Not yet ready to concede defeat, the committee decided to take another, more invasive approach: bring in the wives. In a nod to female modesty, the sisters were made to strip, and their clothing was then inspected for any devices or noisemakers—no such luck. Even among women, this violation must have been searing for the sisters, who were raised in an era when women were expected to be meek and modest in the face of whatever life dealt them. They returned to the stage that night somewhat vindicated but also humiliated and with a new sense of what even wider fame might bring.

That night's demonstration came with the rather unsatisfactory imprimatur of their examiners, who said they could neither prove nor disprove the Foxes' powers. That said, the audience reaction was pretty much the same as it had been the night before. Those who loved it were entranced; skeptics still felt the need to loudly vocalize their disapproval and tossed firecrackers into the crowd and onto the stage to drive home their views. Point taken; the girls eventually accepted a police escort out of there. While the engagement probably wasn't great for their nerves, it was good for business. For all the fuss and fear, their Corinthian Hall booking turned out to be a net good for the Fox Sisters as a property, if not as individuals. Private séance bookings immediately shot up, and they received something that would prove to be more precious in the long run: publicity.

In addition to Greeley's unflagging fandom, word of their powers had begun to spread beyond New York state, and the moment was right for it. Just the thought of what the sisters were doing in the Burned-Over District had struck some sort of collective nerve, and people wanted to see it for themselves. Two weeks after the Corinthian Hall demonstrations, the *Cincinnati Enquirer* wrote, "We have a great city here, and its resources mental, moral, and physical should be made known—its light should not be held under a bushel. Rochester has had its 'knockings' and they have made that place immortal. Why should the 'rappings' not confer a like honor on Cincinnati? That nothing on our part should be wanting to so glorious a consummation: we republish from the *Evening Times*, in which they appear as official the following notes of *rapping* manifestation in our own city."[3] The local-color story that follows is by now familiar: questions are asked about passed loved ones, knocking sounds answer via respectable mediums, and the phenomenon goes national. Ohio: You get a medium…and you, and you. Everyone gets a medium!

RADIANT MATTER

THE SCIENCE OF THE AFTERLIFE

Florence Cook manifesting the spirit of Katie King.

> I look for ghosts—but none will force
> Their way to me; 'tis falsely said
> That there was ever intercourse
> Between the living and the dead.

WILLIAM WORDSWORTH, "THE
AFFLICTION OF MARGARET"

In America, movements (civil rights, pop culture, or otherwise) must find just the right moment to get any real momentum behind them. Rock 'n' roll is bolstered by a large generation of teenagers with pocket money enough to buy records, second-wave feminism comes on the heels of the Cold War's neo-Victorian values and its empty promises to women, the civil rights movement of the sixties grows from seeing the merciless beatings of peaceful protestors in Selma, Alabama, beamed into living rooms via the evening news, and so on. Zeitgeist, technology, and politics meet and make things happen. Spiritualism is no different. It comes to be when America is in its adolescence—first understanding its power and growing into it. In these decades, we'd fight a Civil War, experience a gilded age of money and the arts, witness a boom in science and industry, and become a huge player on the world stage. Collectively it was a lot, and like the milestones in growing children, it came with some regression in search of comfort and the familiar.

The era may not be as sweet and simple as we collectively "remember" it. The Haunted Mansion and the rest of the businesses located around the fantasy land of Main Street USA peddle a collective nostalgia for a "simpler" time that never actually existed as such, because Uncle Walt loved the idea of it and it's how we've agreed to see it. A more accurate metaphor of America in the Victorian era, however, might be the whirling teacups of the Mad Tea Party careening around in the churn of invention, expansion, racism, and political intrigue. Equally exciting, disorienting, and frightening;

every day, citizens could open one of the widely available newspapers and find their world getting both bigger and smaller thanks to a rapid evolution of technological advances and the changing borders of a growing nation. Between the time Samuel Morse tapped out the first telegraph message with the ominous message "What hath God wrought?" in 1844 and Alexander Graham Bell's first phone call in 1876, the atmosphere of the era fairly crackled with the potential power of unseen forces.

So much so that upon accidentally discovering X-rays in 1895, Nobel Prize–winning physicist Wilhelm Röntgen believed for a time that he had stumbled upon proof of ectoplasm[1]—the glowing, mysterious stuff that arose out of mediums' mouths, noses, and other parts and was said to be physical proof of spirit manifestation.* Like ectoplasm itself, the idea of tubes and unseen spectrums didn't materialize from thin air. Röntgen's experiments were building off the work of the respected British chemist Sir William Crookes. Crookes's observations had identified the element thallium and created an early version of the vacuum tube, known as the Crookes tube. This device would eventually be developed into the parts that made radio and television possible. An early pioneer in spectroscopy and fluorescence and a member in good standing of the venerable Royal Society, Crookes's scientific bona fides were nothing to sniff at; he was also dedicated Spiritualist.

---

* Contemporary samples of ectoplasm produced during a séance were analyzed and revealed to consist of everyday substances like muslin and paper cutouts that had been secreted away in the usual human hiding places (which may explain why it was also said to have a horrendous smell), but we'll get to the full lowdown on manifestation in a later chapter.

While the taxonomy of the spirit certainly wasn't the number one priority of most scientists of his day, Crookes would pursue this research with the same passion of any of his past endeavors. Over the course of four years, Crookes created a sort of lab in his home and published the results complete with mechanical drawings of the measuring devices he concocted to quantify the moving of tables, the weight of mediums as they conjured spirits, and such, and—to him anyway—his theorems were borne out and his experiments were a success. Having run his numbers and analyzed his findings, he was convinced that a powerful medium could manifest physical phenomena. Crookes responded to his critics: "These experiments confirm beyond doubt the conclusions at which I arrived in my former paper, namely, the existence of a force associated, in some manner not yet explained, with the human organization, by which force, increased weight is capable of being imparted to solid bodies without physical contact."[2] This should have further solidified his place in physics history, but failing to meet with peer approval or reproducible results, Crookes was roundly dismissed as either, at best, indulging in confirmation bias or, at worst, being a sad old dupe.

The latter was partly due not only to *what* he decided to study but *whom*. Crookes spent a great deal of his prodigious intellect on communing with the medium Florence "Florrie" Cook, whom he described as "young, sensitive, and innocent."[3] She was also attractive and red-hot in London's burgeoning spirit circle scene, a factor that hadn't gone unnoticed by the middle-aged man of science. As a medium, Florrie had gained a following by physically manifesting a spirit named Katie King at her gatherings. No mere sheet-waving apparition, Katie King was something of a celebrity spirit who had been turning up at séances on both sides of the Atlantic since the 1850s. Katie King probably owed some of her myriad séance invites to the fact that she had a pretty sexy background. First off, Katie was a sort of *nom d'esprit*, since it was said that in life, her name wasn't Katie, it was Annie—and not only that, but Katie/Annie was the daughter of a pirate! Aaaaaaar! Her dad was said to be John King (né Henry Owen Morgan*), a formidable plunderer and cutthroat in the era when that was all the rage. Furthermore, Annie supposedly followed her father into the villainy business and had been executed for her own scandalous crimes (the good stuff—adultery, murder, etc.). The good news for the wicked Annie is that after her death, she was sent back to the living as the righteous Katie (the reasons for the rebranding are unclear) and entrusted with the mission of showing the world the truth of Spiritualism and making amends for her wrongdoings. To make Katie's mandate happen for her séance guests, Florrie would have herself placed in a medium's cabinet,† and after a period, the figure of Katie would emerge clad in white to roam the room and answer some questions. All in all, a pretty exciting evening in your parlor in the days without streaming services or delivery pizza.

Crookes was especially fond of these manifestations and wrote excitedly, "Feeling, however, that if I had not a spirit, I had at all events a lady close to me, I asked her permission to clasp her in my arms, so as to be able to verify the interesting observations which a bold experimentalist has recently somewhat verbosely

---

* Very hard to get monogrammed towels in that family, no doubt.

† A medium's cabinet could be anything from a chair surrounded by a curtain to a lockable wooden cabinet depending on the specific demands of the psychic and the observer.

recorded. Permission was graciously given, and I accordingly did—well, as any gentleman would do under the circumstances."[4] Which was exactly the sort of thing that caused other professors and researchers to snicker behind his back. In addition to shoddy methodology and dubious motives, after years of work, Crookes's reputation would be crushed by one of the great scourges of the era—succumbing to feminine wiles. He would eventually drop his Spiritualist studies entirely and return to more conventional pursuits with whatever was left of his reputation. Even so, both his contributions to science and his advocacy of the supernatural were equally at home in an era that was simultaneously rushing headlong toward modernity and looking for divine intervention.

—◆—

Stepping back to the early development of the Spiritualist movement, things were moving very quickly, not just for the Fox Sisters but also for their cause. No longer was it simply a singular phenomenon of the "rappings" or a cult of personality based around one family; instead, displays of mediumship were coalescing into a new widely growing movement based around social progress and public faith. Around this time, the sisters found their way to New York City and a room at the Barnum Hotel,* where

---

* Not to be confused with P. T. Barnum's American Museum, which was nearby and served by turns as a dime museum, freakshow, entertainment venue, and tourist trap. Their lodgings were simply in a hotel owned by one A. S. Barnum, who shared a last name with the impresario but no business attachments. In fact, P. T. was not a fan and declared them frauds in his 1865 book *Humbugs of the World*.

their days would come to follow a similar, increasingly isolating pattern of private readings and public demonstrations interrupted by occasional family squabbles and romantic intrigues (all of which were possibly fueled by excessive wine consumption, sibling rivalry, money woes, and other internal power struggles). For now, let's leave them to it and pick up their thread later. While it must be acknowledged that the Fox Sisters' "rappings" and "knockings" certainly opened things up, they are just one part of the entire dark picture. They had tumbled into a moment Alice in Wonderland–style, but they didn't dig the hole, and they wouldn't be the only guests at the mad tea party that followed.

When measuring the madness that would surround them, it's also important to remember that it was highly unusual for women to become famous or important or notorious at this point in American history. There was no public space that was quite right for them, no statehouse, no pulpit, no courtroom, and even the boards of the theater came with some sketchy associations. Heck, there were almost no public "ladies' rooms"* available to women until the post–Civil War era when the department store began to emerge. By putting women front and center, Spiritualism was about to run smack into the walls of social convention and send them tumbling down.

For all its "We the People" hoopla, the fledgling American experiment really hadn't accounted for what 50 percent of the

---

* Not that there was a huge amount of indoor plumbing anywhere, but grand public buildings generally didn't concern themselves with restrooms for women because they weren't lawyers, doctors, college students, etc., so what would they be doing there?

population were going to do with themselves besides marry and have babies. We weren't against women necessarily; we'd just never really fleshed out what their exact role as citizens might be. Abigail Adams had certainly tried to get her husband, John, to "consider the ladies" in framing the Constitution, but that had gone largely ignored like so many "honey do" notes. Now about seventy-five years into the American experiment, women still couldn't vote, hold property in most cases, serve on juries, attend most universities, or enjoy any number of the rights and privileges that the government afforded to men (white men, really) that had allowed some of them to climb the rungs that made up our promised social mobility. And don't think the fairer sex hadn't noticed that discrepancy.

In fact, returning to the Burned-Over District for a moment, in addition to the "knockings," the summer of 1848 also witnessed the nation's first women's rights meeting in Seneca Falls. For two days in July, around three hundred attendees met to discuss and debate about where women stood and where they could go if even the smallest of restrictions were removed. Noted Quaker abolitionist activists such as Lucretia Mott, (her sister) Martha Coffin Wright, Jane Hunt, Mary Ann M'Clintock, and Elizabeth Cady Stanton joined together and debated what actions could be taken to change things. They agreed that a good place to start was a list of demands and a manifesto. Toward that end, their Declaration of Sentiments (penned largely by Stanton) was modeled on the Declaration of Independence and made it clear that women were more than ready to claim their piece of the American dream and had plans on how they were going to do that, declaring:

Now, in view of this entire disfranchisement of one-half the people
of this country, their social and religious degradation,—in view
of the unjust laws above mentioned, and because women do
feel themselves aggrieved, oppressed, and fraudulently deprived
of their most sacred rights, we insist that they have immediate
admission to all the rights and privileges which belong to them
as citizens of these United States.

In entering upon the great work before us, we anticipate no
small amount of misconception, misrepresentation, and ridicule;
but we shall use every instrumentality within our power to effect
our object. We shall employ agents, circulate tracts, petition the
State and national Legislatures, and endeavor to enlist the
pulpit and the press in our behalf. We hope this Convention
will be followed by a series of Conventions, embracing every
part of the country.[5]

Moreover, the women (and men) of the newly christened
Seneca Falls Convention went on to accuse American men of
something the Founding Fathers didn't even think to level against
George III, head of the Church of England (and they accused
him of plenty)—the women of America had been fenced off from
the grace of God Himself. They declared that the American man
"allows her in Church as well as State, but a subordinate position,
claiming Apostolic authority for her exclusion from the ministry,
and with some exceptions, from any public participation in the
affairs of the Church."

These women were demanding a voice in the government, in
their own families, with society at large, and with heaven itself. It

was a radical move and one that, like Kate and Maggie's rappings, was about to find a national audience. If anyone had the determination and skill to do it, it was this group. Coming from an abolitionist/Quaker background, they were well versed in rallying around unpopular causes. While not all abolitionists were Quakers and not all Quakers were abolitionists, a large, notable number of them had been railing against slavery in both the United Kingdom and the colonies since the mid-eighteenth century. Some of those early activists created a playbook that would give future generations a model for protest and public declaration—and an excuse to say it louder for the people in the back row.

Speaking up was the American way. Rooted in the lofty ideals of the Enlightenment, the Founders believed that man and his systems were perfectible in this life. For all their myriad ethical failings around women, slavery, Indigenous peoples, and so on, they designed a government that inspired the idea in the population that there was always room for improvement. It was a great and egalitarian notion that had come to define the American psyche in a pervasive way. Don't like your looks, your lot, or the laws? For a segment of the population, it was practically dogma that with enough luck, pluck, and hard work, you could change that, or so white men were told. For women, self-improvement was certainly possible with enough dedication and stringent self-denial, but societal change? That was a much more complicated task since there was almost nowhere in the public sphere where you were welcome to even make yourself heard.

Corseted, contained, and silenced practically from cradle to grave, women of the era were hobbled with duty and expectation by everything from the law to the dictates of fashion. In the case of the latter, literally so, since it was not just difficult and uncomfortable to chase young children, tend to domestic duties, and do farm or factory work in the standard issue corset, petticoats, and full-length dress, but the uniform was also literally a threat to life itself. By way of example, one of America's first available plastic surgeries was designed by Dr. Thomas Mutter (of Mutter Museum fame) to remove scar tissue and restore mobility in the jaw and neck of women who'd been burned when their dresses caught fire while tending to their cooking or heating, leaving their mouths permanently open and fixed in a silent scream. Pioneered before anesthesia or sterile surgery, it was so common an injury—thanks in part to the fact that the voluminous shape of the dresses acted like a chimney, sending flames at the hem up toward the face— that doctors sought a solution and patients were willing to endure the surgical nightmare in hope of a cure. Simply put, women were expected to endure a lot and say very little. The spread of mediumship would change all that. In the fullness of the Spiritualism movement, it would be said that women made ideal mediums since these conditions had made them both sensitive and passive vehicles for what the dead had to say.

—·◆·—

This was the atmosphere and ethos that suffragists and emerging Spiritualists were alloyed with by the mid-nineteenth century. In terms of a formalized practice, Spiritualism as a sect was emerging both from the moment and from some more established philosophies—similar to but different from other schools of thought that were then growing to meet the moment. Transcendentalism was, for example, all the rage among the new bad-boy set of the literary world. Authors like Ralph Waldo Emerson, Walt Whitman, Henry David Thoreau, and their circles were exploring and adapting everything from Puritanism to ancient Eastern philosophies into tenets that (in some ways) would come to define the modern American way of thinking. Breaking with the Founder's Age of Enlightenment need for empirical evidence and reason, transcendentalists instead embraced the power in creativity and intuition.* While history remembers it as a profoundly important movement in arts and letters, at the time, it was met with a healthy dose of skepticism.

As *The Knickerbocker* magazine put it in 1848, "Transcendentalism, so long as it keeps itself in the cloudy regions of metaphysics and moral sentiments, may escape confutation or exposure; you cannot *prove* its worthlessness, because you cannot bring it to any absolute and settled test. But when it came down to the *terra firma* of actual life, and gives its views of national interests, and traces the (connections) of human events, and enables us to see it against a background of experiences, we then discover the shadowy vanity of the imposture; for these are matters which sense and reason and logic, only can properly deal."[6] In a manner of speaking, the poets of the age had hit on the very twenty-first

---

* These revelations came, in Thoreau's case anyway, as a result of having the invisible labor of women to smooth things along—in particular, his mom and sister, who ensured that he was well fed and had clean underwear in his nearby wilderness.

century notion of "truthiness."* While the transcendentalists' back-to-nature exhortations and go-with-your-gut rationales would swim against the current tide of industrialization and modernization, they would also help power the spread of Spiritualism, since it allowed people to believe without seeing.

Additionally, American Spiritualists were drawing their own inspiration from popular, feel-good movements that started in Europe, namely mesmerism and the Swedenborgian Church. Emanuel Swedenborg's contributions to the evolution of Spiritualism were myriad. As a scholar, he linked science and the supernatural, publishing works that explored physics, physiology, and theology, and sought to tie them all together in a physical search for the soul. In 1745, according to his writings, the spirits began to visit with him—and he with them, innocuously enough at first, with one joining him at dinner and advising him not to overindulge, and then in a more serious way that allowed him to communicate with spirits on other planets or other planes and to predict the future. Based on his own interaction with these spirits, Swedenborg went on to form a theology that held that the body was temporary (and prone to getting chubby) but that the soul endured forever and remained communicative. He never founded a church during his lifetime, due in no small part to the fact that the Swedish state and its official religion deemed his writings heretical. (A charge that was later dropped down to "clearly mistaken.") But

---

* Attributed to Stephen Colbert, *truthiness* is defined as the quality of seeming or being felt to be true, even if not necessarily true. It currently serves as the basis for a great deal of our political discourse, the existence of trad moms, and dude-with-a-mic podcasting.

his works did get the general "let's talk to the dead" idea out there and cloaked in socially acceptable Christianity, rather than as part of some taboo paganism.

Spiritualism's hands-on approach to séances and healing also had roots in Europe, namely in the metaphysical practices of Franz Mesmer. A German physician and amateur astronomer, Mesmer developed healing methods based on Sir Isaac Newton's theory of tides, which inspired Mesmer to postulate that wellness was an unseeable liquid wave of energy within the body that could be manipulated and realigned to restore health and unlock potential—a property he called "animal magnetism," an antecedent to ectoplasm and similar to the Eastern philosophy of chi. Mesmer would spend hours passing his hands over patients with the goal of manipulating this fluid energy to achieve a state that might be scientifically described as "good vibes only." His work met with limited success, but Mesmer and his followers were convinced it was just a matter of refining the technique and tapping into the right channels, which bolstered the notion that science could eventually catch up with belief.

Both animal magnetism and Swedenborgian thought easily made their way to America and began to find adherents in the new nation. In fact, according to one follower, Swedenborg himself had designated a stateside messenger of his works in 1844, which is incredibly impressive considering he had died in 1772. He appeared, alongside the philosopher Galen, to a young man named Andrew Jackson Davis in Poughkeepsie, New York.* Only the previous year, Davis

---

* Located north of New York City, Poughkeepsie is not quite in the Burned-Over District, but you could still wonder what's in the Empire State's famed water.

had become devoted to developing his psychic skills after attending a lecture on animal magnetism. His conversation with the two deceased sages was a revelation and inspired him to begin lecturing, writing, and offering healings. A charismatic speaker, he soon began to spread the gospel of Spiritualism, traveling extensively and giving talks and demonstrations of his powers. Not long after, his talks started to attract a small but dedicated audience that was eager to hear about the health possibilities of "magnetic healing" and what he referred to as "the Summerland," which was, if not heaven, the home of souls in the afterlife. Within a few years, Davis, who was becoming known as the "Poughkeepsie Seer" or the "John the Baptist of Spiritualism," also began to dictate and publish books that came to him in a trance state. By the time the Fox Sisters arrived on the scene in 1848, Davis was already the more established voice on the subject of mediumship.

In 1845, he had published *The Principles of Nature: Her Divine Revelations and a Voice to Mankind*, in which he laid out some of the initial practices and ideas that would eventually coalesce into Spiritualist theology. While he was touring and "writing" at a prolific pace and picking up adherents as he went, he wasn't exactly an overnight sensation. His work was largely dismissed by the scientific community as drivel, and he was parodied by no less a talent than Edgar Allan Poe, who attended a lecture in 1844 and was impressed with his displays, if not convinced of his powers. Poe would later dub a character in his short story "Mellonta Tauta" Martin Van Buren Mavis (get it? get it?) and write, "There surely cannot be 'more things in Heaven and Earth than are dreamt of' (oh, Andrew Jackson Davis!) 'in your philosophy,'" in his 1846 article "Mesmeric Revelation."[7] Davis may have been a pioneer in the field, but the Fox Sisters were a vibe, a trend, and a controversy. Sure, he would get plenty of snippy criticism from intellectuals and tsk-tsking from religious figures, but the sisters would stir enough fury to face actual violence.

According to Maggie's biographer, Nancy Rubin Stuart, the sisters barely escaped with their lives when an angry mob attacked their lodgings during an appearance in Troy, New York. As sister Leah recalled it: "We had not been in the house ten minutes when several shots were fired and stones thrown... We crouched beneath the furniture and lay on the floor to escape the bullets, expecting at every moment some stray shot or stone would strike us."[8] Which had to be pretty traumatic for young girls out of their home for the first time. Why the violence of the reaction to them in particular, especially considering that Davis was doing the devil's work and challenging the established order of the universe? Why no vigilantes on his tail? It may have something to do with gender. To the culture at large, Davis might be dismissed as another snake oil salesman in a world that was full of them. Before TV or radio, lectures were a popular pastime for Americans looking for "infotainment," and speakers roamed the country holding forth on everything from abolition to poetry, so he could easily be filed with them. The sisters, on the other hand, were engaged in something positively unseemly: women talking in public. Whatever the objections were, the sisters were about to find their place with a growing audience who felt that a link with the next world was what their lives—and America's public policy discussion—were missing.

This is not to say that everyone was excited about the coming séance craze. *The National Era* magazine was, to say the least, skeptical that voices from beyond were necessary in the greater public discourse, stating that "a new race seems to be springing up from buried teeth of old dragons of mythology and goblinology. Psychology, biology, and a host of *ologies* besides, have arisen in flourishing array. An age cannot be called entirely practical, which threatens to exalt Mormonism into the sovereignty of a state; which swallows undigested, by the whole, the 'revelations' of Andrew Jackson Davis and his compeers, and the ten thousand contradictions of Clairvoyance & Co., enshrining their mysteries even within college walls, and which lifts its ear timorously and tremulously at a roguish rap in Rochester or Stratford."[9] But as it turns out, for a huge number of Americans, those knockings were something they wanted and needed to hear in the swirl of an unfolding era that would be defined by both the darkness of war and the light of invention.

In the coming decades, Spiritualism would spread far beyond New York state and present some true miracles, if not in the form of contact with the dead, at the very least in its dedication to putting women front and center as its voice in the public sphere. It would weave itself into the conversations around civil rights, science, mortality, and faith and permanently change the way Americans expressed their beliefs in these things in public. It both moved us forward as a people and introduced some backward notions about the power of personal belief. If its impact goes unappreciated or misremembered, now is an ideal time to ask why it all disappeared into the ether.

What I Did on My Summerland Vacation

A WEEKEND IN AMERICA'S LAST SPIRITUALIST COLONY

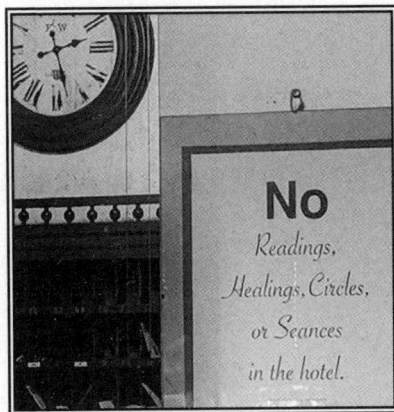

No
Readings,
Healings, Circles,
or Seances
in the hotel.

The Maplewood Hotel, Lily Dale, New York.

AUTHOR'S COLLECTION

> "**A** single death is a tragedy; a
> million deaths is a statistic."

ATTRIBUTED TO JOSEPH STALIN

The town of Lily Dale, New York, is about an hour's drive southwest of Buffalo and so close to Canada that the radio station in my rental car seems to play nothing but Rush and Nickelback. On a bright July day, you can see why Spiritualists refer to the realm where spirits go after they've left this plane as the Summerland. Everything along my route is bright and beautiful with rolling green hills, pleasant temperatures, and minimal traffic; it's just one of those glowing mornings where everything seems okay and you're happy to be off on a little adventure. Specifically, my destination is the Lily Dale Assembly, which is one of the nation's last extant Spiritualist settlements. Not a town exactly, the Assembly within the larger town is more like a lakeside summer camp, albeit one dotted with gingerbread homes occupied by vetted mediums, at least three souvenir shops that sell healing crystals, and a "fairy trail." Its website describes this arrangement as "Western New York's home for mediumship and spiritual healing since 1879."[1]

It may be one of the last dedicated outposts of mediumship now (the Cassadaga camp in Florida also hangs on near Orlando), but at the height of the Spiritualist movement, it was one of many. In 1894, the *St. Louis Post-Dispatch* noted that "Each year adds to the number of Spiritualist camps, and as the sect increases, the camp meeting extends further west, until at present time there are thirty in the United States, many of them in the Middle and Western states, and two in the Southern states."[2] What distinguished these vacation spots from the bungalows of the Catskills or the fishing camps of Florida was that in addition to the usual resort attractions of dances, picnics, and communing with nature, they offered a portal to the other side of the veil with "a roster of the best lecturers in the field"[3] and mediums whose "séance rooms are crowded to their utmost capacity."[4] You can still get those things at Lily Dale even as the other Spiritualist camps across the nation have faded into near oblivion.

I'm there not only for an annual symposium on the links between Spiritualism, science, and the arts presented by my friend, author and photographer Shannon Taggart, but also to do some research for an article that I'm trying to write about Spiritualists dealing with current issues of death and loss and just to see the place for myself. While there, I'm lodging at the Angel Guest House. I booked the Blue Angel room for no other reason than I love the Marlene Dietrich film of the same name. So far, my one plan is to take a nap as soon as I get in, because I've been traveling since before dawn. I do not get la Dietrich's vampy glamour on check-in. Instead, the room is clean, comfortable, and decorated with an eighties-does-Victoriana flare. It also has images of angels everywhere: on the wallpaper, in tchotchke form, as dolls staring down from high places. With all the unblinking surveillance, I can't quite settle down and decide to go for a walk instead.

I end up wandering down one of the woodland paths that lead to the pet cemetery, which is both darling and heartbreaking with its mossy grave markers and sweet tributes to beloved dogs, cats, and horses that have gone to whatever the four-legged equivalent of the Summerland is. At the end of my trip, I'll understand that this is the general appeal of Lily Dale—death is nearby, but there's a warm, homey, even personalized approach to loss. From that burial ground, I manage to find Inspiration Stump, which is the remains of a tree encased in cement and surrounded by a clearing with a good number of wooden benches. It looks like a summer camp meeting spot. During the season, there are daily services here. These services basically consist of mediums introducing themselves and their practice and then "reading" the audience. I don't know what I expected the mediums to look like—Stevie Nicks maybe—but they don't look like that. One sporty one reminds me of Peppermint Patty from *Peanuts*. One guy looks like he's stopped in on the way to a Jimmy Buffett concert. The others just seem like your parents' suburban neighbors: pleasant, casual, and chatty. Their readings begin with the phrase "Can I come to you?" This throws me initially because they don't physically approach the subjects of their readings. They mean it in a metaphysical sense, that is, "Can I read the spirits around you?"

It's hard to put my cynicism aside and just observe. At first, I analyze, since I recognize these as some of the same skills involved in "cold reading," a mentalist skill that allows you to read the subtle nonverbal clues that people give off so you can build guesses about them until it looks like you are discerning personal facts about strangers in an otherworldly way. Then I move on to amusing myself with a game of "what would my departed loved ones say?" I imagine my friend Rachel's (lost to cancer) spirit coming through the medium with "Is there a John here?" and then throwing her head back and laughing when he figures out what he just said. My dad (who never even read his horoscope) would not have time for this nonsense and would just fold his ghostly arms and mumble, "I don't want to talk to this schmuck," and the witchiest of my friends, Kenwyn (seriously, fuck cancer), would kid about not being picked, good-naturedly transmitting, "What am I, chopped liver?"

Turns out your spirits may actually be hilarious. A visitor in 1895 described his experience thus: "Laughter and jest abound with the company, the mystery of the grave has ceased to be, the veil rent from top to bottom—but no God speaks. To the objection I raised with the Sage, I was told 'This man was a buffoon in his life on the earth-plane. What will you have? To amuse was his trade and it still is.' To me this is horrible."[5] I have to chalk up that last line to the author's sense of Victorian propriety, because I'd hate to imagine people who made me laugh so hard in life were suddenly immune to dopey jokes in death. It's fun for me, but it's also cheap and sneering, so I try and refocus and just let things happen.

People all around me are in tears—actual heartfelt tears. One medium tells a young woman he "sees a leather jacket," and she is just beside herself with the recognition of that object. Other people are told their loved ones are proud of them or that they should travel or there's a motherly energy surrounding them, which is nice but nothing that strikes me as uncanny. Almost all readings end with the phrase "Thank you for letting me be of service," which I really like because it seems very kind, and it's often hard to feel useful in offering comfort to the grieving. I'm not more convinced when the service is wrapped up, but I do understand the craving. In just the two years leading up to this postcard summer day, I'd lost my precious father, two beloved "aunties" (natural causes and a rare skin disease), a cousin (guess what, cancer), and a good friend (yup, big C), and I'd love it if someone could just get word to them that I'd published my first book and I miss them terribly. I don't believe but I can empathize, and I'm not here to yuck anyone's yum. Sure as death, grief comes for us all, and she's a real bitch.

This constant communication with the dead is at the heart of Spiritualism, and by doctrine, it generally takes two forms: physical and trance. Physical mediumship is generally what you see in movies and magic shows: Ouija boards, ectoplasm, crystal balls, musical instruments played by unseen hands, etc. It's a physical manifestation of those who've passed on to another realm. These practices have been forbidden in Lily Dale since the 1940s, so you won't generally get that during your visit. They're too easy to fake and can invite trouble in a state where "fortune telling" is still technically illegal. More likely, you will have a more intuitive reading. This was originally referred to as trance mediumship. It is characterized by the spirit (or spirits) speaking through the medium, often after the practitioner has fallen into a trancelike state. This was probably an attractive feature to women of the nineteenth century, since it created a space where they could be the ones speaking. While not all mediums are or were women, at the outset of the movement, the "weaker sex" was thought to be particularly suited to mediumship, because their mommy-lady nature made them passive and attuned to souls crying out to be heard. These speakers were not dubbed psychics, fortune tellers, witches, or oracles but simply mediums. They were not regarded as powerful conjurers or holy shamans; instead they sat modestly as mere conduits to be used by departed souls with something important to say.

But no worries if you're not a natural. According to current practitioners, mediumship is a skill you can cultivate. As a full-time resident of Lily Dale and professional medium, Rev. Celeste Elliot explained it to me: "I will say in the Spiritualist tradition, since the formation of spiritualism in the 1800s, after they got over the idea that mediums were born instead of trained… Because it was one of the early beliefs. As the Victorians were sitting in séance for inspiration and information, the spirit people were coming through and going, 'No, you can study this. We'll help. Everybody has it to some degree, and we'll help get you there.'"[6] This tenet especially continues to appeal to Americans because it democratizes miracle working. In the same way you could win the lottery or become a movie star, you could also be revealed to be a formidable medium (or, in current parlance, *empath*) at any moment.

Lily Dale is not all chatting with the dead. That first evening, Shannon invites me to medium Lauren Thibideau's house for dinner and to meet with other attendees. Lauren is warm, gracious, and fun, and her house is soon buzzing with scholars and attendees enjoying wine and chili. I try not to make too much of the fact that she looks very much like one of the aunties I was missing earlier. Talk is mostly of people we know through Morbid Anatomy, a museum we used to work with, our travels, families, and whatever earthly things are going on with us. I mention to Shannon's husband, Ralph, that I may go to bed early because I couldn't sleep the night before and am tired, and he says something to the effect of "yeah, that happens here." It's a perfectly lovely evening, and when I do tap out and head back to my B and B, I'm struck with what a cheery place it is.

The gingerbread houses are a canvas for the owner's sense of style, and there's no preciousness about keeping them white and spare, Martha Stewart style. Colors abound, and gardens are trimmed with angels, gnomes, and frog figurines. One of my favorite home designs spills out from the front step and onto the sidewalk, where its keeper has created a little fairy land complete with twinkling lights, fake flowers, and a tree with a tiny door for any visiting sprite that might come knocking. I didn't get to see the inside of the human house, but I can't imagine it was any less whimsical.

That said, I also feel somewhat privileged to be there and talking to these people. In truth, Lily Dale's human residents are warm but also cautious. I've been warned by both scholars and mediums that the people of Lily Dale are hesitant to talk to the media, since they've been burned in the past by people eager to either debunk the mediums' powers or make them look like vultures who prey on the weak. Over the course of a couple hours in their company, however, I feel safe in saying that's not who they are and that dismantling their work is not part of my job any more than it's my job to scream "people are statistically unlikely to win" at anyone who buys or sell lottery tickets when I pop into any magazine stand or 7-Eleven. I swear to myself that in all my dealings, I will be respectful, interested, and kind as I try to do my little history thing.

Lily Dale has always been not just a lively and sociable place but also a hub of social justice in keeping with its declared principles, which hold things like community and development in high esteem alongside the more esoteric ideas of the eternal life of the spirit and theism without dogma. Laid out by the movement's chronicler in 1887 (and reprinted in the Sunday Service program I received), Emma Hardinge via the spirit of Welsh social reformer Robert Owen, the principles of Spiritualism are as follows:*

1. The fatherhood of God.
2. The brotherhood of man.
3. The immortality of the soul and its personal characteristics.
4. Proven facts of communion between departed spirits and mortals.
5. Personal responsibility with compensation and retribution for hereafter for all good or evil deeds done here.
6. A path of eternal progress open to every human soul that wills to tread it by the path of eternal good.

Understandably, the hard-and-fast rules are a little hard to grasp through the Victorian phrasing but can be parsed to mean that we believe in God, community, the immortality of the human spirit, communication with the dead, and a form of karma. It doesn't exactly have the formality of a religion, but it has a few more theological requirements than a school of philosophy or a self-help method. For a lot of versions of Protestantism, Spiritualism could be used as a plug-in to enhance an existing practice. Obviously,

---

* Some current congregations have updated some of this language to more modern, less gendered language, for example, *the infinite spirit* rather than *fatherhood*, but this varies from church to church. These tenets have also been split up differently, so sometimes they're listed as the Seven Principles, sometimes Nine Principles.

I'm sketching broadly here for a modern audience, because even at the time, there were endless tracts and debates about how to put these things into practice (or why you shouldn't), but those are the agreed-upon starters for anyone wishing to follow the path of Spiritualism.

Given this progressive-minded structure, it follows that the messages the dead sent to the living contained warnings to right society's wrongs. Before the Civil War, for example, there were a number of Spiritualists involved in the call for abolition and a subset of early suffragists. After the war, Spiritualism would have a place on its platforms for women* radical enough to demand their equality as citizens. Not that belief in the beyond is or was a requirement for admission to Lily Dale. Famously, Susan B. Anthony took to their stage many times to make the case for suffrage, financial independence, family planning, and other forms of social equity for women, and she was largely agnostic on talking to the dead—publicly anyway. One story I heard both in books and shared by mediums in the Dale goes something like this: when Anthony was presented with a message from an aunt who'd passed over, she'd responded with "I didn't listen to her in life, bring me someone more interesting." Allegorical or not, it makes me feel a little better about my own jokes.

Back in my own blue heaven of a room that night, I toss and turn. Nothing supernatural; I just can't settle. Given that, I'm willing to believe that I'm a little fuzzy on things when I begin to

---

* Just to be clear here, they pretty much mean white women. As with most feminist movements, intentional intersectionality would have to wait a long time, if at all.

hear voices while waiting for the next day's lectures. I know that they're not in the meeting hall where I'm sitting and that they're female, but beyond that, I can't really make out the specifics of what they're saying. After a flashing moment of being both amused and, I don't know—flattered, maybe?—it dawns on me that the gentleman sitting next to me has left the phone in his pocket on speaker. I can safely go back to my default "girl reporter" mode.

Between talks, I wander around looking for coffee and generally taking in the sites. Built in 1880, the Maplewood Hotel is a particular favorite of mine for its charming porch, instructive lobby sign ("NO Readings, Healings, Circles, or Seances in the hotel"), and collection of "precipitated paintings" of Napoleon, Lincoln, and a spirit guide named Azur the Helper that all allegedly appeared fully formed on canvas to the mediums known as the Campbell Brothers.* There's also a large tapestry that was trance embroidered by Mollie Fancher, also known as the Brooklyn Enigma. For a movement that was always on the lookout for signs and wonders, Mollie must've seemed like a godsend.

Accounts of her bad luck vary, but the general consensus is that while riding in Brooklyn's Prospect Park one fine day in 1864, her horse was startled and Mollie was thrown to the ground, causing a head injury that left her with headaches and fainting spells. By some reports, she was also injured not long after her fall when one of the hoops under her skirts was caught in a trolley car, which led her to being dragged for a block. Whatever the cause, blind and

---

* They weren't really brothers; in fact, they started life as Allen Campbell and Charles Shourds. Lifelong friends and business partners, they lived together and may have presented themselves as family members to hide a forbidden romantic relationship.

crippled with pain, she took to her bed and would periodically fall into "trances" for the rest of her life. While in the grips of these spells, she would demonstrate incredible abilities such as mind reading, clairvoyance, and needle arts. (I'm a hobbyist myself and can barely embroider and follow a TV show at the same time.) She was also one of several famous "fasting girls" who practiced a form of holy anorexia,* their pure, virginal bodies uncorrupted by anything so worldly or base as food or drink. It was said they could go weeks without so much as a sip of water. Her fame would blend mysticism and the tropes of Victorian womanhood of purity, chastity, and the ability to suffer silently. This also stirs thoughts of Goop because it strikes me as sort of a metaphysical version of the fashionable "cleanse" or "detox," where dieters are encouraged to practically starve themselves to get rid of whatever modern life "toxins" are swirling around in their bodies, making them impure.

In modern times, a lot can happen in less than a generation. Spiritualism and its rapid growth were directly tied in to that particularly busy chapter in American history. In between the Hydesville rappings of the Fox Sisters in 1848 and the psychic crafting of the Brooklyn Enigma of 1864, America had gone through a Civil War, had a new wave of immigrants flowing on to her shores, and added several new states. There's a reason we split a lot of our past into antebellum and everything else. That war in particular would forever be intertwined with and bound to Spiritualism by the sheer

---

* The Vatican referred to this phenomenon as *anorexia mirabilis*, literally "miraculously inspired loss of appetite."

amount of loss it left behind. Writing in 1870, Emma Hardinge estimated that "About the opening of the year 1861 Spiritualism had attained a numerical strength and popularity little anticipated by either its friends or foes. The latest statistics estimated at nearly nine millions [*sic*]."[7] It's hard to say how accurate that statistic was since according to the official 1860 census, there were just over thirty-one million Americans in total, which would've made almost a third of white men, women, and children self-identified Spiritualists.* So take her number with a grain of salt, but suffice it to say that the movement entered the war in great numbers and picked up a number of new converts as a result of the loss of nearly 2 percent of the population. According to writer Drew Gilpin Faust, the casualties were "generally estimated at 620,000, [which] is approximately equal to the total of American fatalities in the Revolutionary War, the War of 1812, the Mexican War, the Spanish American War, World War I, World War II, and the Korean War, combined. The Civil War's rate of death, its incidence in comparison with the size of the American population, was six times that of World War II. A similar rate, about 2 percent, in the United States today would mean six million fatalities."[8] To put it bluntly, it was a boom time for death and the culture that surrounds loss. Spiritualism would see a hole in that particular market and find a different way to fill it.

—·◆·—

---

* Also, don't forgot that during that particular census, enslaved people were still counted as three-fifths of a person, and Indigenous people weren't counted at all until 1890.

By the time I'm ready to check out on Sunday, I'm a little afraid of driving back to the airport. I spent yet another restless night, and I'm a little tired. I can't say I wasn't warned in some way; when I told my friend (and editor of my first book) Jake Bonar that I was going to be in the area for a Lily Dale visit, he described the place as having "such a distinct vibe and energy." Whatever that force is, it's one that keeps me awake more than the usual Manhattan traffic outside my window. Of course, he lives in Buffalo, the "City of No Illusions," so I'm willing to believe him. Sleepy but determined, I forge ahead with my morning of trying to hit up all the things I didn't see or do in the last couple days: buy myself a souvenir coffee mug, see the museum, attend Sunday services, and go to the Healing Temple.

I love the museum. It's housed in an old schoolhouse, and its jumbled curation reminds me of my favorite kind of antiques store. Glass cases are chock-full of bent spoons, spirit paintings, slates, meeting badges, and spirit trumpets. The walls are hung with photographs of mediums long since gone to the Summerland and channeled watercolors, and every last corner has a spirit typewriter or phonograph. It also contains holy relics from the Fox Sisters' cabin. Saved from abandonment, the house where it all began was purchased by a believer and moved to Lily Dale, where it stood as a memorial to the origins of their faith until it was struck by lightning on September 21, 1955; only the sisters' family Bible was saved from the ensuing fire. For pilgrims seeking an actual artifact, you can visit the stones of its storied basement, which are preserved at Hydesville Memorial Park in Newark, New York.

From there, I cruise over to the nearby Healing Temple for the service. It looks like a small, simple chapel on the outside; the inside reminds me of a yoga studio. The walls are a peaceful blue, and people sit quietly in rows of chairs waiting for their turn with the healers. The day I visit, the healers are all women and they're dressed in white smocks like they're at a cosmetics counter. When I'm called up, I don't wish or ask for anything; I just take my seat and wait to see what's going to happen. A nice blond lady of a certain age puts her hands over my shoulders and…nothing. I sit there with her like this, listening to my own breath and trying to tell if my hands are tingling or anything. When she's done, she whispers something in my ear that I can't quite make out, and I say thank you and head back to my spot without any particular reaction. Either way, I can say I tried it.

The second I sit down, the thought floats up through my head—*I miss my dad*—and I begin to weep. Not cry. Weep. I am not dabbing away a stray tear as I sometimes do when something reminds me of him; instead the water is flowing like a bathtub was left on inside my head. The warm, fat tears well up in my eyes and overflow down my cheeks. I am shocked. Shocked. I remember in the moment just being absolutely thunderstruck by it. It came from nowhere and it emptied me out. I don't even make excuses for it. I just let it happen. I weep these tears until I feel like I don't need to cry anymore. When I'm able to, I excuse myself and begin wandering back to my car by way of a ladies' room to make sure my mascara hasn't run down to my chin.

Along the way, I run into Asti Hustvedt, an author who was also attending Shannon's weekend and is an expert in the Victorian fascination with women's "hysteria." I tell her I was just coming from my psychic healing. She asks how it was. I say something like "It was…" and then I can't find an adjective. She nods understandingly; she was one of the attendees who encouraged me to experience it for myself. We don't really talk about it much further, and I have to get on the road to make a lunch appointment in Buffalo and my flight out of the Burned-Over District.

When I return home, I will unpack this particular moment (and the hearing voices thing, because that's just funny) with friends, jokingly with a doctor before a minor surgery a few months later, and my mom. Everyone has their own take on it. I tell my therapist the story and try to rationalize it, but she wisely says, "You know what? It doesn't matter," and I decide she's right. It is what it is, it was what it was, and for a moment, I felt untethered from the small but constant, leaden weight of grief that I had dragged around with me even in my good times. Sometimes you forget you've been carrying something heavy until you accidentally drop it. It gives me a sense of empathy for the widows, mothers, sweethearts, friends, and others who found themselves in circles and séances and churches looking for a sign that would free them from the burden of loss. This doesn't change my position. I am still not a true believer, but it does give me a new insight. If you told me there was something simple and easy that could take the pain of loss away and purify my psyche like a "cleanse," I'd be there every week. People need that like they need to breathe, because they need permission to go on living and laughing. I get it.

In the end, my drive goes well, my lunch with Jake is lovely, and on the way back to drop off the car, I remember that I need to gas it before I turn it in. I ask Google where I can find a station.

A disembodied voice guides me expertly through the side streets around Buffalo Niagara International Airport toward a nearby Mobil station and calmly advises, "Take a left on Dick Street." I slap the wheel and giggle like a Muppet. I'm going to take that as a sign.

GIVE MY REGARDS TO BROAD STREET

SPIRITUALISM IN THE PUBLIC SPACE

Woman in mourning dress with a picture of a soldier.

UNKNOWN, UNIDENTIFIED WOMAN WEARING MOURNING
BROOCH AND DISPLAYING FRAMED IMAGE OF UNIDENTIFIED
SOLDIER, SIXTH-PLATE TINTYPE, HAND-COLORED, 1861,
LIBRARY OF CONGRESS ONLINE CATALOG, LILJENQUIST
FAMILY COLLECTION OF CIVIL WAR PHOTOGRAPHS.

> "Knowledge is a fine thing,
> and Mother Eve thought so;
> but she smarted so severely for
> hers, that most of her daughters
> have been afraid of it since."

ABIGAIL ADAMS, 1791

Throughout American history, where are women in the public spaces? I don't mean that in some fancy academic sense. Literally, where are the women? In America, there are over five thousand roads named for George Washington, which makes sense; as a Founding Father and the first president, he is a big deal. There are significantly fewer named for notable women. You can ask Google Maps, but it will probably not tell you to take the Rosa Parks Expressway to the Ruth Bader Ginsburg Exit and then merge onto the Dolly Parton Turnpike. In New York City, you can sit in traffic on the Hutchinson River Parkway, biding your time, singing along to the radio, and cursing the SUV in front of you. Named for Anne Hutchinson, a preacher deemed "heretical" by the Massachusetts Bay Colony and exiled to an area north of Manhattan (now the Boogie Down Bronx), the road itself meanders by the stream where she and her family were killed by Indigenous people who were at war with the Dutch colonizers. But that's about it. And while we're still asking for our proverbial place at the table, a number of mediums would at least help women emerge from literal obscurity and into the spotlight.

For several enterprising women, the platforms movement would provide both comfort and the tools necessary to forge their own roads into politics, finance, and other spheres of influence. The spirits would lead them to the offices of the most powerful men in America and set a new standard for women as pundits, counselors, and celebrities. Not that the timing for that leap was perfect—in fact, it was pretty awful. In the run-up to the Civil War, the experts on both sides were convinced that the country was going to heck in a handbasket and that the silly women (and their duped male counter-parts) talking to spirits were not helping matters. Additionally, because Spiritualism was associated with the radical notions of aboli-tion and suffrage, it was an easy target for critics in both North and South. An 1859 women's rights convention in Buffalo was described by a syndicated column in the papers as a public nuisance.

> *The Convention of self-styled reformers has been sitting in this city for two days past, comprising the leading abolitionists, spiritualists, free-lovers, infidels, fanatics, and women's rights men and women of the country. They have been assiduously searching for the origin of evil and its cure, while their speeches, for the most part, have been disgusting and blasphemous. The Convention closes its session tomorrow (Sunday), and the public generally will experience a feeling of relief when the city is rid of these reformers.*[1]

This seems harsh, but to be fair, any large gathering of progres-sive women is still viewed in some corners of this country as unladylike, hysterical, and potentially dangerous. Don't forget the panic of the "pussyhat" era when a peaceful mass turnout of women struck fear into the hearts of men.

One of Spiritualism's deepest impacts on America was its insis-tence that women be heard in the halls of power, even if it equivo-cated on who was actually speaking. While the movement's numbers were growing, its connection with both radical causes and female

leadership made it a somewhat threatening and discrediting association for men in power. To add to Lincoln's other troubles during the
Civil War, accusations were lodged against him that not only was
he a warmonger and race traitor, but he was also a "spirit rapper."
According to the anonymous pamphleteer who went by the pen
name "A Citizen of Ohio," we were a "A Nation Demonized," and
Spiritualism was at the dark heart of it. This citizen argued passion-
ately that the rappings and table turnings of the years leading up to
secession made the nation vulnerable to war, and Lincoln, the big
dope, had fallen under Spiritualism's spell.

> *The war, which is upon us, these spirits have induced, by prepar-*
> *ing the minds of men for its inauguration, and now, through a*
> *president and his adviser, whom they control, they are hurrying*
> *the country on to its destruction... Mr. Lincoln is not only a*
> *Spiritualist of the abolitionist school, but has his media around*
> *him, and has been from the beginning of his term directing the*
> *war under the direction of spirit rapping.*[2]

Before there was the "lost cause" myth, there was the "lost
souls" gambit. The cause of the Civil War is, was, and will always
be slavery. That said (and it still sadly seems to need saying), at
the time, by aligning Lincoln with Spiritualists, his enemies could
make him look like a weak, henpecked, and even insane leader.

However, because the Union won and he tragically died a
martyr, you can also make any cause look better by associating
it with Honest Abe. The image of Lincoln, almost more than
his actual words and deeds, remains something of a totem for

every generation that has come since. Permanent but mutable, he's reinterpreted on all sides to stand for the promise of self-made American ambition and "the better angels of our nature," particularly in pop culture, where almost every generation gets the cinematic Lincoln that they deserve. Movies from *Birth of a Nation** to Spielberg's *Lincoln* tend to cast him as something of a down-to-earth deity who appears in troubled times to broker peace and comity—or kill the occasional zombie or vampire as needed.[†] To claim a piece of Lincoln's image is to place oneself at the center of America's history, zeitgeist, and mythology.

Given all that, it's no small wonder Spiritualists claimed him as one of their own, even if he wasn't really one of their number. It's more likely that his wife, Mary Todd Lincoln, was seeking out its comforts, so he was around for it, if not hunting down a personal experience. Plus, given the amount of loss that life had thrown the Lincolns' way, you could understand their desire to reach across the veil. By 1863, Mary had already buried two of her four sons: Edward, who was taken from them by tuberculosis at four years of age, and twelve-year-old Willie, who was lost to typhoid fever just the year before. The latter was so devastating to her that she was unable to attend his funeral or move from her bed for three weeks. Willie was also said to be reaching back. According to medium Fanny Conant's 1873 autobiography, the Lincolns' child came

---

* For as insanely racist and "lost cause" as this silent movie is, Griffith does have a weird soft spot for Lincoln, whom he regarded as a friend of the South. Also, no word if Lincoln's ghost attended Woodrow Wilson's 1915 screening at the White House.

† Granted this incarnation is more of a recent phenomenon, since 2012 saw the release of both *Abraham Lincoln: Vampire Hunter* and *Abraham Lincoln vs. Zombies*.

through during her regular circles in the Boston area. According to her recollections, "Among the spirits who regularly controlled the medium at this place was the little spirit son of the then president of the United States. By him, through the mediumistic organization of Mrs. C., the reelection of his father to the Presidency, and his subsequent tragical death at the hand of an assassin were also correctly predicted."[3] Mary Todd Lincoln's own image has also changed somewhat over the years, from a grief-mad spendthrift to someone suffering with genuine loss and mental illness. Modern medical historians have postulated that she may have suffered from everything from bipolar disorder to pernicious anemia, both compounded by head injuries from a carriage accident. Whatever the root cause, Mary was not handling her grief with the stoicism expected of a First Lady.

The need to relieve her unshakable sorrow was probably what brought mediums like Fanny Conant, Nettie Colburn Maynard, and others into the First Lady's orbit. While it is possible that Abe attended one or more of the circles Mrs. Lincoln held in the Red Parlor, there are no definitive writings from him on the subject, so his level of interest and involvement in those readings depends on whom you ask. Colburn Maynard was instrumental in building part of this mythology. In the medium's telling of it, Abe hung on every word; historians are a bit more circumspect about the influence of the spirits. Whatever the truth of his innermost thoughts, in America, any association with Lincoln could always prove useful in spreading your message. Colburn Maynard's 1891 memoir titled *Was Abraham Lincoln a Spiritualist?* (spoiler alert: the answer is a resounding yes) provides one such account. In particular, an impromptu reading at the White House would turn into an opportunity for the spirits to change the course of history. Describing her trance that night, she said, "For more than an hour I was made to talk to him, and I learned from my friends that it was upon matters that he seemed fully to understand, while they comprehended very little until that portion was reached that related to the forthcoming Emancipation Proclamation." Further the spirits advised Lincoln that he "must stand firm in his convictions and fearlessly perform the work and fulfill the mission for which he had been raised up by overruling providence." To be clear, Colburn Maynard makes the distinction that it was not her (a silly young woman) advising the president; it was the sage spirit of a man of accomplishment. "Those present declared that they lost sight of the timid girl in the majesty of the utterance, the strength and force of the language and what was said the importance of what was conveyed and seemed to realize that some strong masculine spirit force was giving speech to almost divine command."[4]* This scene represents a snapshot of the doors that Spiritualism opened to some women. It created proximity to power but draped it in the layers of demure modesty that the era required. Women's ambition had to be some sort of discretely shared secret.

What Colburn Maynard and Conant were doing was revolutionary—in a quiet way. They were inserting themselves into the narrative of history and power; they were normalizing the presence

---

* She hints that it might have been the spirit of former Secretary of State Daniel Webster but never goes so far as to outright say it.

of women as advisers and experts (albeit in a roundabout fashion) to male decision-makers. They couldn't vote, they couldn't hold property in most cases, but here they were suggesting that they could be believed and considered in matters of the utmost importance to the nation, not merely as conduits for the dead and consolers of the bereaved. To state their importance and declare their access—even if it was indirect—was a way of developing and standardizing a new form of soft power.

Of course, for some people, soft would not do. Victoria Woodhull was one of those people. If the arc of history wasn't bending fast enough, she was going to reach up and yank it down with her own hands. Woodhull not only spoke to the dead, but in a practical sense, she also saw the future of American women in politics, mass media, and business and was determined to speed up the process through the force of her own will—critics, pearl clutchers, and laws be damned. In modern terms, she would be a girlboss or a diva or whatever current phrase we use to both praise and deride women in power. Woodhull is marginally remembered as the first woman to run for president when she couldn't even legally vote for herself, which should make her the sort of feminist icon we teach little girls about, but the totality of her life was (as the kids say) complicated. In truth, she's the absolute Birkin of mixed bags. The good included her sex-positive stance, financial savvy, and a singular devotion to some women's rights. The bad: She was a big fan of eugenics, which means she wasn't just racist and ableist for her era, she was actively peddling a new "scientific" form of racism. She was also prone to trimming her beliefs to the prevailing winds of public sentiment, vengeful maneuvering, and

self-mythologizing. In short, some of the behaviors that made a lot
of male CEOs American heroes.

Whatever her faults (and there were some big ones), her story
also follows the contours of the classic rags-to-riches narrative.
Born in 1838 in Homer, Ohio, she was practically destined to be a
medium and an entrepreneur. She was the seventh of ten children
born to Reuben "Buck" Claflin, a drunk, self-styled lawyer, and
con artist, and Roxanna, an illiterate, possibly mentally ill follower
of mesmerism. Because the family was large, messy, abusive, and
perpetually broke, the Claflins moved often and engaged in various
get-rich-quick schemes to ensure their survival. Young Victoria
was, for a period, pressed into service as a child prodigy preacher,
which would provide her with a profound knowledge of the Bible
and a persuasive public speaking style. Since she was raised in this
environment, it's impossible to say what her level of sincerity was
in her mediumship, but suffice it to say she started early and would
spend much of her life communing with the spirits. As she was
becoming established, she would claim that the main spirit who
spoke through her was the ancient Athenian orator Demosthenes.
Famous for his political and legal arguments, he would be a great
muse for her because of his anti-authority stances and encour-
agement to citizens to speak out against injustice, opining to one
jury, "You stand revealed in your life and conduct, in your public
performances and also in your public abstinences."[5]

By the age of fifteen, Victoria had about three years of formal
education, a career as a magnetic healer, and her first husband, Dr.
Canning Woodhull. Dr. Woodhull was not the knight in shining
armor she'd hope for; instead, he was a neglectful alcoholic and not

much of a physician.* Before they split, they had two children, a boy, Byron (who had developmental disabilities that she blamed on her husband's drinking), and a girl, Zulu (who would later go by Zula). With little support available from her husband and mouths to feed, Victoria established her own business as a Spiritualist healer. In 1864, she was working in St. Louis when she met client Colonel James Harvey Blood;† among her predictions for him was that they were to be married, never mind that there was already a Mrs. Blood. Self-fulfilling or not, that prediction materialized in 1865 when the couple (along with her sister Tennessee Claflin (sometimes written as Tennie C. Claflin) *and* her ex, who didn't really have any bright prospects), took off for New York City. This second, common-law marriage, if not forever, was for the better.

Victoria learned something important from the failure of her first marriage: for women, matrimony was an absolute requirement, but it was also a tremendous gamble. Not just romantically but with little to nothing available to them in terms of rights and opportunities, their unions were financially and socially risky as well. In marrying, women might gain security, but they also legally lost all identity, self-determination, and freedom. The same could not be said of their husbands, who were still pretty much free to philander, drink, gamble, bankrupt, and leave without much backlash.

---

* To be fair to the good "doctor," there really wasn't much formality in what constituted an appropriate medical education until the later nineteenth century with the founding and growth of the American Medical Association. So one could conceivably hang out a shingle without the hassle of things like licensing, apprenticeships, or knowledge of gross anatomy.

† He was an actual colonel; he'd served in the Union Army.

This painful realization would become the kernel of her "free love" advocacy. If the phrase *free love* still conjures ideas of polyamory or seventies-style swinging, you can imagine how shocking it was in the era when middle- and upper-class husbands and wives were encouraged to keep separate bedrooms. This is partly because free love is one of those terms, like *woke*, that shifts meaning depending on what the speaker *thinks* it means. In Woodhull's case, she was not just advocating for sexual exploration (although there is an element of that in there); she was talking about female agency and a very modern approach to marriage. Today we'd call her goals clear-eyed common sense, but in a time when divorces were difficult to obtain, child and spousal support rare, and physical abuse de facto legal, what she was calling for seemed like anarchy. She was tired of the double standard and wanted women to have the freedom to marry for love and to leave those marriages if they failed.

Pretty quotidian stuff now (if personally painful), but declaring these things in public got her labeled "Mrs. Satan" by the powerful political cartoonist Thomas Nast.* In an 1871 speech at Steinway Hall in New York, she declared:

> *The proper sphere of government in regard to relations of the sexes is to enact such laws as in the present conditions of society are necessary to* protect each *individual in the* free *exercise of his or her* right *to love, and also to protect each individual from the forced interference from* every other *person that would*

---

* Not for nothing, but Nast pretty much invented the image of a white-bearded Santa Claus that we're all now familiar with, so his word carried a lot of weight.

compel him or her to submit to any *action that is against his or*
her wish or will… It is therefore a strictly legitimate conclusion
that where there is no *love as a basis for marriage there should*
be no marriage, and if that which is the basis *of a marriage is*
taken away that the marriage *also ceases from that time, state*
law to the contrary notwithstanding.[6]

Emphasis all hers. She also went so far as to compare a loveless
marriage for financial security to a form of prostitution, which
drew much harrumphing from the self-appointed defenders of
middle-class propriety. For her contemporary public, this was not
unlike the recent fight for marriage equality. As it turns out, freaking out about legal changes to "traditional" marriage is a time-
honored American tradition.

Woodhull was also encouraging women to gain control of
one of the nation's most-recognized sources of freedom: money.
Particularly since she was one of the first women to have a public
reputation for financial management, a skill her trance clients
attributed to her close relationship with the spirits. Moreover, when
she and her sister Tennessee* decided to add a brokerage to her
portfolio of businesses, her primary backer was no less than one of
the richest men in America, Commodore† Cornelius Vanderbilt.

---

* Tennessee was the youngest of the Claflin siblings and also a medium. She was
  rumored to have been Vanderbilt's mistress, but that's never been proven and may just
  be gossip aimed at discrediting her.

† Not an actual commodore! It was a nickname. Vanderbilt started out as a ferry boat
  captain between Manhattan and Staten Island and then made his fortune in shipping
  and railroads.

The Commodore was a very public advocate of taking market advice from the spirits and had turned to the sisters as a reliable source. American women would not be allowed to have so much as a credit card without a husband's permission until 1974. Still, in 1870, Woodhull, Claflin, and Co. opened an office on Broad Street near the Stock Exchange and became the first brokerage house owned and run by women. Naturally, it was a news sensation.

Dubbed "the Queens of Finance" by The *New York Herald*, the sisters netted a great deal of coverage, most of which took the form of curiosity about how their lady brains handled the intricacies of finance. As one syndicated story put it, "Our reporter [from the *New York Sun*] remarking that it was quite an innovation, the lady [Ms. Claflin] replied with much energy: 'Why should it be an innovation? If I had engaged a little fancy store along Broadway and sold ribbons and thread, it would have been perfectly proper… (and) no one remarked on it; but because I have brains sufficient to carry on a banking house people are astonished.'"[7] Again, the Claflin Sisters, like the Fox Sisters and Nettie Colburn Maynard, were claiming their place in the spheres outside hearth and home. In addition to the help that they received from the Commodore and the spirits, Victoria and Tennie got some choice stock tips from an unusual place that would go ignored by most men. According to biographer Barbara Goldsmith, Victoria turned to her connections with high-end sex workers to see what they had gleaned from their Wall Street clients.

The world of high finance and the low life of [sex workers] seemed totally separate, but in fact they converged in the elegant

*brothels that Victoria visited. At these establishments women
entertained the richest and most powerful men of the day in
their beds, and yet they were considered insensate and invisible.
Some madams, including Annie Wood, undoubtedly made the
most of the opportunity this provided. As Wall Street traders, city
officials, businessmen, and politicians, gathered in her parlor,
Annie listened carefully to what they said. She also trained her
"girls" to encourage the men to boast of their financial maneuvering, instructing these women in both the art of extracting
information and in seeming ignorant of what they heard.*[8]

The brokerage of the "first firm of lady stockbrokers that civili-
zation has dawned upon"[9] did well enough on this sort of insider
information to bankroll Victoria and Tennie's next passion project,
Woodhull and Claflin's Weekly. No mere lifestyle newsletter, this
publication was an absolute rocket launcher.

It mainly contained Victoria's speeches on marriage, women's
suffrage, and thoughts about other issues of the day, but it was also
a shrewd move for her next act—theoretically anyway. Already a
media darling, Victoria must've had some grasp of the power of
the press. By controlling her own corner of it, she was hoping
to move toward a sort of Oprah status, whereby she could exert
wider influence and mold public opinion in her favor. An alliance
one would need if one were to throw their bonnet in the ring
for the nomination of the president of the United States*—and

---

* Incidentally, her nominee for veep was the venerable Frederick Douglass, which was
not just newsworthy, it was also news to him, since he didn't attend the nominating
convention or even publicly acknowledge his candidacy.

despite not having a legal right to vote for herself,* Mrs. Woodhull intended to do just that. Before Gracie Allen,† Shirley Chisholm, Hillary Clinton, and Kamala Harris, Victoria was the first woman to run for president. The media response was not as glowing as she might have hoped.

Playing stockbroker was treated as adorable and novel, but this was a step too far. Not cute. Reaction was swift and ugly. *The New York Times* ripped into her, proclaiming that she was "a lamp without oil" and "of no possible consequence," declaring that "she fancies that she is capable of illuminating the dark places of politics and social ethics without the light of reason."[10] The newspaper also, as is traditional for all liberal candidates since then, accused her of being a communist. She wasn't, although she was advocating some pro-labor socialist policies. *The Philadelphia Inquirer* piled on with a swipe at her living arrangements. In discussing the 1872 race, it said, "There are other candidates, however, about whom the public do not hear so much; and yet, if other people think their chances doubtful, they have different notions. Mrs. Victoria, if she could get *all* her husbands to vote for her, would probably be a dangerous competitor, but it is doubtful if she could manage so large a poll."[11] As if two guys could possibly be a mathematical advantage. The religious press was not any more charitable in its critiques.

---

* Also one of the first women to testify before a congressional committee, she testified that according to the Constitution, she was a full citizen and was therefore entitled to vote. She was just thirty-four, which disqualified her under the Constitution to take the office, but in the context of things, that was the least of her worries.

† Half of the comedy duo of Burns and Allen, Gracie started off her campaign as a joke and ran on the fictitious "Surprise Party" ticket.

The New York Evangelist snarked her candidacy was an effort to "put this free country under the despotism of Demosthenes, who has never taken the oath of allegiance, nor, so far as we know, been naturalized."[12] And so on and so on. Newspapers nationwide lined up to snicker at Woodhull's personal life, her spiritual beliefs, her convictions, her brains, and her looks—all of which sadly created the pattern we still see today. Needless to say, Woodhull's candidacy would become a footnote in history, Ulysses S. Grant would be elected, and we still haven't managed to get someone of the so-called fairer sex into the Oval Office while we quibble about likability and pantsuits.

Newspapers were, on the other hand, talking about her, and that was no small thing. As later presidential candidate Shirley Chisholm would say, "If they don't give you a seat at the table, bring a folding chair."[13] Colburn Maynard, Conant, Woodhull, and the other women of the Spiritualist movement were—in ways that both whispered and screamed—showing up with their own chairs, and not just to the tables that tipped. They were demanding to be seen, heard, and considered in the halls of power, the boardrooms, and the bedrooms of America. Finding a place for women in the public sphere was a revolution within the American experiment, since they were paving a road that had not existed before. Of course, some of them might have their reputations run over in the process, but as historian Laurel Thatcher Ulrich put it, "Well-behaved women seldom make history."[14] In fact, some of them make inroads, and some, judging by Victoria Woodhull's next move, make powerful enemies.

SALEM

—◦◦—

MASS. HYSTERIA

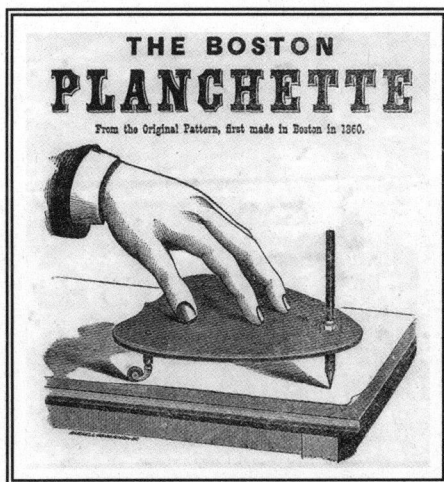

An 1860 ad for an auto-writing device.

> Admittedly I err by undertaking
> This in its present form. The baldest prose
> Reportage was called for, that would reach
> The widest public in the shortest time.

JAMES MERRILL,[*] *THE CHANGING LIGHT AT SANDOVAR*

---

[*] As dictated by his custom talking board.

I'm one of those tourists who wants to know where the best cemeteries or historic crime scenes are in any given city, so I *have* to love Salem, Massachusetts. Because somewhere along the line, between 1692 and the present, the city decided to embrace its reputation for dark weirdness. Synonymous with a certain colonial "hysteria," everything from municipal vehicles to souvenir shops is now labeled "Witch City USA," and while Salem has some pretty grand Victorian architecture, a real literary pedigree, and some fine restaurants, it all comes back to witches. You can shop for candles at Witch City Wicks, enjoy a meal at Witch City Hibachi, and check out a movie at the Witch City Mall. Witchery is a big business, and you can get all manner of spells, charms, hex removers, and wands from a range of different retailers that want to fit in with your lifestyle, whether that's Ren Faire, Pastel Goth, or Intersectional Eco Feminist. Slightly less well-known and celebrated is the fact that Salem is also home to the only museum in the world dedicated to the Ouija board,* which arose from the practice of Spiritualism and continues to bring mediumship into living rooms and slumber parties the world over.

Spiritualism and witches are arguably related, but they are not the same. Witches are not necessarily mediums, and mediums don't have to practice witchcraft. They can be twisted together in the popular imagination because of their association with the

---

* Actually, several months after my visit, another Witch Board Museum opened in "Charm City," Baltimore, Maryland.

occult, but Spiritualism and witchcraft are discrete practices. That said, Spiritualists did build on—and suffer from—some of the factors that brought about the ugliness of America's original witch hunts, namely religious intolerance, mental illness or "hysteria," politics, and/or just plain old misogyny. Unpacking the causes that plagued this colonial outpost is also something of a gingerbread-cottage industry, and there's no shortage of fascinating theories ranging from ingesting a rye crop infested with a hallucinogenic mold, mass hysteria, and a carefully orchestrated land-grab plot. Whatever the cause of the trials, I think it's important to look at the before and after pictures.

Let's start by remembering that Salem was not then located in the great state of Massachusetts; nay, it resided inside the Massachusetts Bay Colony, which was an entirely different thing. A weird mix of commerce incubator, cult compound, and halfway house, the whole place was run by religious fanatics for the profit of the British royal family, all while giving the side-eye to their neighbors in Providence Plantation (now Rhode Island) and the Indigenous peoples who already lived there. Those in power were Puritans,* which meant that while they did business with the Crown, they were vehemently opposed to the contemporary form of the Church of England, which they felt had retained too much Catholic frippery and needed purifying. The roots of their theology were also decidedly Calvinist, which held that who was going to heaven and hell was pretty much predetermined and you should try to stay pure

---

* Pilgrims and Puritans shared a love for basic black wardrobes and a strong suspicion of anything that brought them joy, but unlike the reform-minded Puritans, Pilgrims thought the Anglican Church was beyond saving and needed wholesale replacing.

and holy, but no promises either way. So not exactly party people, and now they were living in an untamed, unfamiliar wilderness rife with disease, cold, starvation, backbreaking labor, and any other number of things that could kill you on a daily basis. Let's just say that tensions were high, and there was little relief in sight.

Additionally, while these circumstances were not exactly paradise for anyone, they were especially hard on women, who were expressly told they were not God's favorite and yet still had to keep their families going and populate this new land. In this context, it's not hard to imagine why a few teenage girls would flip their bonnets. For our purposes, I'm not going to conjecture as to why they did it, and I'll just deal with the fact that they did. Over the course of fourteen short months between February 1682 and May 1683, somewhere between 144 and 185 people were accused (78 percent of them women), 54 people confessed, and 19 were executed (14 women and five men).[1] In the aftermath, what did we learn? Well, not to stop persecuting witches. We did much less of that, but we would actually keep trying to drag alleged witches in front of judges in the greater Salem area all the way up until 1878.

The last case fortunately didn't amount to much, but it does have an oblique connection to Spiritualism and did have the distinction of accusing a man of being a bad witch. The last recognized witch trial in America* came about when poor Lucretia Brown of Ipswich, who had suffered back troubles since a childhood injury, got better—and then got worse again. This

---

* There's a 1928 trial in Pennsylvania, but the victim there is the alleged witch, who was murdered by his neighbors because they believed he was hexing them.

improvement coincided with her conversion to Christian Science and its form of Bible-based mesmerism, which is not unlike Reiki or what Spiritualism called magnetic healing, where the healer runs their hands over the patient in an attempt to rebalance bad energies. Her relapse happened after an alleged remote visit from self-proclaimed "Doctor" Daniel Spofford of Salem and New York. If good mesmerism could cure her, she figured, bad mesmerism* could undo her progress. Spofford was also an adherent of Christian Science but had since been kicked out of the official church due to some disputes with Asa Eddy, husband of the church's founder, Mary Baker Eddy. Incensed at his interference in her recovery, Brown instructed her lawyer to file an injunction against Dr. Spofford. According to a contemporary legal newspaper, "It does not appear that Mr. Spofford† was ever called professionally to Miss Brown, but that he exerted his influence from a distance and does now from New York. The issue of the application will be watched with great interest."[2]

The court proceedings did not go well for poor, afflicted Ms. Brown (or the Eddys). More to the point, they didn't go anywhere. The presiding judge dismissed the whole thing because of "defects in the writ," and further appeals languished into nothingness. This result must've been incredibly frustrating to Asa Eddy, who, tired of waiting for either the wheels of justice to turn his way or his remote mesmerism on Dr. Spofford to take effect, went to Boston

---

*   Christian Scientists have a phrase for this. Church founder Mary Baker Eddy labeled it *malicious animal magnetism* or MAM.

†   He went by "Dr. Spofford," but as we saw with the Woodhulls, that's almost a nickname at this point in medical history.

with a friend and "bargained with a Portland Street 'bummer' to put Dr. Spofford out of the way—in other words, to murder him in cold blood."[3] The conspiracy charges were ultimately dismissed, and the First Church of Christ Scientist continues today as a descendant of Spiritualism thanks to its roots in Mrs. Baker Eddy's practice of mesmerism and other Spiritualist teachings that she picked up along the way concurrently with developing her own doctrines (although she'd later distance herself from the term *spiritualist*). Not exactly a Perry Mason moment all around, but going forward, the courts had quietly indicated that they were largely out of the supernatural business.

After the adoption of the First Amendment's Establishment Clause, the American justice system could still have the occasional satanic panic–tinged trial or the "devil made me do it" murder defense, but we would generally err on the "free exercise thereof" side of things. Those fourteen months, however, continue to mold us as a cultural touchstone, favorite metaphor, and inexhaustible well of lessons about public faith, womanhood, and group psychology. We still have plenty of public tensions about how much religion and where it goes, but we're not actually hunting witches,* which both allowed the Spiritualist movement to rise without criminal punishment and continues to mean tourist dollars for the current residents of Salem. Returning to the latter, back in Witch City, I can enjoy a couple days in a boutique hotel with complimentary sparkling water and a big fluffy bed while I explore one of the darkest periods

---

* Any claims to the contrary of former presidents caught in the legal system by their own actions notwithstanding.

in American history. Again, I'm traveling with a couple of the same friends, Meirav and Eddie, that I went to Disneyland with, and we've made a list of things we want to do: check out the Satanic Temple and get our picture with Baphomet (they're more metal than I am), get a protective spell for my mom's house (she's having repairs), and maybe one of the walking tours. Number one on my list is the Salem Witch Board Museum.

One of the things I found in my research that was news to me is that America's fascination with Ouija grew from its roots in the Spiritualist movement. Its connotation as a portal to hell mostly comes much later* via Hollywood. As for those playing the home game, the board itself is a "witch board" or "talking board." The name Ouija is a trademark of its manufacturer, Kennard Novelty Company of Pittsburgh, but—like Kleenex or Google— it's become a part of the vernacular for anything of that sort. The heart-shaped object that moves to pick out letters, numbers, etc., is a planchette, which comes from the French for "little board." This "Curious and Inexplainable Little Instrument"[4] was developed to help the spirits get their messages through quicker and more directly. With mediumship in the mode of the Fox Sisters, the departed could only be asked either yes/no questions or sitters could count up the medium's raps and align them with the letters of the alphabet (e.g., a=1, b=2, c=3, and so on) in order to write out full words. This method took forever and could be very labor

---

* The Catholic Church did worry about this in the Victorian era, but they were at war with Spiritualism altogether as a forbidden form of necromancy and also came out against "church picnics" in the same 1868 missive. Mainstream Protestantism didn't seem to concern itself much with these items at this time.

intensive if the spirits were chatty. The planchette was originally fitted with a pencil at its center so it could achieve the same results more easily by allowing the medium to glide it over paper to draw or write the spirit's intended message. The lettered and numbered board was added a bit later and gives the whole thing a widely usable design that's suited to domestic or professional use.

It was kind of the gaming system of its day, catching on instantly and receiving mixed reviews. In 1869, The *New York Times* marveled at its "wonders" and recounted the story of a young woman in Battle Creek, Michigan, "who draws with crayons the portraits of deceased persons, as they appeared to their friends while living." The writer otherwise stops short of declaring a miracle, simply positing, "The young lady cannot account for any of these mysterious workings of the planchette. She has never taken lessons in even the rudiments of drawing, and of herself cannot, undirected draw even the roughest sketch. We submit the case to the curious."[5] The *San Francisco Chronicle* was equally impressed but hedged its bets on the game's mysterious perfor- mance, declaring that the "planchette writing as entertainment can do no harm as long as the experimenter does not let go of his common sense and put a superstitious faith in its revelations."[6] Additionally, the question of its potential dark powers was briefly considered and was just as quickly dismissed as unserious with one reporter grousing in 1868 that "Upon the whole, we have come to the conclusion that if planchette is inspired by an evil intelligence; it must be a very blundering and incoherent demon indeed."[7]

So how did this harmless little amusement become a horror movie staple? The answer to that and pretty much every question you could possibly have about talking boards can be answered at the abovementioned Salem Witch Board Museum, which is located on the main drag of Essex Street behind a souvenir shop that specializes in items from a certain preteen, English wizard franchise.* Your host in the museum is John Kozik, a serious collector and punk musician. I'm kind of surprised that we've never met before my visit; we share tons of mutual friends and tastes. I immediately love the whole place and that John greets us with the sort of nerd energy that I'm sure I radiate into the world.† I can't speak for him, but I actually prefer to think of that level of actual scholarship with the Japanese phrase *otaku*, which roughly translates to "having very specific interests that impact your social life," rather than nerd, which encompasses anyone who consumes pop culture these days. No, I gather from our conversation that he's done the homework and read the footnotes.

As John explains it, the origin of the board and planchette as a household item occurs at the crossroads of capitalism and the fantastic. It's the ghost story of Helen Peters Nosworthy, who was rediscovered and retrieved from obscurity by Robert Murch, chairman of the Talking Board Historical Society. Murch found references to her in papers of the time and soon realized that it was Helen who gave the Ouija board its name, or rather asked it what it wanted to be called. When a Pittsburgh outfit, the Kennard Novelty Company, was looking for a catchy name for their version of the talking board, one of the co-owners, Elijah Bond, turned

---

* Rhymes with Schmarry Sotter.

† My personal *otaku* includes American sideshow history, pre-code Hollywood film, and a bunch of other subculture figures that sadly don't rate their own action figures.

to his sister-in-law Helen, who was a "strong medium."[8] Helen in turn politely asked the board how it wished to be known; the planchette spelled out O-U-I-J-A. When asked what it meant, the board cryptically responded G-O-O-D L-U-C-K and left it at that.

Additionally, it was Helen who helped the company secure its patent on the "most wonderful invention of the nineteenth century,"[9] which would ensure its place as a household name. According to the Talking Board Historical Society's account, "Helen and Elijah then traveled to Washington, DC, where they were denied by multiple patent inspectors until the chief patent officer took an interest in the device. As the story goes, he assured the pair that if the device could spell out his name, unknown to Bond and Peters, he would award them a patent. The board apparently did exactly that, and the rest is history."[10] Helen married a Shakespearean actor and moved out west to the Denver area, where she lived quietly and eventually faded from the picture as the Ouija patent changed hands via corporate acquisition. When she went to the Summerland in 1940, her name went unrecognized by even a small grave marker. In 2018, the Talking Board History Society arranged for her to be memorialized with a large headstone that acknowledges her contribution to history.

One of the reasons her contribution was obscured has to do with business. As John explains it, when executive "William Fuld takes over production, he wants to market this board and sell as many of these as he can. So he starts telling people, well, Ouija means German and French for yes-yes or it's Egyptian for good luck."[11] And that little myth has been printed on the box for over seventy years. The trouble with that is modern Egyptians speak

Arabic and that doesn't track, but as John explains it, "You want these boards to seem more mystical, more worldly," not otherworldly. In the end, Fuld believed it would be more salable if it were exotic rather than if it were the work of a woman's mediumship. It's a minor change in the grand scheme of things but another brick in that large wall that separates women from their place as active participants in histories large and small.

Back in the museum, John's own collection of boards began with his grandmother's, which was well used and much loved. In addition to that heirloom, he has managed to fill an entire room floor to ceiling with boards, planchettes, movie posters, valentines, sheet music, albums (including the much-played Morrissey song of my youth), and every other bit of related ephemera an obsessive could want. He points out early decoder-style boards that were too clunky for easy communication, Depression-era planchettes that lit up when they hit the right letter but were too expensive for most households, recent merchandise tie-ins for bands,[*] and movies like the *Child's Play* sequels. All along the way, he sprinkles in little factoids: the band Mars Volta claims to have had their entire 2008 album *The Bedlam in Goliath* composed via a cursed Ouija board, poet James Merrill (who's quoted at the beginning of this chapter) used a self-created version complete with punctuation to write an epic poem and won the Pulitzer Prize in 1977 for his efforts, President Grover Cleveland and his wife were gifted a board in 1886 at their White House wedding, and so on.

---

[*] I covet the one from the seminal punk/goth band the Damned, but the Misfits one is pretty cool too.

John also wants people to understand that the Ouija board's dark reputation is much more recent. This is because pop culture rewires our brains.* "I think a lot of people are pretty surprised to learn this early history, where it's just not viewed by most people as an evil or negative thing. I think most people today are aware of the Ouija board, because of the five-hundred-plus horror movies that have come out. So most people really only tend to know the negative side to them, but this board wasn't viewed that way by most people in mainstream media or pop culture." The same way that as a horror fan, I can't look at a chainsaw—no matter how practical and safe an item it may be—without thinking about the splatter of *Texas Chainsaw Massacre* or *Motel Hell* or *Get Out*. Before its inclusion in *The Exorcist* movie (and *not* the book), the board and planchette were not considered to be any more of a threat than the risk of Monopoly turning your kids into tone-deaf finance bros. In fact, Ouija boards were wholesome enough to have appeared in everything from Norman Rockwell paintings to ads for "shirts to toothpaste to cigars to alcohol."

A more recent wrinkle on the familiar form is 2008's Ouija for Girls. In form and function, it is the same board used by players of all genders for decades except that this one is, of course, pink. Shocking pink. Not Barbie pink, because that color belongs to Mattel, and Hasbro currently owns Ouija, but otherwise yet another candy-colored, pointlessly gendered plaything. There is nothing specific on whether only lady spirits come through or if it

---

* In case you were wondering, the semiotics term for this phenomenon is *cross textualization*.

allows all gender identities and expressions into the borderlands. Ouija for Girls was quickly discontinued and is now a collector's item that will run you about $250 on eBay. It's one of those things that's both silly and speaks to the way we still talk about young women. Ouija boards are still making panicky headlines, including one from the summer of 2023 from Colombia proclaiming: "Hysteria at School as 36 Students Hospitalized after 'Playing with Ouija Board.'"[12] The cure in that case was a little holy water and some time off from school, but as we've learned, you can't be too careful with large groups of frantic young women.

If you hang around Salem enough, you're going to hear the word *hysteria* a lot. It's a way of describing the craziness around the witch trials, the behavior of the afflicted, and even a deal on tickets offered by one of the local sightseeing companies (Hysteria Pass— Discounted Admission to 2 Attractions*). On our way back to the hotel that afternoon, I noticed that there's a brick monument to a different era's persecution of hysteria, namely the late nineteenth century when Spiritualism and women's hysteria would intertwine in the field of medicine. Salem is also home to the Lydia Pinkham Memorial Clinic. Lydia E. Pinkham, a practicing Spiritualist and wellness pioneer, was the queen of all things patent medicine and the fight against women's tendency toward hysteria. To understand her importance, it's crucial to understand the world of health care she was up against that made alternatives like magnetic healing and dodgy elixirs seem like good ideas.

The science of the day was getting better at important things like

---

* Good for the Salem Wax Museum and Salem Witch City.

germ theory, anesthesia, and improved surgical technique, but even so, there still wasn't a lot on offer for those whose bodies and minds were aching. Doctors were little regulated, irregularly trained, and expensive; hospitals were a last resort. For most people, especially people in rural areas, all but the most drastic treatments were done at home and could involve some sort of folk remedy. Into this void of care drops patent medicines that were cheap, widely available, and made with enough intoxicants to take your mind off the hurt. Because they were unchecked and made wild claims, these "medicines" were kind of the wellness supplements of their day. Pitched with the promise of youth, vigor, and good health, these pills, drops, and ointments could contain just about anything— and I don't mean beet extracts or essential oils. I mean moms were passing out spoonfuls of medicine that contained things that would make the in crowd at Studio 54 blush. We are talking about opium, cocaine, arsenic, lithium, lead, mercury, and radium swirled into alcohol and ladled out for everything from teething to cancer. The best-case scenario was the same as today: placebo effect or nothing at all. Worst-case was death, poisoning, cancer, and addiction.

The market was willing and the varieties were endless, but for decades, Lydia E. Pinkham was the grand dame of them all. Her signature formula was perhaps safer but no more effective than the rest of the bottles that crowded drugstore shelves. It contained (among other things) unicorn root and 18 percent alcohol.* But

---

* By way of comparison, most wines contain 11 percent to 13 percent alcohol per serving. Despite the fact that Lydia was also a major proponent of temperance, she viewed the spirits in her product as necessary to extract the active ingredients and not party fuel.

unicorn root may not have been the draw; the kicker for her Vegetable Compound was that it was designed to treat a host of whispered "female complaints." Female complaints were not "equal pay" or "do your share of the housework"; they were a delicate Victorian euphemism for just about everything wrong with women's bodies, such as cramps, anemia, exhaustion, pain, and heavy periods. Attending to these issues, Pinkham figured, would also address the most dangerous female problem of them all—hysteria.

Hysteria is a euphemism within a euphemism for anything affecting women's moods, whether that's mild PMS, severe mental illness, or just having a strongly held opinion. The word comes from the Greek for "uterus," and that organ was thought by early physicians such as Galen, Hippocrates, and Plato to "wander" within the body and cause all manner of problems. It was understood as a matter of science that men seldom became hysterical, but when they did, it was from a lack of sex. This theory would be upended by later studies, which came to different conclusions, particularly "throughout the Dark Ages until the 13th century, when it began to be replaced by the theory of demoniacal possession leading to treatment by exorcism and finally to torture."[13] Different but certainly not better.

In the Victorian era, hysteria was very much in the eye of the beholder, and its causes could be anything. One mid-nineteenth-century expert worried that "Anything that gives an undue prominence to the emotions tends toward hysteria. Hence, young ladies who subscribe to the circulating libraries, and people their brains with heroes and heroines, who weep all day over imaginary distresses or rejoice in real prosperity, who are instructed alternately in superhuman virtue and satanic vice, such young ladies see always the things that surround them as superlatives and are superlatively affected by them."[14] Another doctor suggested that scent might have a role. "In some persons certain kinds of perfumery excite hysterical symptoms. This is especially true of bergamot, ambergris, fresh hay, rose, and lilac."[15] Success could also turn a woman's head. Even Pinkham's biographer's thought so. Writing in the twentieth century on her company's growth, Robert Collyer Washburn asserted the belief that "after the Compound began to sell, this became the dominating passion of her life. She even developed a somewhat hysterical belief in herself as the savior of her sex."[16] This was no small barb. As with witchcraft, the mere accusation of being hysterical could ruin your life. Women had little agency over their lives and could easily be dismissed, institutionalized, and marginalized if they were seen to be difficult, melancholy, or any of the other things the term could cover.

For what it was worth, Pinkham was arming women to keep up necessary appearances with her homespun formulas and her books on the care of the female body. Women were not only a headache and enigma to doctors, but they also didn't know much about their own bodies. Modesty, piety, and a lack of good resources kept a large number of them in the dark about the most basic changes and functions from childhood to old age. In addition to her elixirs, Pinkham provided straightforward answers in the forms of pamphlets, books, and a bureau of assistants who answered letters in her name* on a wide range of intimate concerns.

---

* They actually kept up this practice for years after her death until *Good Housekeeping* pointed out the discrepancy—and Pinkham's obituary—further soiling the company's reputation for honesty.

As a businesswoman, her lasting genius was in following the then radical idea that was synonymous with suffrage and Spiritualism—the notion that women were people who wanted to be heard. If you're asking yourself how one magic, unicorn-root-powered bottle could solve all those things, it's important to look at the context of the day's understanding of lady physiology. Even in the current, objectively more advanced practice of medicine, "research suggests that women are twice as likely as men to be diagnosed with a mental illness when their symptoms are consistent with heart disease."[17] So you can imagine how often women were dismissed when bleeding and leeching* were still somewhat reputable treatments. Women like Pinkham tried (and continued to try) to stand in that gap between women's fear of medicine and their need for treatment. As scholar Anne Braude puts it, "In medicine as in religion, Spiritualists took the opposite extreme from the orthodox, turning for healing not to men with training but women with vision."[18]

In 1941, F. Scott Fitzgerald wrote, "There are no second acts in American lives,"[19] but the field of marketing was still pretty new then, and a modern sensibility might leave room for "rebranding." When I look around, I see that the Ouija board is having a boutique fashion moment, and even the trappings of witchcraft are hot again—both as a lifestyle and an accusation. As an accusation, it's increasingly ridiculous—to me anyway. If you've lived through the original Satanic Panic of the 1980s/1990s, you want your evildoers to have leather pants and guitar solos; Taylor Swift

---

* In all fairness to leeches, they're still used in the treatment of some wounds, which they're very good at because they improve circulation and introduce some anti-clotting factors.

singing about "Folklore" in a rhinestone catsuit is just not going
to do it. Besides which, witches declare themselves these days.
It's even a whole beauty subgenre that my friend and traveling
companion Meirav has covered as a journalist (and metalhead),
including crystal-infused products, black lipsticks, and "13 Witch-
Inspired Beauty Products to Celebrate the Halloween Season."[20]
I asked her why she thought witchcraft was so chic a while back,
and she said something like, "No one has good health insurance,"
which is sad but true. Between the "wellness" trend, our increasing
loss of reproductive agency, and our place in the world of business,
we may as well have a Pinkham's Vegetable Compound* smoothie
and a CBD chaser and rethink our trajectories.

After a day and a half of rolling around Salem in the cold, we
pack up our magical souvenirs and head back to New York. Back
home and staring at the blank page of this chapter-to-be, I wonder
for a wishful moment if I could coauthor with a talking board. I
then remember that my contract forbids AI, wonder if the talking
board falls into that category, and decide that it's hard enough to
be taken seriously as someone dealing with women's histories. I
don't need to add that element. I have my answer. Y-E-S. N-O.
G-O-O-D L-U-C-K.

---

* For what it's worth, you can still get it on Amazon, and it's down to 10 percent alcohol.

WOKE FROM A TRANCE

—◦⟨⟩◦◦⟨⟩◦—

RACE AND SPIRITUALISM

> "I am not a spook* like those who haunted Edgar Allan Poe; nor am I one of your Hollywood–movie ectoplasms."

RALPH ELLISON, *INVISIBLE MAN*

---

* It's worth noting that "spook" was once a slur along the same lines as the N-word.

Content warning: all kinds of slurs and bigotry forthcoming. For the purposes of this chapter, I've chosen to leave in words like "negro," "slave" versus enslaved, and other outdated, offensive terms in these historical texts rather than blunt their impact by bringing them up to date. They don't need a revival or reexamination any more than measles does.

From my experience in writing about it, I feel sadly comfortable in saying that American history is a gumball machine of racism. That is, you know that if you put in your quarter and you spin the handle, it's inevitably going to spit out some glob of stale, hard-to-digest prejudice, and since you know just what you're getting, the surprise entirely lies in guessing what flavor you're going to be given. This will probably get me banned from some choice Florida libraries and could be a function of my own worldview, but if you spend enough time going through the newspapers, personal scribblings, and books of America's past, you're bound to find something that's both shocking and familiar in terms of institutionalized racism. Don't get me wrong, America definitely has its brilliant moments, and I love elements of it, but prejudice is absolutely baked into our shared apple pie. Why should Spiritualism be any exception? The easiest way to link Spiritualism's relation to racism is to split it into two eras, antebellum and postbellum. They're both ugly, just in their own unique way.

While the Spiritualism movement has a deserved reputation for being forward-thinking, the truth is slightly more complicated than all its members marching forth in one direction. As a movement with no singular governing body, there was no doctrinal obligation by its adherents to agree on the role of race and the spirits. In the years before the Civil War, the fiction of white supremacy was necessary for maintaining the reality of slavery, and Spiritualists were not immune to that mindset. Even among more progressive Spiritualist circles, the attitudes toward Black people as sentient humans ranged wildly from patronizing white concern to a drive for actual equality. Moreover, not everyone who advocated for communication with the spirits called for the end of slavery in the States; many people just folded their prejudices into their practice. These differences would create internal tension among those who viewed mediumship as a tool for progress and those who viewed it as a strictly personal practice as well as external criticism from outsiders who viewed it as everything from frivolous to racist.

Even before and after the first shots at Fort Sumter, volleys would be lobbed across the pages of the leading abolitionist and Spiritualist papers, *The Liberator*, the *Spiritual Telegraph*, and the *Banner of Light*. For example, *The Liberator* detailed the sign on the door of one Spiritualist church in Connecticut, where leadership refused to even discuss the issue of abolition during the height of the Civil War by posting a sign that warned all entrants:

> *Notice. We the undersigned, being a Committee of the Spiritualists Society, are appointed to take charge of the church, hereby forbid, any person or persons using or speaking in said church, except for the discussion of Spiritualism, that being the purpose for which this house was built and specified in the deed to said society.*[1]

The author of the article was quick to label the undersigned

"Copperhead* Spiritualists" (meaning they were anti-war) and level this criticism: "It is a noted fact, that Members of the Society are so pro-slavery that they will not listen to an anti-slavery discourse, even though it come from an entranced medium."[2] He closed by adding that the secretary of the society was "a negro-hating rumseller" and concluded this could mean that either "Spiritualism was our old enemy" or "that these people were not true spiritualists." The latter at least allowed some room for forging alliances. While not all interactions between the two factions were this contentious, there would be back-and-forth between the two camps about where the movements should overlap from the beginning and after a peace was negotiated between North and South. The debate on the Spiritualist side largely amounted to "What can we do for abolition?" The questions on the abolitionist side included "Do we need the Spiritualists for anything?"

Even for a radical movement that needed to court public support, abolitionists were hesitant to align themselves with another possibly even more radical group. In an 1858 *Liberator* article, one author posited, "If spiritualism is good—good for anything—it is to impress us with the more thorough conviction that all men are brothers; that there is not distinction of rights; that wrong done to the poorest, weakest is only made the basest by its cowardice; that only the base and coward soul will apologize for the oppressor, and sneer at the oppressed."[3] This wasn't a compliment; this was an accusation. The author noted

---

* Anti-war Democrats were labeled "Copperheads." They weren't so much peace-loving hippies as they were avowed racists and/or ex-pat Southerners who disliked Lincoln and didn't see a point in the war.

that there were those in the Spiritualist press that defended slave owners.

This, of course, was yet another round between Spiritualist readers of *The Liberator* and abolitionists who felt the movement and its mediums were too tainted by these associations to be part of the anti-slavery movement. In their defense, one practitioner wrote a letter to the editor, William Lloyd Garrison, encouraging abolitionists to avoid purity tests for Spiritualists.

Friend Garrison,

By your leave, I purpose [sic] to offer the readers of The Liberator a few thoughts suggested by three articles, mainly on the subject of Spiritualism, touching its relation to anti-slavery, to be found on the fourth page of The Liberator Last Week. It seems to be assumed throughout those articles that spiritualism is to be held responsible for all of the vagaries and shortcomings that may be traced to the dozen of any and all who claimed to be called by its name. This, it seems to me, is quite unjust; for, until spiritualism takes the form of an organization (which may Heaven forbid!)…it cannot justly be held for the moral delinquencies of its adherents.[4]

Part of this friction is due to the fact that Spiritualism itself was still deciding what its public role was going to be: Was it there to comfort the grieving? Or was it there to make this world a better place for all the living?

In the pre–Civil War era, it could be said that mediumship was steered by what the medium hoped to accomplish in a larger sense. The Fox Sisters offered a personal, comforting vision of the spirits; Victoria Woodhull's messages could be businesslike and authoritative; Achsa Sprague wanted to free the enslaved. Born in Plymouth Notch, Vermont, in 1827, Sprague's path to Spiritualism reads like so many other tales of saintly devotion that take a simple farm girl through a miraculous recovery to become a well-known spreader of the gospel. Unlike the Burned-Over District—which had a pretty lively social-political scene thanks to its prosperous cities, handful of famous residents, and connection to mass transportation—that corner of Vermont was (and remains) fairly bucolic. And until President Calvin Coolidge was born there in 1872, Sprague was probably the Notch's most famous citizen. A bright and inquisitive girl, she showed early signs of intelligence and began teaching younger students by the age of twelve. Her sense of the afterlife was precocious as well;* as the town's historical society recalled in 1941, "She created a local sensation at the time of her father's death by compelling all the school children to file over to the funeral, at which she stood and said 'These are only the remains—he is only a shell—he is with God.'"[5] Sadly, her teaching career was cut short around age twenty when she was struck with an inflammatory disease (probably a form of arthritis) that left her bedridden and racked with pain.

With a lot of time on her hands, no medical solution in sight, and a doctor who dismissed her as merely being spoiled (read: hysterical), Sprague turned to prayer for healing. After about five

---

* She also was a firm believer that dogs go to heaven, which I can't argue with in any way.

years of being an invalid, she experienced a remission of sorts that she interpreted as divine intervention. As writer S. E. Porter explains it, "[Sprague] experienced a rapid recovery and attributed her healing to the spirits. What the spirits asked in exchange was the unthinkable: that she go forth and speak in public—an act forbidden to women, according to the dictates of her time, by the Apostle Paul*... In following the directions of her spirits, Achsa joined other Spiritualist trance speakers, some of them girls as young as twelve or thirteen, in ascending stages across the country to preach a new Spiritualist doctrine, not only of communication with the dead, but of absolute human equality. Achsa's surviving diaries prove her passionate sincerity."[6] Sprague, like Victoria Woodhull, felt she had a divine mandate not just to speak for the dead but to educate and elevate the living. In 1854, she began her career as a trance medium for gatherings of Spiritualists and soon thereafter took her message on the road, speaking to audiences of believers and skeptics across America of the absolute necessity of abolition. By 1857, she was traveling as extensively as she could and became involved with conductors on the Underground Railroad. Sprague noted in her diary, "Horrible indeed is the necessity that compels the poor Negro to fly like a hunted deer to the land of kings for that freedom he cannot find amid 'the land of the free & the home of the brave.'"[7]

In 1858, she would find herself back in Vermont, intent on

---

* According to 1 Corinthians 14:34, he's pretty specific on this point: "Women should remain silent in the churches. They are not allowed to speak, but must be in submission, as the law says. If they want to inquire about something, they should ask their own husbands at home; for it is disgraceful for a woman to speak in the church."

addressing a convention of what abolitionist William Lloyd Garrison's paper, *The Liberator*, referred to as a "friends of Free Thought"[8] and The *New York Times* called "Free Lovers-Spiritualists-Trance Mediums-Abolitionists-and All Sorts of Queer People."[9] In addition to that anarchic bunch, the *Times* also noted that a number of the women who were asked to speak were "invariably unbonneted."[10] The messages of that day—from speakers talking on behalf of the living and the dead—called for prison reform, marriage based on love, free trade, and other then radical reforms. For her address, Sprague stood still for five minutes and waited for the spirits to direct her; when she did finally summon them, they spoke through her on the importance of abolition. At least one visiting journalist was not impressed with her stagecraft or message, dismissing her and another medium as "the usual dose of trance stuff, both being a very weak imitation of Mrs. Cora Hatch."*[11]

One thing that Hatch and Maggie Fox had going for them in getting their messages across was, as the press often noted, they were hot—or whatever the cool kids were calling it in those days. Sprague, however, was allegedly not, and as one contemporary account put it, "We thought she was haggard, as though the 'trance state' in which she spent part of her existence, was not congenial with the corporal system and we were disappointed at the outset,

---

* Cora Lodencia Veronica Scott Hatch Daniels Tappan Richmond, known professionally as Cora Hatch, was a renowned beauty and one of the preeminent trance mediums
  of the day working to sellout crowds in both England and the United States. Her first
  husband/manager, Benjamin Franklin Hatch, was a stage mesmerist, but that's a
  scandal for another chapter.

for we knew that the magic of a woman's tongue is scarcely effective with a mixed audience, unless there is the important adjunct of personal beauty."[12] To a great extent, women like Sprague were caught in the gears of the rising machinery of mass media. While some segments of the press were willing to coo over the rappings of the Fox Sisters, others remained skeptical or even hostile to what Spiritualists had to say, especially when viewed through the lens of the male gaze.

When not speaking, Sprague would also find her voice—or at least a voice—in the written word. She employed a technique Spiritualists call "automatic writing" (or trance writing), which involves the medium entering a trance state and transcribing the spirits' prose, poetry, personal messages, or other missives. Not unlike the use of talking boards, it was a means of allowing the spirits' messages to flow through the medium. Through this method, she dictated poetry on subjects including her own illness, patriotism, and abolition. Before the Emancipation Proclamation of 1863, she commemorated the government's "Emancipation in the District of Columbia" with a poem of the same name.

> *No longer at my feet shall crawl the slave,*
> *While high in air my starry banners wave;*
> *No longer will I list their clanking chain,*
> *Or on my garments wear this loathsome stain.*[13]

Unfortunately, Sprague wouldn't live to see the national Emancipation Proclamation on January 1, 1863, and the conclusion of the war in 1865. In July 1862, she succumbed to her long-term illness and died. While not as sensational as the Fox Sisters or Victoria Woodhull, Achsa Sprague was one of a myriad of Spiritualists who believed that social justice was a divine imperative and used mediumship to drive their message into the public's consciousness. Buried in her hometown, her headstone reads "I Still Live," echoing the title of her epic poem celebrating the Civil War and the cause of liberty.

—•◆•—

For Spiritualism, the medium was the message in more ways than one. In addition to the public speakers, having their own publications within the ecosystem of the mass media gave Spiritualists a chance to reach a wider audience with the messages from beyond they felt the living needed to heed. Periodicals like the *Spiritualist Telegraph* and the *Banner of Light* would print the text of speeches, poetry, and other missives that outlined their worldview on what one writer called "harmonial philosophy." Among the elements of modern society writer William H. Mantz decried was institutionalized inequality and slavery, declaring, "If all be free, why do we continue to tighten the letters about our fellow man? If all be free, why not turn our declaration into practice, and break at once the ponderous chains that bend human flesh and blood in life-long slavery? Go ask the leaders of public sentiment, go ask the council of the nation!"[14] It was a fair question and one of the central questions of the day, and it was one Spiritualists were literally trying to give voice to.

Outlets like the *Banner of Light* were incredibly generous in giving bylines to the dead, including messages from spirits who had been enslaved in life. This is where we get into some of the uglier territory of Spiritualism's white savior work. In a Spiritualist society debate titled "Is Anything Wrong?" one speaker postulated, "Slavery appears wrong, but it may be a means for good; it will have an end; and it is Spiritualism that shall bring about its abolition."[15] Which is a pretty strange, self-serving way to look at abolition. Another device that all the abolitionist press employed to great effect was the slave narrative, which presumably allowed formerly enslaved people to tell their own stories of the horrors they faced. Because they regularly published notes from spirits on the other side, the Spiritualist press could provide these narratives from multiple dimensions. While the intent in sharing these messages was to highlight the evils of slavery, the relating of these stories for white audiences followed a formula that allowed readers to reinforce their own preconceived notions of what even disembodied Black voices should sound like and concerned themselves with. Namely, the spirits of the enslaved continued to speak in dialect, a fate that other spirits, even non-English speakers, escaped when crossing to the Summerland. For example, one Italian spirit named Pizzaro was able to say things like "I lived in Genoa and was a baker's boy" and had no trouble communicating to his American medium but suggested he'd also like to have a medium to speak to in his native land, because "I speak good there."[16]

Sadly, Black spirits were somehow not as articulate. Like the white mediums of today, who assure us that George Floyd wanted us to back off on civil rights, what the pre–Civil War spirits had to say also seems insanely insensitive and miles off the mark. And sure, this is partly a function of an era when there were almost no constraints on what was considered acceptable public language (e.g., frequent use of the N-word), but the Black spirits that appear in these pages are cyphers. They're a stand-in for all Black people, and their communications were designed to appeal to Northern readers' ideas of what an enslaved person's inner life might be like and to make them feel good or guilty about their own actions. For example, "Sam, a Slave from Richmond" claimed in the *Banner of Light* that he could read and write in his lifetime but had difficulty communicating with his medium in anything more than childlike, patois terms and addressed his words to his former enslaver.

> *Oh, bress do Lor, massa, I'se free, free, free… Massa say I should b free when I ' dead—so I'se dead and free too.*[17]

Bress, b, massa, and so on are not my typos; that's the way the words appear in print to drive home the idea of this man's degradation and ignorance. Even freed from his earthly troubles, Sam concerns himself with his master's approval and day-to-day operations. Some Spiritualists may have supported the notion of abolition, but that didn't always translate to recognizing the agency or humanity of Black people in a deeper sense.

In the pages of their papers, it would appear that some souls are more equal than others. A similar story, from "Tole, an Alabama Slave," is prefaced with this disclaimer: "As we allow all grades of spirits to commune through our medium, it may not be uninteresting to our readers to peruse the following from a spirit who, when in the earth form, was an Alabama slave."[18] A story like Sam's follows, wherein a slave defends their enslaver and asks whites advocating for abolition to examine their own actions.

> *Dere's bad massas, but you white folks what got no slaves, you say all bad massas. It's large, confounded lie, and I come to tell you so too.*

Warnings about hypocritical or cruel behavior were a constant theme in these missives. All spirits had a message to send back to the living, but what varied was how they communicated with the listener. The spirits of people of color had wisdom to impart, but it came detached from who they may have been in life.

Native Americans fared little better than their Black counterparts in what they had to say and how they said it.

> *Good moon to you, pale face. The Indian Scio wishes to send message to the pale face brave, John. He wishes to tell him many Scios come, but the Great Spirit send me, and me only, to guide him through the little hunting ground. He wishes to tell him to bow low before the Great Spirit when the sun sink low and the moon rise high, and Scio, the Indian, will kneel also; and together we will pray to the Great Spirit, and together we will receive blessings from Him.*[19]

This was probably not unlike the current-day practice of smudging with sage to remove bad energy or hanging a souvenir dream catcher in your home. It's a kind of popular American notion about having a generic Native American archetype without any actual tribe or clan affiliation as a personal shaman or talisman. It's the same sort of spiritual fast food as "manifesting" abundance or banishing negative vibes that gives the practitioner the impression that they're tapping into something "authentic" and profound.

This push and pull from within and without the movement would continue to determine which voices were heard in the wider world. If it was hard to locate genuine Black voices before the Civil War, in some ways, their existence would become even more precarious with the accomplishment of abolition. Beyond their spirit forms, there were Black trance mediums, but their role is minor in the pages of publications like the *Banner of Light*. Despite having some known Black figures, like activist Sojourner Truth, involved in the Spiritualist movement, people of color were seldom asked to speak for themselves outside the context of the slave narrative in these spheres, and when they did, they often didn't reach wide audiences. Moreover, for less well-known figures, these perspectives are especially fragile and easily lost. One such voice within the movement's orbit was that of Northern-born author Harriet E. Wilson.

She first appears post–Civil War in an 1867 letter to the *Banner of Light*'s editor from a Boston-area parishioner.

> *I cannot resist the impulse to send you a few words in relation to the good cause in this place. We are not dead, neither sleeping. By the efforts of a few, fearless souls, we have been favored with public meetings since January. We have had some excellent lectures, some fine circles, and the last two Sabbaths we have*

listened with rapt attention to the influences controlling Mrs.
Wilson, the colored medium. Truly she has not handled her
subjects with gloved fingers, and we have been led to exclaim
almost audibly: Thy dusky skin shall prove no bar to the light
that beams from Truth's radiant star.[20]

Wilson's story is a painful example of how these narratives can
be eclipsed by the passage of time and imbalance of power. Born
to a white mother and a Black father in 1825 in Milford, New
Hampshire, she was abandoned by her mother as a small child.
She spent much of her life in absolute poverty and would eventually end up as an indentured servant for a local from ages five to
eighteen. During her childhood, she had very little schooling but
clearly a thirst for knowledge and need to express herself, since she
was published as a poet by the time she was twenty-two. During
this time, she would also marry and have a son, only to lose both
son and husband to disease before she was thirty. Alone in the world
again, she would face destitution and ill heath for the rest of her life.

Despite all this hardship, in 1859, Wilson managed to write
and publish a novelized version of her own life story. Called *Our*
Nig: or, Sketches from the Life of a Free Black, it would go largely
unnoticed for over a hundred years. While she was technically free,
she details the range of abuses she suffered at the hands of her New
England employer, particularly her mistress. Recalling a life of
unending defeat, she paints a picture of someone who was primed
for the comforts that Spiritualism offered.

Stung by unmerited rebuke, weak from sorrow and anxiety, the tears rolled down her dark face, soon followed by sobs, and then losing all control of herself, she wept aloud. This was an act of disobedience. Her mistress grasping her raw-hide, caused a longer flow of tears, and wounded a spirit that was craving healing mercies.[21]

Sadly, her work never found much of an audience. Even in an era when Harriet Beecher Stowe's *Uncle Tom's Cabin* was a hit, Wilson's novel didn't connect with readers in either the North, where audiences were still seeking slave narratives, or the South, where reading a work by a Black woman would be unthinkable. Professor Dick Ellis, editor of the UK version of *Our Nig*, noted the following:

It is true to say that Harriet Beecher Stowe shows some under-standing of northern failures to tackle slavery and racism, but Harriet Wilson brings a much fiercer analysis to bear upon the USA's and especially the North's racial, racist record. Harriet Beecher Stowe presents, more or less unaware, a confused, deeply flawed and messy story of always already compromised white opposition to African American enslavement and white racism (so laying herself open to a justifiable charge of racism)—a story quite digestible to her mostly northern readership. Harriet Wilson represents, wholly aware, the confused and repeatedly racist messiness of white northern American attitudes to slavery, as she experienced these, full force. Perhaps consequently, where Stowe more or less finally settles upon a belief that migration back to Africa constitutes the best future for African Americans,

Harriet Wilson's history, and to a degree, that of (her protago-
nist) Frado, exhibits a belief that persistent resistance, however
etiolated by the darkness of racism, is essential in the struggle to
obtain a proper position for African Americans in US society.[22]

Despite her book's failure to achieve mainstream success, Wilson would have some platform to speak to audiences. Not long after the publication of her first and only known work, she would become a full-fledged supporter of Spiritualism and would remain so through to her death in 1900. During this time, she'd share stages with no less a celebrity than Victoria Woodhull, be a national delegate to their movement's convention, and start her own Sunday schools and assemblies. Despite all this, her work would remain largely unknown to and unheralded by historians working on the social justice elements of the larger Spiritualist movements, who instead focused on the accomplishments of better known and documented white women. Even Wilson's novel would fade from public memory for over a century until scholar Henry Louis Gates Jr. rediscovered it and restored her place in history as one of the earliest Black women ever published in America.[*]

Professor Ellis's own research, however, shows the limited distance her voice carried in a post-slavery society and a movement now even more divided on the course of its future. "Harriet Wilson's life after the Civil War showed how, despite her success

---

[*] Wilson was thought of as the first published Black female novelist from when Dr. Gates republished her work in 1981. In 2001, the discovery of a work by a formerly enslaved woman named Hannah Crafts was found. Scholars believe that Crafts's novel, *The Bondwoman's Narrative*, was written as early as 1853.

as a Spiritualist, continuing racism and discrimination limited her achievements. For example, the radical Spiritualist Sunday school she established, though successful, attracted negative attention from powerful white spiritualists and soon closed down."[23] By the time Reconstruction took effect, the movement itself was discussing where or if people of color belonged in the Spiritualist movement.

With abolition accomplished and the nation still grieving the mass casualties, the next steps were up for debate. Should Spiritualists press forward on equality for Black people? The vote for women? Did the future lie in the adoption of temperance? Or would they simply work toward expanding the number of faithful? In particular, the introduction of the Fifteenth Amendment, which gave the vote to Black men (nominally anyway) but not women of any sort, would cause friction between suffragists/Spiritualists like Elizabeth Cady Stanton and civil rights activists like Frederick Douglass. Stanton in particular would react like some Karen from the Summerland at having to wait longer and would do some slur-inflected ranting in her memoirs about how white women were entitled to be first in line when rights were handed out.

In the same years that all this chatter was swirling around, the publication of a book from a formerly obscure English natural-ist would add a whole new faction. In 1859, Charles Darwin published *On the Origin of the Species* and introduced a world-wide audience to the study of evolutionary biology. Putting aside the debate swirling around God's role in creating the universe and its contents, what started with an observation about the adaptive nature of different turtle shells and bird beaks would soon be co-opted to suggest that some humans were just better bred than others. Moreover, it wasn't just some random yahoo who kicked off the "scientific" idea of a Westminster Dog Show for human babies; it was Darwin's cousin,* Sir Francis Galton. While Galton was a very smart and prolific creator, helping the development of things like hearing tests and fingerprints, he also coined the term *eugenics* and was one of its earliest disciples. His "scientific" approach to white supremacy would become so ingrained in mainstream thought that the magazine *Nature* was still addressing it in editorials in 2022, when scholars of color declared, "So how do we know that science has advanced racist ideas? We know because it is detailed in the published scholarly record... Such ideas came into their own when colonization was at its peak in the 1800s and early 1900s. In 1883, Francis Galton, an English statistician, coined the term eugenics for the study of human improvement through genetics and selective breeding. Galton also constructed a racial hierarchy, in which white people were considered superior. He wrote that 'the average intellectual standard of the negro race is some two grades below our own (the Anglo Saxon).'"[24]

His crackpot, pseudoscience theories would filter through American society and affect everything from segregation to mental health for over a century. Spiritualism, which was grounded in a love for progress, was not above embracing these notions. This makes sense according to scholar Christine Ferguson, who wrote that "Adherents of both belief systems held a worldview in

---

* BTW, I'm living proof that being the cousin of an influential scientist is absolutely no guarantee of smarts in the same subject. My cousin, Marshall Nirenberg, shared a Nobel Prize in chemistry for his work on RNA; I just squeaked through high school science.

which the dead, whether for good or evil, and whether through bioplasm or the disembodied will, controlled the deeds of the living. It is as a result of these deep affinities between spiritualism and eugenic utopianism that one can struggle to differentiate between their written expressions."[25] This was especially true of prominent Spiritualists like Victoria Woodhull, who was churning out materials on such subjects as "Scientific Propagation of the Human Race" and "The Rapid Multiplication of the Unfit," which is sort of amazing when you consider the Woodhull family's own reputation for insurance fraud and drunkenness.

All snark aside, it's easy to say these views were a product of their time—and that's true—but it's also cold comfort and an excuse that makes things too simple. These views were at some point a somewhat complicated choice. If you were involved in the conversations that were occurring around Spiritualism in those years, you had to understand on some level the nature of slavery, you had to understand and accept the nature of women's right to participate in the republic, and you had to accept the unprovable existence of the human spirit. And yet even with all this understanding, you still felt that some souls were more equal than others. This is not to say that we've solved these issues. We are as a nation still struggling to find intersectionality, give people the agency to speak for themselves, and even acknowledge that we have a problem. It is, so to speak, a lot to chew on, but it's an element of the Spiritualist movement that needs to be acknowledged if we're going to see it as anything deeper and more important than a novelty postcard from the past.

8

NOT HAUNTED

NEW ORLEANS AND SOUTHERN SPIRITUALISM

Your results may differ.

GARY J. WOOD, WIKIMEDIA COMMONS/CREATIVE COMMONS 2.0

> "So which is real, the grief or the celebration? Both, simultaneously, and that is why it is profound."

TOM PIAZZA,
WHY NEW ORLEANS MATTERS

During daylight hours, the French Quarter is pretty much just Cajun-spice Vegas or cornbread Times Square. It's a sticky plastic mess of beads, booze, and overly exuberant bachelorettes on ghost tours. Some nights, however, when the sun goes down and the foot traffic thins, the fog rolls in, and shadows dance across the dueling grounds of St. Louis Cathedral, it's easy to believe this city stands as a toll bridge at the crossroads between dimensions. It's a town on a bend in a river and in the liminal space between extremes: heaven and hell, black and white, piety and debauchery, slavery and freedom. Like the witchy allure of Salem, the Big Easy has turned a dark history of oppression into a glittery form of tourism. This peppery blend of the supernatural and the dead serious is an ethos that's in the cooking, the music, the literature it's produced, and the weird way we've turned its dark history into sparkly tourism, particularly in putting voodoo on the American map.

Meaning "to serve the spirits," voodoo was, like much of early America, built by enslaved people. Voodoo (also written out as *voudou* and *hoodoo*) isn't exactly a singular belief system. It was instead smuggled into America inside the hopes and prayers of Africans and Haitians as they arrived in Louisiana in the early nineteenth century, some of whom were forced onto ships in the name of the slave trade and some who were seeking refuge from the recent Haitian revolution. Voodoo's form in the West is derived from a blend of traditions created by the forced emigration of the African diaspora. Made to work and live together, members of tribes such as the Yoruba, Fon, Kongo, and others blended their traditional beliefs together to create something new and precious that would adapt to and survive in the oppressive environment of the cities and plantations where they were forcibly settled. It is, however, wildly different from New England's homemade brand of feel-good hocus-pocus. Because Louisiana's charms involve our fears and entitlements around race, voodoo did not benefit immediately from the passage of time and the First Amendment. Rather, it would become even more open to voyeurism and exploit.

Forbidden by the white masters from being practiced openly, voodoo was also occult in the original sense of the word, meaning "hidden." Moreover, because it was developed in the crucible of slavery, voodoo is both a mix of faiths and a syncretic religion. Syncretism is a nifty trick developed over millennia by conquered peoples to hide their traditional religion inside their subjugators' faith, or alternately, to let conquerors add elements of local beliefs in order to make forced conversion a little more palatable. It's the religious equivalent of a hollowed-out Bible with a whiskey bottle secreted inside, but instead of a little nip, it's another, entirely different holy book. It works especially well with the holidays and intercessor saints of Christianity: the feast of Saturnalia becomes the celebration of Christmas, Celtic goddess Brigid becomes Saint Brigid of Kildare, the Aztec deity Coatlicue becomes Our Lady of Guadalupe. The many Catholic saints of Louisiana's French colonizers provided an ideal cover for the forbidden orishas of voodoo, and over the years, the two practices and their people would become intertwined to the point of fusion.

This arrangement allowed voodoo to exist both behind closed doors and out in the open—so much so that there developed an outer façade of public mythology around the inner sanctum of private practice. From the eighteenth into the nineteenth century, voodoo was practiced largely in secret by the enslaved, slightly more openly by free people of color, and then somewhat more freely after emancipation. With people of color being free but not equal after the Civil War, however, the practice would remain marginalized even while more accessible to onlookers. Additionally, because the law prohibited large numbers of Black people from assembling, in the consciousness of white citizens, voodoo was primitive, forbidden, and reviled, which of course served only to make it that much more exotic and alluring. These are the deeply twisted roots of New Orleans's own version of religious tourism.

By the reasoning of those in power, if you wouldn't participate in it and you couldn't eliminate it, what was the harm in stopping by for a quick looky-loo and a small souvenir for your own amusement? As historian Michelle Y. Gordon notes, by the late 1800s, press reports of public gawking were so widespread that "one [Black-owned] New York newspaper complained, 'It seems as if each [newspaper] had a special agent to work in this particular field.'" Further, she explains: "In newspapers, national magazines, travel narratives, city guides, histories, folklore journals, and expositions on the 'Negro,' both slave and free, Voodoo narratives and semipublic spectacles confirmed for many whites what they presumed to be true about black savagery, feared about losing social control, and fantasized about."[1]

It was an arrangement that would create a booming cottage

industry that allowed dabbling in someone else's faith and the creation of some prominent civic saints, particularly Marie Laveau, a.k.a. the Voodoo Queen, a.k.a. Marie Laveau I,[*] a.k.a. la Veuve Glapion.[†] Marie Laveau was born to a white father and a biracial mother on September 10, 1801, and died as a respectable local figure on June 15, 1881. She is said to rest entombed, but hardly undisturbed, in the world-famous cemetery St. Louis No. 1. These are the bare bones of her life story; the more accurate nuances of her life, her faith, and her accomplishments are still being teased out from real but ephemeral records and from mythology created by tour guides, novelists, and generations of general *gumbo yaya*,[‡] that is, the Creole word for gossip. She was an actual historical figure and religious leader, but she's also a cypher for people's notions of race, religion, sexuality, and good copy.

Most of her life's work slightly predates the Rochester rappings, so she didn't exactly connect with the movement, and even with her passing, it's telling that Spiritualists didn't claim her in the same way that they embraced Greek philosophers or Indigenous spirit guides. As a priestess, she does share a common thread with the Fox Sisters as to whether a belief in the supernatural was a source

---

[*] Her daughter is referred to in a lot of the literature around her legacy as Marie Laveau II, and it's been suggested that the younger Marie took over Marie's practice when she was too old to continue.

[†] Her name is actually not listed on her tomb; instead she's marked as The Widow Glapion. Her first husband, Jacques Paris, a free man of color and carpenter, abandoned her and their young daughters in the early 1820s. Soon after his departure, she entered common-law marriage with a minor French nobleman, Christophe Dominick Duminy de Glapion, until his death in 1855.

[‡] Literally translated as "everyone talks at once," it's also used to describe the sound of jazz.

of local pride or a civic embarrassment. She was such a mysterious figure in her hometown that even her obituaries varied as to her age, worldly accomplishments, and reputation. *The Daily Picayune* declared her saintly, saying, "A woman with a wonderful history almost a century old, [was] carried to the tomb yesterday evening… Besides being charitable, Marie was also very pious and took delight in strengthening the allegiance of souls to the church. She would sit with the condemned in their last moments and endeavor to turn their last thoughts to Jesus."[2] The *New Orleans Democrat* was a little more skeptical of her legacy in its perhaps sarcastically titled obit "A Sainted Woman," saying, "The fact is that the least said about Marie Lavoux's [*sic*] sainted life, etc., the better. She was, up to an advanced age, the prime mover and soul of the indecent orgies of the ignoble Voudous; and to her influence may be attributed the fall of many a virtuous woman."[3] With her passing, accounts of her powers—in this life and from the next—would become even more sensational and allegorical depending on the teller of the tale. If New Orleans were to become the Disneyland of Voodoo, Marie Laveau would be cast as its star mascot.

Like the Fox Sisters, she was more than the sum of her parts. Within fifty years of her death, there was little distinction made in the popular press between what was true about Laveau and what was hype designed to drum up tourist dollars. In her anthropological essay "Hoodoo in America," Zora Neale Hurston acknowledged that "It is difficult to say how much of hoodoo in Louisiana today stems from Marie Laveau," but "It is probable that she sums up traditionally a whole era of hoodoo; she was the great name in its Golden Age."[4] While the academic Hurston was sure to balance the claims around Laveau with tempering phrases that put her reputed powers in the area of folklore, such as "She is traditionally said to have been consulted by Queen Victoria, who was so pleased with the results that she sent her a shawl* and a large sum of money,"[5] other biographers were a bit less circumspect. More sensational writers skipped the folklore caveat and went straight for the old razzle-dazzle of the miraculous. Herbert Asbury, of *Gangs of New York* fame, for example, claimed that Laveau had delayed the fate of a pair of condemned men by whipping up a storm that caused the hangman's noose to break, and even if that wasn't her handiwork, "the Voodoo Queen was quite capable of engineering bizarre effects without the aid of Nature."[6] Asbury painted Laveau as the original spooky goth girl bent on freaking out the squares with her macabre antics.

With all this press, her reputation as a miracle worker and granter of wishes would soon enough be enshrined as fact, thereby making it a small leap from Voodoo Queen to shadowy saint and local intercessor. In 1947, the *State Journal* in Lansing, Michigan, noted for its readers that

> *A New Orleans housewife who found three pieces of cake under her doorstep didn't even look back. She went straight to St. Louis cemetery No. 2 [sic] and scratched a sign of the cross on the tomb of Marie Laveau. It was the only thing to do, she said. Her neighbors and certain policemen agreed. The cake meant*

---

* Oddly enough, Asbury claims that she had a shawl from the emperor of China, which begs the questions, Is there a kernel of truth in there? and Why fancy scarves from crowned heads?

Voodoo. The cake was gris-gris, or a manifestation of the kind*
of hocus-pocus brought by slaves from Africa. Police figured at
once that since the housewife was a landlady, one of her tenants
was trying to Voodoo her because she had filed an eviction
notice. Marie Laveau practised Voodoo in the 1830s. But she
was still a power in her tomb today, still able to overcome the
power of a bonafide gris-gris.[7]

When you put it that way, voodoo was intriguing, benign, and involved delicious cake. Stripped of its racial charge and its sinister connotations, an entire faith becomes an object of human interest to white audiences, like a Ripley's Believe It or Not or a new muffin recipe or the latest trend in hats.

So hallowed ground becomes a tourist attraction: come to New Orleans, have a beignet at Café du Monde, enjoy the jazz, and easily invoke the favor of the famed Voodoo Queen. No harm, no foul, no ritual blood sacrifice. And ta-da, generations of tourists have trucked on over from the French Quarter to a once sketchy tract of Basin Street, made their wish, carved their crosses into her tomb, and went home again. Which sounds fun and inclusive, until you realize that while her resting place is noteworthy and historic, the cross-carving ritual itself is about as sacred as waiting in line for Magic Mountain.[†] In fact, carving (or knocking or

---

* A less dismissive definition of the Cajun word *gris-gris* is "charm or talisman," but it can also mean a curse or spell placed on someone.

† Not surprisingly, the origins of the crosses and the knocking are murky but are generally believed to come from the imagination of a tour guide or security guard looking to spice up their spiel for visitors.

kicking five times) on Marie Laveau's vault not only has no roots in the actual practice of Voodoo, but it has also been so destructive to the tomb that it had to undergo an extensive preservation effort in 2014. The city declared after 2015 that visitors could only visit under the watchful eye of a licensed tour guide, and even that only slowed people down. According to Michelle Duhon of Bayou Preservation, charged with repairing the years of damage, "the most frustrating part was trying to stop people from marking up the fresh layers of plaster and lime wash with Xs. In the beginning we hoped for the best and put caution tape around the tomb but that didn't work," Duhon said. "Then we wrapped the tomb in plastic but that didn't work either. People cut through the plastic."[8]

The meaningless but popular ritual had been transformed by repetition and sense of entitlement into a strange sort of colonization of Laveau's resting place. One local carriage driver feared that rude visitors and guides looking for a good yarn would ensure that the repairs won't last long. "I hear tour guides…telling people to knock three times, spin around three times, draw three Xs and she'll grant your wish," Nancy Landry said. "It doesn't make any sense. You wouldn't travel to Egypt and do some hokie-pokie with King Tut's pyramid, so why would you do that with a queen or a Voodoo priestess?"[9]

This is a fair question. Who are we visiting with when we visit America's holy places? In Salem, you can commune with witches; in Sedona, it's a mix of New Age and Indigenous traditions with a sprinkling of Eastern traditions; in New Orleans, it's ghosts and voodoo queens. America is not expressly a Christian nation by legal design, but there are also not a lot of Last Supper–themed buffets and casinos. There's Christ of the Ozarks and the Salt Lake Temple, but those are parts of actual churches, and the setup is less sensational and more reverent. It's some religions outside the Christian mainstream that are prone to becoming tourist traps, largely due to their tantalizing association with exotic occult powers. Outside the mainstream is open to exploitation. Sort of. As a Jewish New Yorker, I try to envision an equivalent where Katz's Deli has a souvenir stand that offers novelty yahrzeit memorial candles or sacramental bottles of "Part the Red Sea" pinot noir. It's hard to imagine selling what's truly sacred to us. The culture and cuisine, yes, you can certainly get commemorative T-shirts and salamis, but the trappings of actual practice? Not so much. This may, however, speak to our integration into America. No longer recent immigrants, our religious trappings are left alone. More recent arrivals, like those from Latin America and Asia, are still seeing their holy objects repurposed into celebrity votive candles and designer yoga mats. Religion, culture, and tradition all touch in this world, and in America, we're all up in each other's business as part of the social contract, but what we treat as sacrosanct and what we feel free to borrow is tied into our complicated boundaries around race, class, faith, and gender.

This may be one of the legacies of Spiritualism: the democratization, rightly or wrongly, of the spirit world. This includes a wide selection of religions but also things that fall into the gray area between religious belief and secular superstition. Spiritualists' belief in making the supernatural a part of the everyday opened a channel to the other side for some and a whole tourism industry into the hallowed for others. We're not just a nation of "temporarily embarrassed millionaires"; we might also be undiscovered mediums. Given that possibility of a quick brush with the super-natural, ghost tourism is a strong industry throughout the United States, and in NOLA, it's big business. So much so that when I casually asked the desk clerk at my boutique hotel if my room was haunted, she responded, "Darling, this is New Orleans. Every inch is haunted." I didn't see anything spectral during my stay, but the mini fridge did occasionally make a distinct rapping noise that would rouse me from a deep sleep with a start.

According to local real estate broker (with an amazingly Dickensian name) Finis Shelnutt, "Ghost tours is a very large business in the [French] Quarter—very large. I mean extremely large. You can't imagine. Thousands of people a night doing ghost tours. It's, like, real big."[10] So big that he began to list his properties with prominently placed "Haunted" or "Not Haunted" signs swinging from the underside of their wrought-iron balconies. Shelnutt himself is neither a firm believer nor a hardcore skeptic, so there's no rigorous claims testing; instead, he's done this purely as a businessman. According to one article, "he says he thought what better way to edge out the competition than with creating a buzz about ghosts. All the signs say 'Haunted' and 'Not Haunted' because [he] was once a bond broker and believes in hedging his bets." Like the Winchester Mystery House or the Haunted Mansion, it doesn't even matter anymore if there are ghosts—just the suggestion of a haunting is enough to draw in audiences. Here ghosts have become another commodity available for public consumption. Also, real or imagined, it's worth noting which spirits we (or our tour guides) tend to see and celebrate. In New Orleans, they tend to be romanticized figures of the old

quarter: pirate Jean Lafitte is still swirling through his eponymous Blacksmith Shop and piano bar; author William Faulkner,
eternally, is pensively smoking a pipe at his desk at Faulkner House
Books; and Marguerite, a famed Storyville madam, is still stalking
the halls to seek revenge on the lover who spurned her in what was
the Old French Opera House but is now a Sheraton.

On a recent trip, I paid a visit to a dissipated gambler, Pierre
Antoine Lepardi Jourdan, who took his life after a losing poker
hand in what's now the Séance Lounge of Muriel's Jackson Square
bistro. The lounge is a comfortably appointed room above the bar
with reproduction Egyptian sarcophagi, an LED crystal ball, and
plush couches. I rambled in with several other performers during
a sideshow convention* for a cocktail and a look. As we chatted,
three little girls (and their kindly, exhausted moms) came through
looking for their own answers from the afterlife. Hopped up on
pralines and youthful verve, they shouted their questions about
their cheerleading futures and who was going to be killed. Naturally,
we loved them and tried to encourage their interest in the occult by
providing them with an impromptu séance. I told them the name
of the resident ghost using my research notes, but my seven years
of French instruction made his name too hard to understand, so he
just became "Mr. Jordan." We improvised a talking board out of the
strongwoman's Ouija-print sweatshirt and a wineglass planchette

---

* As I mentioned, I'm a sideshow professional, and like every profession, we have a
yearly conference to encourage the newbies and let the elders tell stories, complain
about the state of the industry, and just generally goof around. Present that day were
friends and colleagues Sally the Cinch (she can squeeze her waist down to 12 inches);
Juliette Electrique, sword swallower; Krystal Younglove, strongwoman; and Carmen
Getsum, an escapologist.

and let them slide it over her back—with the help of Mr. Jordan, of course. We had them close their eyes, put their hands in, and ask yes or no questions, and then I tapped on the table with my feet. "You're using your feet," they cried. I managed to nonverbally get my friend Juliette to do it on the other side of the table, so the sound was at least coming from a different direction. No sale. Eventually they lost interest and took off. We had to be at a workshop soon, so we broke up the event and wandered off. We all agreed kids are a tough audience, and I wondered if there's a connection between the TikTok generation and the dwindling impact of physical medium-ship, but I also admitted my skills need—as the kids say—rizz.[*]

Whether for after-school activities, abolition, or suffrage, ghosts could seemingly be enlisted to speak whatever plotline was necessary. Haunting has been rendered somewhat pragmatic in the wake of the Spiritualist movement's channeling of its messages as it was in the pages of *Banner of Light*. For New Orleans, these deaths are a tourism booster. They are tragic but not horrific; moreover, the ghosts are largely white or Creole[†] and were usually colorful characters in life. The notable exception to these rules being the victims of alleged serial killer Madame Delphine LaLaurie,[‡] who

---

[*] I think they say that. They could be saying something else by now.

[†] Marie Laveau's spirit falls in this category and is said to haunt at least three locales: St. Louis No. 1 Cemetery, the Old Absinthe House bar, and the site of her home on Rue St. Ann.

[‡] Madame LaLaurie was said to have killed and tortured the enslaved people in her household in service of weird medical experiments. The absolute truth is hard to determine with the available records, but those accounts seem to be later pulp stories piled on top of her actual cruelties. The building that now stands there is said to be one of the most haunted spots in the city and was once owned by the actor Nicolas Cage.

are said to haunt the apartments that now occupy the land on Royal Street where her mansion once stood. The city itself is stalked by the dualists who met at Exchange Alley who are said to still call out there, but notably not by the tortured cries of enslaved people being sold away from their families on the same street. It's not the unresolved, day-to-day horror of our nation's history that plagues us; it's quasi-fictional monsters. It's literally the stuff of *American Horror Story* subplots. What, where, and who we are haunted by has become one of the ways we make our priorities and our sense of our own history known. As author Colin Dickey puts it in his book *Ghostland: An American History in Haunted Places*, "If you want to understand a place, ignore the boastful monuments and landmarks, and go straight to the haunted houses."[11] We speak loudly for ourselves when we speak for the dead. And in every haunted inch of New Orleans, there is a lot to say.

Prone to plagues, wars, and natural disasters, the swampy parishes of Louisiana have long lived side by side with their beloved dead in their own unusual way. This is one of the reasons the city seems so ghostly; bodies simply do not stay buried in New Orleans. If placed in the earth, the departed will rise again. Literally. Not in the sense of resurrection, but in the past, corpses have been known to pop up after interment because the water table is so high that water-logged coffins will be ejected from the ground. The solution was to build cemeteries full of aboveground vaults, so brick and plaster cities of the dead were erected practically side by side with the palaces of the rich and the shotgun shacks of the poor.

For all its lush greenery, not everything takes root in the swamps of Louisiana right away. In the years before the Civil War, the South was already giving the side-eye to anything imported from the North, since it bore the taint of unpopular and radical movements such as feminism and abolition. Cultivating Spiritualism in New Orleans was not a huge success at first, largely due to the grip that Catholicism had on the population and the fact that citizens were already used to a certain amount of spooky in their everyday. It also didn't help that Spiritualism was held in contempt by the local press who sided with both the cynics and the church. In 1853, as the movement was spreading like wildfire in the north, the *New Orleans Picayune* declared as a point of hometown pride,

> *We are very far from sympathizing with those individuals who believe in what are termed spiritual manifestations. The rappings, the knockings, the moving of tables and upsetting of chairs, the independent moving of lead pencils and unaccountable performances of inspired quills, we either do not believe, or else believe to be humbugs... The fact that Yankees themselves believe it goes for nothing.*[12]

The *Picayune* later felt it necessary to mention that the Vatican agreed with it on this point and that "They...find that 'modern spiritualism' including mesmerism, clairvoyance, spirit rapping, and somnambulism to be a superstition and a delusion, and issue an 'evangelical letter' accordingly, handing it over to anathema and the devil."[13]

In that environment, launching a Spiritualist church was a hard sell—tough but not impossible. According to Melissa Daggett, author of *Spiritualism in Nineteenth Century New Orleans: The*

Life and Times of Henry Louis Rey, Spiritualism was initially championed in the Crescent City by socially prominent Creoles and French émigrés, who began to form their own mediumship circles in 1850s as they were beginning to break away from the strictures of the Catholic church. The features that made New Orleans unique among American cities also made it special among Southern cities in terms of welcoming Spiritualism. As Daggett puts it, "The city's cosmopolitan nature, the more relaxed Creole culture, and its Gallic connections are partly responsible for New Orleans being the most important southern center for spiritualism in the 1850s and, earlier, of mesmerism in the 1840s. New Orleans developed into a desert island of Spiritualist activity in a sea of southern conservatism."[14] It was a small but devoted French-speaking following with ties to the earlier mesmerism movement in France and nourished by a steady stream of Yankee visitors eager to spread the latest wisdom on their movement from both up North and beyond the veil. Not quite the throngs of followers that the Northeast was developing, but a presence was there.

This was, of course, before the Civil War. The Civil War would both change the direction of the nation's fate and force it in the actual direction of its promise to be a "more perfect union"; it would unleash an unprecedented tide of bloodshed and death that would stain every aspect of American life and create an insistent need for comfort in a world of mourning. In the North, this would create the perfect hothouse for an even greater spread of Spiritualism with its comforting promise of reunion and everlasting souls. The need for this kind of comfort was profound due to the sheer number of lives the Civil War consumed. Approximately

620,000 men, or 2 percent of the entire population North and South,[15] died of disease, injury, or other misadventure, thereby plunging webs within webs of friends, family, and associates into years of mourning. It was a tear in the fabric of the everyday that was so disruptive that "The Message Department of the [Spiritualist magazine] *Banner of Light*, which continued to carry communications from dead soldiers for more than a decade after the war, affirmed for its community of readers that individual soldiers were neither dead nor lost."[16] Whatever form they took, their absence would continue to haunt those they left behind, creating a vacuum that the living would try to fill with séances, spirit writing, and trance lectures. It was an ideal environment for Spiritualism to thrive; massive loss creates a need for comfort and a way to make sense of the modern world.

Even if Spiritualism isn't literally a tourist trap in the Crescent City, it enabled the kind of environment that lets its beloved spooky, schlocky businesses thrive. Spiritualism opened the door to the occult and allowed Americans to vacation with manageable ghosts, postcard interpretations of voodoo, sassy witches, and New Age wellness. The city of New Orleans continues to benefit from these changes and is now far enough removed from the pain of the initial injuries of slavery and early death to turn the afterlife into a seasonal haunted house. Spiritualism itself lurks in the background of these travels like the spectral presence of Lincoln "captured" behind his widow in a spirit photograph. Additionally, whatever the cultural hangover is from the war between the states (and it's massive), the Civil War itself is not a major draw in New Orleans. There are some fortifications outside town and a

Confederate Memorial Hall Museum in the Warehouse District stuffed with various cannons and tunics, but it likely sees less foot traffic than the literal Museum of Death in the Quarter with its serial-killer clown paintings and bloody crime scene photos. There's some interest in that moment in the history of these United States, but these days, more people are stalking the vampire-themed cafés and souvenir stores for the fictional wraiths of Anne Rice novels and local-color ghosts than the problematic specters raised by the Confederacy.

While its central belief in an ongoing cultural conversation with the dead faded from the mainstream, its impact remains in America's visits to the resorts and neighborhoods located within arm's reach of the other side of the veil. So we can freely flock to New Orleans to enjoy the cuisine, raise a glass, groove to the music, and connect with the dead in a way that's neither frightening nor challenging. Decades of inviting the dead into our parlors and churches opened us up to the possibility that we may be untapped mediums and that faith can be a pick-and-choose affair, if only while we're on vacation.

Mediums and the Media

SPIRITUALISM, SCANDAL, AND POWER OF THE PRESS

Spirit photo of Mary Todd Lincoln.

MUMLER, WILLIAM H, MARY TODD LINCOLN WITH ABRAHAM
LINCOLN'S "SPIRIT", 1872, OSTENDORF COLLECTION LINCOLN
FINANCIAL FOUNDATION COLLECTION/PUBLIC DOMAIN.

Towering in the public square,
Twenty cubits in the air,
Rose his status grand in stone;
And the king, disguised, unknown,
Gazing on his sculptured name,
Asked himself: "And what is fame?
Fame is but a slow decay—
Even this shall pass away."

THEODORE TILTON,
"THE KING'S RING," 1858

I walked into a small basement bar in the East Village not long ago, and a stranger recognized me and asked if I was the author of a particular book on lipstick. It so happens that I am, and I was thunderstruck to be recognized. In that moment, I was both excited to be downtown famous at Japanese garage rock night and also slightly creeped out to be recalled from a one-inch author's photo. Any inflation in my ego was quickly tempered by the worry that I had something in my teeth or that the back of my skirt was tucked into my underwear or something. Given my general awkwardness, I feel that being genuinely famous would be nerve-racking for me. On the other hand, I see the appeal. As a sword swallower, I've also been a featured extra on a few TV shows. People really treat you like a pampered pet while you work, it's pretty cushy, and the money can be good. Then again, I can roll out in streets of Manhattan looking like I slept in a laundry bin, and no one at TMZ will complain that I've let myself go. It's a modern conundrum.

We live in a world driven by the concept of fame. According to a 2023 Morning Consult poll, some 57 percent of Gen Z respondents want to be "influencers."[1] Whether we covet riches, adulation, or power, Americans put a lot of stock in fame and the famous. Part of this is due to the fact that there are a lot more ways to be a celebrity than at any other time in human history: film, music, politics, journalism, activism, and social media all have their stars. Of course, this isn't an entirely new phenomenon; there have always been princesses and poets and popes with far-reaching reputations, but celebrity in a modern context is really dependent on the existence of mass media and a somewhat literate population. Spiritualism, of course, did not invent fame and mass media, but it would come along at a great time for those wishing to be known far and wide, and some of its people would learn how to pull those levels of power.

Technological innovations in printing, the Civil War, and a growing population desperate for news and vicarious adventure resulted in a boom for the press. As a nation, what would follow wasn't our first sex scandal and certainly wouldn't be our last, but it would open up a model that continues to this very moment. Also launching in earnest in New York in 1848, the wire services had grown up alongside Spiritualism. For newspapers clamoring for readers and readers seeking sensation, the scandals that would follow (particularly the Beecher-Tilton scandal) would be a lesson in both yellow journalism and the mythological hunt for objectivity. The proliferation of telegraph wires would allow just-the-facts reporting and color commentary to wing their way across all corners of the Union for print in papers that could then embroider if they wished and further fuel American's appetite for news as entertainment.

The growth of nationwide media would coincide—for better or worse—with the rise of Spiritualism and would provide the nationwide platform it needed to grab hold of the popular imagination. It would create and destroy lives for public consumption in a way that is now familiar but was then quite novel. This relationship between famous Spiritualist practitioners and the mainstream press would be a high-tension tango of praise and damnation that would add to the skill set on either side in managing public image.

Some people were very good at this particular dance, and some would get tripped up by it. Women were especially vulnerable to falling out of step. The notorious Victoria Woodhull was one of those women. When last we met our erstwhile heroine, she was running for president. As we know well, politics is an ugly business even (or especially) if the media likes you or, in the case of Mrs. Woodhull, you control a news outlet. Again, in a different time, *Woodhull & Claflin's Weekly* could have been a Goop or a Poosh or an InfoWars,* but just as the wounds of the Civil War were scarring over, Woodhull would use her paper to launch a less important, more personal little war that would set the stage for sex scandals for centuries to come. Before we launch into the fabulously sordid details, it's important to know the players.

- Henry Ward Beecher: Celebrity preacher, evangelist, abolitionist, suffragist, secret womanizer, and member of the famous Beecher clan, which included his sister, novelist Harriet Beecher Stowe, and half sister, suffragist Isabella Beecher Hooker.
- Catharine Beecher: Writer, educator, sister of Henry and Harriet, anti-suffragist. She was an unmarried tradwife. and her tomes on housekeeping and child rearing would set the standard for domestic drudgery for years to come.
- Theodore Tilton: Editor, poet, all-around civil rights activist, best friend of Henry Ward Beecher, husband of Elizabeth "Lib" Tilton, Spiritualist, and Team Victoria Woodhull.

---

* Let's be real, Victoria was fond of some fringe theories and had a strong sense of "us vs. them."

- Elizabeth Cady Stanton: Leading suffragist, religious critic, reproductive freedom advocate, newspaper publisher, and kind of a blabbermouth.
- Horace Greeley: Political operator, powerful editor of the *New York Tribune*, Team Fox Sisters, progressive activist, presidential candidate, popularized the phrase "Go West, young man, and grow up with the country."
- Anthony Comstock: Postal inspector, anti-pornography crusader, and absolute anti-sex sex pest.

At the time, these people and their overlapping circles of friends and colleagues were some of the most famous and influential names in America, touching everything from literature to theology. The Beecher women were particularly influential: Harriet with her famous abolitionist novel *Uncle Tom's Cabin*, Isabella with her suffrage activism, and Catharine with her women's education advocacy. Catharine was actually not a suffragist; in fact, for someone who never married, she was a huge advocate of what we'd now call the "trad wife" and women's access to education. In fact, she'd go so far as to argue that since women control the important spheres of rearing of children and teaching the young, they already have a huge amount of power and didn't need the vote. Which was, indeed, a take for someone who didn't have kids.

Additionally, starting with their patriarch, Lyman Beecher, the Beecher men were incredibly influential religious figures who would argue for moving their church away from the strictures of Calvinism and toward a more personal evangelical foundation. Of Lyman's thirteen children by two wives, Henry Ward Beecher was

really the breakout star and would become the Victorian equivalent of a televangelist of a megachurch with a national presence
and the ear of politicians and businessmen. Known and respected
nationwide, he was gathering quite a large flock to his Brooklyn-
based Plymouth Church by developing a new, more entertaining
style of preaching with humor, performance, and the inclusion of
current events packing 'em into the pews. Theodore Tilton was the
man behind the man, helping Beecher spread his messages through
the *Independent*, the progressive newspaper where they were both
editors, and serving as his assistant/sounding board. They were
such close friends that Beecher even presided over Tilton's 1855
wedding to the shy, sweet Elizabeth "Lib" Richards. Together the
two men would become huge figures in the movements for suffrage
and abolition. Their various advocacy works kept Tilton constantly
busy and away from home a lot; fortunately, Beecher would visit
Lib often. If you think you know what happens next, you're not
wrong. The reverend and Mrs. Tilton had engaged in what Mr.
Tilton would euphemistically refer to as "criminal intimacy."[2]
The affair, while heartbreaking for all involved, should have been
a domestic problem. Instead, through a series of betrayed confi-
dences, it became national news.

In 1870, after divulging the infidelity that Mr. Tilden would
later call a "crime of uncommon wrongfulness and perfidy,"[3] all
three decided the best course of action was just to keep things
quiet to avoid any ensuing scandal or public judgment. Privately,
however, Lib was tortured by what had happened. Seduced by her
trusted adviser and alienated from her husband, she quite naturally
decided to unburden herself to a few trusted friends, and tight

circle that it was, word spread. Those in the know included the famous suffragists Susan B. Anthony, Isabella Beecher Hooker, and Elizabeth Cady Stanton. So without tarring some of America's most famous feminists with the gendered label of "gossips," people do talk, and the story eventually got around to the infamous Mrs. Woodhull via Elizabeth Cady Stanton and Isabella Beecher Hooker. Woodhull had met Stanton and Hooker during their time in DC lobbying for women's rights. Stanton and Hooker thought the Rev. Beecher and Mr. Tilton were wobbling in their crucial support of women's suffrage, and they may have been a little vengeful about it. They probably had no intention of publicly destroying Rev. Beecher but were just venting and trying to impress the feminist scene's new cool girl, Woodhull, when they dished the dirt about the affair in a couple letters to her.

Unlike poor Lib, Woodhull was not naive in the ways of the world. She knew that she was not just in possession of some hot gossip, but she was also now in a position of power, and it's easy to imagine her wickedly tenting her fingers at her big desk in her plush brokerage office and laughing maniacally to herself, Batman-villain style.* So on May 22, 1871, Woodhull published a letter to the editor of the *World*, where she called out the hypocrisy of some of her critics in a veiled way. "My judges preach against 'free love' openly and practice it secretly; their outward seeming is fair [but] inwardly they are full of 'dead men's bones and all manner of uncleanness.' For example, I know of one man, a public teacher of

---

* I obviously have no proof of this, and Batman wouldn't be invented for another sixty-plus years, but it's fun to think about.

eminence, who lives in concubinage with the wife of another public teacher of almost equal eminence."[4] It was a warning shot. That same morning, poor Theodore Tilton was summoned to her brokerage on Bond Street in downtown Manhattan, and Woodhull laid out her demands for her silence: she wanted Tilton and Beecher's public backing. And for a while, she got it, or at least a portion of it.

Tilton would release a glowing tract titled *Victoria C. Woodhull, A Biographical Sketch*, wherein he declared that "A more unsullied woman does not walk the earth. She carries in her very fact the fair legend of a character kept pure by a sacred fire within. She is one of those aspiring devotees who tread the earth merely as a stepping-stone to Heaven, and whose chief ambition is finally to present herself at the supreme tribunal 'spotless, and without wrinkle, or blemish, or any such thing.'"[5] Chafing at being hoisted on his own petard, Beecher would try and stave off Woodhull by doing nothing (that is, neither praising nor damning her from the pulpit) rather than making any public endorsement of her. This did not sit well with Woodhull. In addition to her irritation with the Rev. Beecher's hypocrisy, Woodhull had a beef with Beecher's sisters, the aforementioned Harriet Beecher Stowe and Catharine Beecher. They were inveterate pearl clutchers and viewed "Mrs. Satan" as a radical. Stowe even went so far as to publish a novel satirizing her,* which resulted in Woodhull firing off a letter to the right reverend that was the equivalent threat of "Nice reputation

---

* It's called *My Wife and I* and features a female reformer named Audacia Dangyereyes. Stowe swore it wasn't a portrait of an actual person; rather it was part of "the author's purpose to show the embarrassment of the young champion of progressive principles, in meeting the excesses of modern reformers."

you got here, shame if something were to happen to it." Again, Beecher did nothing, or more to the point, he did nothing to further Woodhull's ambitions.

His timing couldn't have been worse, since in 1872, her aims included (among other things) the office of the presidency. Since she couldn't even guarantee her own vote, she could definitely use the publicity bump from one of America's favorite men of God in her battle against the odds-on favorite General Ulysses S. Grant and powerful newspaperman (and Fox Sisters' fan boy) Horace Greeley. Since Woodhull couldn't beat a Civil War hero, outfoxing Greeley was her next best move. So the die was cast: Beecher had better bestow an endorsement on her or face her wrath—inaction was not an option. Tilden tried to soothe her, but she had made up her mind. Victoria Woodhull did not make idle threats.

Appropriately enough, she spilled the beans during a Boston convention while speaking in one of her trances, recalling later, "They tell me that I used some naughty words upon that occasion. All I know is that if I swore, I did not swear profanely. Some said, with tears streaming from their eyes, that I swore divinely."[6] Nice move, but in a world before newsreels or press conferences, it didn't go far. Furthermore, while it's hard to imagine now when even the mainstream press will (and has) covered the alleged details of a president's so-called manhood, there was a time when the press was reticent to print the sordid details of an important man of God's affairs. Unless, of course, they were merely reacting to another outlet's story. Woodhull soon realized that if you wanted to air someone's dirty laundry in a very public way, you had to do it yourself—and as luck would have it, she had the means to do so.

On November 2, 1872, in *Woodhull & Claflin's Weekly*, Woodhull would lay out her case on page nine and pull no punches in her "aggressive moral warfare," stating plainly that "I intend that this article shall burst like a bombshell into the ranks of the moralistic camp."[7] Kaboom!

It exploded all right, but it also backfired spectacularly. When news of the article spread, newsstands could not keep up with the demand for copies of the salacious paper, and all the juicy details and her printing presses went into overdrive trying to turn out enough scandal sheets for titillated readers. This was hot stuff... by Victorian standards. It's not exactly a *Penthouse* letter; in fact, most of the missive is Woodhull recounting various slights and explaining why she decided to spill the tea, but she does directly state that there was an "affair" and (ahem) "criminal intimacy" and that Lib's marriage to Tilton was a form of "prostitution."[8] Sure, it seems tame today, but her indelicate language was enough for postal inspector and anti-smut warrior Anthony Comstock to come calling.

Comstock* is a strange figure in American history and one who is having an undeserved second act thanks to his insanely backward views on sex, women's health, and abortion care.† He

---

* Seriously, Comstock could find smut anywhere and hounded his quarry literally to death, with at least three of his subjects committing suicide rather than face his public humiliation. That said, his diaries revealed that he was a chronic masturbator and, of course, kept an "exhibit" of dirty materials he had confiscated for "educational purposes."

† Notably, the Arizona State Supreme Court ruled recently that all abortion care without exception could be outlawed, because it was considered obscene in 1864. Not obscene under the same law: setting the age of consent at ten years old.

was another form of puritan on his own personal witch hunt, and his personal form of hysteria (as it often is with these guys) had to do with S-E-X. He's a definitive character in Victorian America, and his spiritual descendants pop up every generation to combat the evils of comic books, heavy metal records, "woke" YA fiction, or whatever else they imagine threatens to turn our poor innocent children into debauched libertines. Even in those more modest times, portions of the press mocked him as a monomaniacal prude by printing cartoons of him bathing in a three-piece suit and hat or putting pants on naked pets.* The penultimate accomplishment of his career was the passage of eponymous laws that were put on the books to keep "obscene, lewd or lascivious" items out of the U.S. postal system. And what constitutes an "obscene, lewd, or lascivious" item? Well, if you were to ask Mr. Comstock, it was pretty much everything; the man was profoundly weird and probably would've ticketed the Statue of Liberty for flashing her ankles if allowed. In this case, it was the revelation of an extramarital affair. He, of course, had had the free-love lady in his crosshairs for some time before this, and now he believed he had the goods on her. He promptly had Woodhull and her sister arrested on obscenity charges for sending dirty stories via the mail. The Beecher-Tilton scandal and the presidential campaign would have to roil on without her.

While not an exact mirror, it turns out that America does have some experience in seeing a presidential nominee brought

---

* Obviously, one only does that now because it's frigging adorable. Pets are otherwise the original shameless, body-positive activists.

up on charges around a sex scandal during campaign season. In Woodhull's case, though, six months in the prison cells of New York's notorious Tombs would indeed have a chilling effect on her would-be campaign, since it would leave her unable to either publish or tour as a speaker. Whatever her odds were, and they weren't that great, she didn't even get to make her point. In fact, she didn't even get the chance to be arrested for trying to vote that year because she was still locked up on obscenity charges when election day rolled around in 1872. Susan B. Anthony would get that glory and catch charges for her attempt to vote at a Rochester, New York–area barbershop, which would go down in history as such a milestone moment in the struggle for women's suffrage that in 1920, the Nineteenth Amendment granting women the vote would be called the "Susan B. Anthony Amendment."*

No one involved would come out ahead. Woodhull would be sprung from jail after a few months and cleared on First Amendment grounds. The board at Plymouth Church convened a committee to assess Rev. Beecher's guilt. Lib, now completely split from her husband, testified that it was all in Tilton's head since he was a jealous beast. Witnesses were paraded before the assembled panel to speak to Beecher's flawless character (including big donors), and the elders debated. Finally, in 1874, the church declared Beecher was innocent and Tilton should be the one to go. Tilton countered in 1875 with a $100,000 civil lawsuit against Beecher on the grounds that he had "wholly lost the comfort,

---

* President Trump would actually pardon Anthony's charges in August 2020 much to the ire of the Susan B. Anthony Museum, which rejected it as antithetical to the whole damn point of her civil disobedience protest.

society, aid, and assistance of his said wife."[9] The proceedings in a Brooklyn court were naturally a media sensation, with scores of reporters hanging on every word and the public clamoring for the few available gallery seats. The Associated Press alone sent dozens of reporters to cover every aspect within and without the Brooklyn courthouse, including Mrs. Beecher's stiff upper lip and all-black wardrobe. The case would take six months, in part because the right reverend would employ a fleet of lawyers, call ninety-five witnesses, and testify uninterrupted for four and a half hours. Jurors apparently didn't know what to do with all that information and deadlocked twice.

What started with a "bombshell" would end with a bunch of smaller legal skirmishes and the four main parties retreating to different corners. Mrs. Tilton would move in with her mother and live quietly; Mr. Tilton would continue to lecture some and eventually move to Paris; Beecher would, although slightly tarnished, continued to preach; and Woodhull, having had quite enough of the American press, would take off for England where she would marry a well-to-do banker* and advocate for women's education with her daughter until her death in 1927, by which time American women had the vote and she was reinvented as a pretty respectable figure. She's popularly remembered as the first woman to run for president, but that's just a part of the picture. It's worth looking at her impact on both Spiritualism and women in the public sphere given how far we've come and how much we've remained the same.

---

* Her sister Tennessee would become a Lady. An actual Lady, not like a doctor or a reverend or something you could just name yourself. She married a baronet, Francis Cooke, and died as Lady Tennessee Celeste Claflin, Viscountess of Montserrat.

—•◆•—

The whole sordid, front-page affair also speaks to the powerful hold that Spiritualism and its practitioners had on the public imagination. Rather than diminishing it, the Beecher-Tilton scandal kept the conversation around both women's rights and Spiritualism in the spotlight. The 1870s were prime years for the Spiritualists, buoyed by the long-standing collective grief over the war dead and high child mortality. It was a movement that was flourishing because it was a movement that was needed. It was also a crusade that was helping to make sense of a rapidly changing world, particularly as people were adapting to the new technologies of mass media—specifically, the advent of photography, which would also lead to a scandal splashed across the pages of the daily papers. While the delicate images captured on the silver-coated copper plates of daguerreotypes look quaint and stiff now, at the time, they were an extraordinary breakthrough that allowed everyday people to keep friends, family, and heroes in their pockets. The world was not yet electrified, and it was getting smaller and faster by the day thanks to these rapid advances of the somewhat mysterious forces of the telegraph and the camera.

Much like the current examination of the potential powers of AI, the popularization of the camera was met with both wonder and confusion about what it could and couldn't do. *Scientific American*, which would spend decades trying to debunk Spiritualism, was early in its dismissal of spirit photography (and spirits), quoting a contemporary article from the *London Review* that flatly stated: "A ghost can hardly be less material, if it wears a crinoline, is helped twice to beef, drinks claret and wants a portrait taken. The photographer's plate was liable to no delusions, has no brains to be diseased, and is exact in its testimony."[10] While the article's verdict seems pretty final, it neglects to factor in that all those plates had to pass through human hands, and we're prone to all kinds of mischief in pursuit of making a point (or a buck).

The advent of affordable, widely available portrait photography would reflect the human impact of the Civil War in all its facets: as tokens left with loved ones, as news flashes from the battle-field, and as memorials to those lost. Even the era's most famous photographer, Matthew Brady, seemed to grasp the profound permanence of a picture and advertised his Manhattan studio with the admonition, "Never delay the important business of getting your Portrait; you cannot tell how soon it may be too late."[11] The deadline of mortality itself was being extended slightly by the practice of memorial photography, that is, taking one last photo of the deceased just before they were buried—often already laid in their coffin.* Spiritualists, of course, wanted to ensure that it was never too late. If spirits were coming through talking boards and trumpets, capturing them on film seemed like a natural next step.

Much like the rappings of the Fox Sisters, spirit photography started off as a way to cover up one small misstep. Credited to amateur, Boston-based photographer William H. Mumler, these

---

* This sound gruesome to current audiences, but it was fairly common at the time, especially since people usually didn't own cameras for personal use, and it could be the one souvenir image that loved ones had. We've also pathologized death and the dead and just generally have less contact with and ritual around the body.

pictures of the living and the dead could be described as a meme*
that arose from an early attempt at a selfie that then quickly swept
the nation and accounted for some of the era's most talked-about
celebrity portraits. While not a scam exactly (at least in the beginning), Mumler's first spirit photograph was undoubtedly not a
chimera; it was almost certainly chemical. In the days before plastic
or digital negatives, photographers used chemical-coated glass
plates to capture images. While cumbersome and fragile, these
plates did have the advantage of being reusable since they could
be cleaned and recoated. Mumler's initial photo may have been
an accidental double exposure on an insufficiently cleaned plate
or a layering of negatives during the developing process, or it may
have been a combination of methods. Whatever it was, it worked,
and his celestial portraits would soon cause a media sensation. It
was what a later American artist might call a happy accident...or
Mumler had done it on purpose to impress a Spiritualist friend.

This is where the story of Mumler's intentions gets a little
blurry. Mumler was a silver engraver by trade and something of an
amateur inventor; at the time of his first spirit photo, he was also
learning the science and art of photography from Mrs. Abernathy
Stuart, or Hannah. Mr. Stuart seemed to be out of the picture,
and Mumler was entranced by the young businesswoman, who
was running her own photography studio in Boston. Hannah was
a Spiritualist and a serial entrepreneur in the death sector, and
business was booming, with one scholar listing her occupations as

---

* Before modern internet usage, *meme* was a word coined by academics to denote units
of information that pass by imitation within a culture.

a hair worker,* clairvoyant physician, and photographer. As it turns out, Mumler captured more than a ghost with that self-portrait. He also seemed to have captured Hannah's heart, and they were soon married. News of Mumler's miraculous pictures spread quickly around town, and soon both believers and skeptics were finding their way to the newlywed's studio on Washington Street.

They were soon garnering attention from locally based publications such as the Spiritualist *Banner of Light* and the abolitionist *Liberator*, the latter quoting the former on the subject. This conveniently allowed both parties to skip taking a final position. Quoted in the article, Dr. A. B. Childs, who had a chance to observe Mumler at work and the resulting images, took the Solomonic position, "I have a desire not to be too credulous in believing this new phenomenon, which seems almost too good to be true—and I also have a desire to not appear like an obstinate fool by shutting out the perception of palpable, tangible facts, and deny that they exist when I know that they do."[12] This was the general response the couple received to their mediumistic portraits, and their business began to boom, attracting attention from both believers and skeptics. Things in Boston went very well for the Mumlers, but they soon decided that their future lay in moving the photo business to New York. Whether they thought they were getting too much attention from skeptics or law enforcement or it was just the next big step is unknown.

In New York, they set up shop on a busy stretch of Lower

---

* This is not a hairdresser. These are artisans and amateurs who created jewelry, plaques, and other tokens of affection and remembrance from locks of hair snipped from both the dead and the living.

Broadway in Manhattan just a mile away from P. T. Barnum's legendary American Museum and photographer Matthew Brady's portrait studio. Soon they were doing a brisk business in reuniting the dead and the living. Additionally, like Brady, they were capturing some of the era's most famous faces. It wasn't just locals and tourists that stopped by the Mumlers' to have their pictures taken; their clientele included some DC luminaries, such as our old friends Fanny Conant and Mary Todd Lincoln. They also captured the attention of the tabloid press, and despite what we've been told, all publicity is not good publicity—particularly when it gets you arrested on fraud charges. A science reporter named P. V. Hickey suspected some kind of shenanigans were afoot at the Mumlers' studio and swore out a complaint to Marshal Joseph H. Tooker, who "was sceptical [*sic*] as to believing that likenesses of deceased persons could be produced by photographic processes"[13] and opened an investigation by putting down a deposit and sitting for his portrait. Upon delivery, there appeared to be the faint likeness of the deceased father-in-law that Tooker had mentioned.

Impressed but also certain he had been bamboozled, Tooker had Mumler and his former partner arrested and sent straight to the Tombs* to await a trial. Naturally, a media circus ensued.

And I do mean circus in the truest sense—it was a carefully calculated spectacle. As someone with an extensive background in sideshow as a writer and performer, I want to emphasize the

---

* Formally named the New York City Halls of Justice and House of Detention, the original Tombs were designed in an Egyptian Revival style, so that may be the initial reason for the nickname. It probably didn't help that they were (and are) also a living death for those confined there.

fact that people misuse the word to mean scrum or chaos or something seedy. This is not how a circus or sideshow works; rather, it's an exacting presentation of skills or bodily difference intended to evoke an audience reaction. Toward this end, the prosecutor literally trotted out none other than P. T. Barnum. Barnum didn't actually know anything about photography; instead, his area of expertise was in the production and distribution of "humbug." He was for it when it came to having a taxidermist sew a monkey and a fish together and displaying the resulting creature for audiences as "the Feejee Mermaid"* or having a public autopsy in a saloon for an elderly Black woman,† Joice Heath, whom he had claimed was George Washington's wet nurse. He was opposed to it when it came to Spiritualism, which he felt exploited the grieving. He wrote in 1866 that "some correspondents ask me if I believe that all pretensions to intercourse with departed spirits are impositions. I reply, that if people declare that they privately communicate with or are influenced to write or speak by invisible spirits, I cannot prove that they are deceived or are attempting to deceive me—although I believe that one or the other of these propositions is true. But when they pretend to give me communications from departed spirits, to tie or untie

---

* Probably from the same genus as the mink fish or the jackalope, the industry term for this sort of fake is a "gaff."

† Just to be clear, I am 100 percent pro freak. Displays of bodily differences are not in and of themselves exploitative; to boil down a mountain of discourse to a footnote: it's all about the agency to decide for yourself if you want to take the stage. That said, Barnum's treatment of Heath, who he literally enslaved, was just undeniably awful. Like most famous men, his legacy has a lot of dimensions to it: some good, some really bad.

ropes—to read sealed letters, or to answer test-questions through spiritual agencies, I pronounce all such pretensions ridiculous impositions, and I stand ready at any time to prove them so, or to forfeit five hundred dollars."[14] For Barnum, if an exchange of money was involved, it was certainly a scam,* and he testified to this belief under oath.

What he couldn't speak to was *how* Mumler did it, but neither could the prosecution, instead offering jurors no less than nine options for how he achieved the effect. In the end, the case was too weak to convict, and Mumler was acquitted. In turn, he ultimately decided he wasn't a New Yorker and headed back to Boston, where he would quietly continue to sell photographic souvenirs of the Borderlands.

Mumler would also return to his original skills of inventing and engraving and, ironically enough, create something that would revolutionize journalism, particularly the sort of tabloid media that pilloried him. The Mumler process would allow newspapers to print actual photographs rather than illustrations, so readers could feel like they were seeing the absolute truth of a situation with their own eyes. Unless, of course, those pictures had been cropped or doctored…and around it goes. At the end of his life in 1884, a trade obituary emphasized this latter part of his career and reduced the whole spirit business to one line, noting that "The deceased at one time gained considerable notoriety in connection

---

* It must be remembered that "humbug" was not Barnum's only revenue stream. He displayed tons of people and objects that were absolutely "as advertised." His real skill was in the power of good copy, so between that and some hokey movie musicals, modern audiences are a little skeptical of everything with his stamp on it.

with spirit photographs."[15] Fittingly, this passing acknowledgment made the whole scandal appear as though it were a mere shadow on an otherwise bright picture.

The modern media and Spiritualism would grow up together and feed off each other's successes, sensations, and failures. As the years passed into the twentieth century, Spiritualism may have faded into the background, but its impact continues to haunt the way we take in the news that we're constantly bombarded with. Given the profound impact the news has on our lives in this moment, now is a good time for this sort of ghost hunt.

A Haunting We Will Go

GHOST HUNTING IN CHARM CITY

Late check out.

IMAGE OF GHOST, PRODUCED BY DOUBLE EXPOSURE,
1899, THE NATIONAL ARCHIVES UK/PUBLIC DOMAIN.

> "Ghosts, like ladies, never
> speak till spoke to."

RICHARD HARRIS BARHAM

When we talk about great American cities, poor little Baltimore seldom gets the respect it deserves given its outsized contributions to our history and culture. "Charm City"—home of the "Star-Spangled Banner," Cab Calloway,* Colt 45, *The Wire*, the linotype machine, and (for my money) America's greatest cultural critic, John Waters—has packed a lot of wit and weirdness into its tumbledown streets. Not surprisingly, the final resting place of Edgar Allan Poe is also thought to be extremely haunted. It's one of the reasons I've picked it for my crash course in modern ghost hunting. When I arrive for a quick, spooky weekend trip, it's raining mercilessly, and while atmospheric, I am grateful that several spirits have decided to spend eternity where I am spending the night. Originally opened in 1928, the Lord Baltimore Hotel has a very grand lobby, and it's easy to imagine an era when fancy patrons came sweeping in with matched luggage and chic hats. It's a lot less formal now with a run-of-the-mill sports bar at the back and lots of plastic signage.

My room on the eleventh floor is off a long hallway that gives definite *The Shining* vibes and is beset by a miasma of Fabuloso cleanser fumes. I assure myself this means clean, but I also worry what needed so much scrubbing that the room still stinks of chemical flowers. I'm not a big believer, but I am an insomniac,

---

* Okay, *technically* he was born in Rochester, but he was raised in Baltimore after age twelve, and the city stakes a claim to his greatness as well as his older sister, Blanche, who was a successful singer and bandleader.

and I hate to be awakened, so for years I've performed a little ritual whenever I check into a hotel that may have spectral visitors. I go into the bathroom, brush my teeth, and telepathically assure any nearby entities that I respect this is their home and I'm just passing through, and I ask them to kindly just let me sleep. I started doing this many years ago at the Boulderado Hotel in Boulder, Colorado, which is said to be wildly haunted, and I slept well, so I stick with it. Now, if I'm tossing and turning, it's just because I'm stressed about something earthlier.

Among the unique offerings at the Lord Baltimore Hotel is Poe's Magic Theater and the ghost tour on Saturday evenings. The proximity of these two specific activities in the popular imagination may be an unintended side effect of Spiritualism. Rooted in the supernatural, ghosts make for good theater, and magicians have always dealt in the gray areas between the miraculous and the ridiculous. The rise of Spiritualism and its central tenet of communication across the veil would feed the narratives of both skeptics and the faithful sometimes in ways that were very human. For example, Cora Lodencia Veronica Scott Hatch Daniels Tappan Richmond* would mix mediumship, showbiz, and more than a dash of sex appeal to create one of the most successful and controversial careers in the history of Spiritualism. Born in Cuba, New York, in 1840, she was an early bloomer, starting as a trance speaker at age twelve. After her father's death in 1853, she relocated to Buffalo in the heart of the old Burned-Over District to continue

---

* Victoria Woodhull took a lot of heat for remarrying, but Cora really takes the Liz Taylor Prize for Hopeless Romantic here.

her career development. Just three years later, she married her first husband, Benjamin Franklin Hatch, who claimed that he was a well-respected and successful physician. He would be instrumental in taking her career from local attraction to internationally known sensation before trying to punch a giant hole in her world on the way out of their marriage.

Needless to say, their honeymoon phase did not last long— about two years, which may have seemed an eternity for Cora, who was only sixteen on her wedding day, and the blink of an eye to her husband, Dr. Hatch,* who was in his forties. In that brief period, they managed to tour the country extensively and establish Cora as a celebrity medium. Blond, attractive, and seemingly innocent, she was basically on track to be the Taylor Swift of trance talkers until a Britney Spears–type fight about legal control over her career broke out. Exhausted and yearning to get free of her controlling husband, in 1858, she let him know that she wanted a divorce; naturally, this did not sit well with him. It also made news up and down the East Coast due to the wild nature of the complaints they lobbed at each other and the media's overall skepticism of Spiritualism. *The Baltimore Sun* reported on the supernatural manner of their conflicting claims:

> *Cora V.L. Hatch, who, a year or more since, gained a wide notoriety as a trance speaking medium, and her husband, Dr. Hatch have separated. The cause of this separation is differently*

---

* He claimed to have studied medicine, but at this point, who knows if he graduated or practiced. Either way, he often signed his correspondence "B.F. Hatch, M.D."

stated. According to the New York Post the doctor's theory of the
matter is that his wife is possessed of a demonical influence, and
he further believes that this is the result of such mediumship
as hers. Some of the friends of Mrs. Hatch, however, do not
hesitate to express their conviction very freely that all the devil
in the matter belongs on the other side of the house.[1]

This dispute probably rang a bell with tabloid readers. Undoubtedly at that moment in American history, there were any number of domestic disputes going on in their own households that had Spiritualism (and its associated hot-button issues like ghosts, free love, temperance, abolition, and women's rights) at the root of the conflict. When added to the classic scandal factors of money, showbiz, and a contentious divorce, voilà, you have all the makings of a tabloid blockbuster that would put Spiritualism itself on trial.

The Hatches' he said/she said complaints boiled down to who was in charge of their marriage: Cora claimed that Benjamin was exploiting her as a money maker, and Benjamin claimed that Spiritualism had turned the fourth Mrs. Hatch into a free-loving, devil-possessed tramp.* Despite his previous enthusiastic involvement in her trance speaking career, at some point (probably moments after she left him), he concluded that most mediums were homewreckers and that the world should be made aware of this. To wit, one journalist received his list of "forty trance speaking mediums, of both sexes, which

---

* It sounds cute now, but it must be remembered that stepping out on your marriage was still technically illegal in this era and a social death sentence for women.

will soon be made public, who have either separated from their husbands or wives, or are now living in extreme unhappiness." But wait, there's more! "Some women have abandoned their husbands for other 'affinities.' One who has featured in the most recent Free Love Conventions is set down as abandoning two husbands, both of whom are still living—and one woman who traded husbands with a sister spiritualist."[2] Pre–Anthony Comstock, you could get away with some pretty racy assertions.

Going into court, the good doctor may have had gravitas and experience on his side, but Cora had beauty, youth, and popularity. She also quickly gained sympathy by filing first and painting her husband as a shiftless brute who lived off her earnings and gave her nothing in return. She even alleged that when she needed money for warm underwear, he "made reply by asking her if she could not make said garments out of an old flannel blanket which he had, but was entirely insufficient for the purpose required." Literally and figuratively chafing at his control, she wanted the court to know he "left her destitute of suitable undergarments, exposed to the inclemency of the weather, so that her health has been constantly in danger, and has been sometimes seriously impaired thereby."[3] Dr. Hatch countered, of course, with his merits as a husband, stating that "More than a year prior to January, 1858, he entreated Mrs. Hatch to wear flannel underwear and he never refused her the means for their purchase." More to the point, "Mrs. Hatch was young and indiscreet, and at times permitted freedom from men which modest females seem to resent and did not seem to understand that it was improper; and he cautioned her that such things would occasion remarks derogatory to her character."[4]

And so it went...with either side making accusations and counterclaims in different states until a legal decision was reached. Ultimately, Mrs. Hatch was granted her divorce by a judge, and Dr. Hatch lost in the court of public opinion. He was not gracious in defeat, going so far as to self-publish his own missive designed not just to trash his ex-wife but also to take down Spiritualism as a whole. *Spiritualists' Iniquities Unmasked, and the Hatch Divorce Case* not only laid out the couple's dirty flannel laundry for the world to see but also listed by name the peccadillos of various mediums and their marital woes, which he claimed was par for the course for people who communed with the dead. Moreover, in his telling of it, the good doctor was an insider who had returned to Christ after witnessing the "hydra-headed monster, which is now coiling its slimy folds in the bosom of humanity"[5] and would now lay out why people should reject mediumship. In short, like later satanic panics and Ouija boards, communicating with the spirits could possibly open some kind of hell portal and leave one vulnerable to demons, etc., etc., etc.

Further, Dr. Hatch hinted that Spiritualism might be playing tricks on people's minds via hypnosis and other forms of psychology, stating, "I give these examples which clearly prove that a psychological subject (and all mediums are such) may, as in the case of Cora, state things wholly false, and at the same time be irresponsible."[6] Interestingly, he brought up trickery as a possibility but didn't go much further, choosing to spend way more time on why the movement is ungodly, and this raises some questions. He may have pulled a punch here since there has been some suggestion that Dr. Hatch had himself been a stage mesmerist and may have been privy to some of the tricks of the magic trade. Whether he was being oblique to save his own reputation or he had genuinely split with mediumship can only be guessed at, but it would only be a matter of time before men of magic and science would align to eclipse the women of Spiritualism.

Putting the women who reached beyond the veil under the microscope to determine exactly what type of sorcery (if any) they possessed was a reasonable assumption and a logical next step in an era of invention, but it would also soon become a cudgel that was designed to keep some of the higher pitched voices out of the conversation. Cold, logical, and measured, science was roundly and historically considered to be the purview of men. Given their sensitive nature, women, on the other hand, were always prone to that old female complaint, "hysteria." The good news for the ladies was that the scientific field was expanding to include the field of psychology. This meant that there would be fewer Satan-based complaints like Dr. Hatch's accusation and more medical diagnoses based on new, more exacting criteria. According to the 1859 Annual Report of the Superintendent of the Hamilton County Lunatic Asylum, rising admissions or "Exciting causes...are about equally divided between moral and physical. The number of insane caused by 'Spiritualism'* has gradually increased since 1852."[7]

—·◆·—

---

* Other cited root causes of crazy in that report: masturbation, "intemperate use of alcohol," and tobacco.

Currently in the "Hairdo Capital of the World" of Baltimore, these supposedly cold, logical spheres of men and the magical ones for women still both coexist and wrestle across the hallways and stages. When I arrive at the lobby sports bar, Vince Wilson, the proprietor of Poe's Magic Theater and the organizer of tonight's ghost hunt, greets me. He's much taller than I imagined[*] and favors a snap brim cap and novelty tie. He's incredibly accommodating and supportive in all our conversations and gives off a sort of "your favorite English teacher" vibe, so I'm glad we've connected. When I get there, the evening's show has just ended, and a bunch of magicians are hanging out talking shop. I listen in and try to find if I know any of the people being discussed. The fields of magic and sideshow are close cousins, and there's often an overlap of characters. Tonight's feature performer, Meadow Perry, has a rare distinction in the field of magic—she's a woman. Like a dope, I ask her if I know her through Tanya Solomon, the only other female magician I know well. Perry doesn't know her, but I put in a good word for my Semitic sideshow sister and her smart illusions. I feel like they should meet; lady variety artists could have strength in numbers.

According to a 2023 *New York Times* article, only about 8 percent of professional stage magicians can make that claim,[8] and there's an interesting quote in the article that brings me back to the gender disparity in Spiritualism and the magic world. In that piece, magician Nicole Cardoza, who is Black (another underrepresented

---

[*]   Unfair presumption on my part, but I've worked with a lot of magicians who have that stereotypical short guy mentality no matter their height. Also, of course, some really talented, great folks.

group), wisely pointed out "we have to get into the role of who is allowed, historically, to be magical, supernatural."[9] While Spiritualism had both male and female followers, women were often at the front, and that probably didn't sit well with a large chunk of the population who believed that "lady-like deportment is always modest and quiet."[10] Conversely the art of magic has long been a boy's club where most women are merely tools of the trade meant to be seen (and sawed in half) and not heard. The rising mediumship of the Spiritualist movement would upset the supernatural order of things and create a rivalry that endures.

For what it's worth, I'm ready to stifle myself tonight, not out of any sense of etiquette but because I get the impression that ghosts will be scared off by my chatter. Turns out there's no need, because my tour guide that night is Louis Vittorio, and I adore him off the bat. Clearly, I've met another one of my fellow *otaku* travelers. That evening, he's perfectly dressed in a look I can only describe as "college freshman in a speakeasy": sweater vest, tweed cap, wire-rim glasses. He mentions that he looks for the "butch lesbian" styles of every era. I describe my own most recent look as "adventuress who gets killed second in an Agatha Christie murder mystery,"* and our conversation just flows from there. In terms of the living on this hunt, it's also just the two of us, since it's raining so hard that my friends who were going to drive up had to cancel, so we do a lot of talking as we wind our way through the hotel.

We start in the ballroom, which is decorated to look like a little

---

* Dietrich inspired, menswear-tailored for day, satin for evening, over-accessorized always, darling.

piece of Versailles in Baltimore; from there, he challenges me to find the entrance to the long-hidden speakeasy, which I manage pretty quickly from a small gap in the door. Once inside that hidden parlor, I don't see anyone or anything. I'm not a fan of this little room's TGI Fridays decor, but it's still pretty cool, and it lay hidden in plain sight until renovations in the early eighties reopened it. Louis is studying sociology and explains to me that a lot of cultures believe that restoring or redecorating these spaces stirs up ghosts, since their familiar spaces are being changed. I'll recall this about a week later as I'm talking to a contractor who's repairing my mom's house after some flood damage. He says his assistant hears strange noises and doesn't like to be there after dark, and later I'll think "Of course, that's my dad; you brought new tools into his space." My dad had been a mechanical engineer, orthopedist, and amateur Mr. Fixit in this life, and there was nothing he loved more than tools. He also liked to fix things around the house and, failing that, following tradesmen around to observe and learn. If there's a Summerland, I like to think he's still tinkering from the other side.

From the speakeasy, we move upstairs to another ballroom that's used for meetings and such, and Louis introduces me to the ghosts who live there. There's a boss man who observes people from the balcony and a vortex in a smaller room that is said to result from mirrors being placed directly across from each other. There's also a female apparition in old-timey formal wear who is known to float across the room toward the windows. She doesn't appear that night, but it allows Louis to raise an interesting point about specters and fashion. "Close your eyes and imagine your ghost outfit," he instructs. I take a deep breath and conjure my look: I'd like to haunt people in my fifties, one-shoulder, baby-blue sequin cocktail dress that made me feel like the glamorous weirdo I always wanted to be. Once I see it in my mind, he asks, "What shoes are you wearing?" I hadn't thought of any. That's a pretty universal answer, he informs me; when we picture ghosts, they almost never have feet. This is both convenient and fascinating, the former because I've largely given up on high heels and just the thought of wearing them for an eternity makes my lower back ache, the latter because this is another unit of cultural information that we've absorbed by osmosis.

The final stop on the tour is the most heartbreaking. The nineteenth floor is thought to be haunted by a little girl known as Molly who bounces a red rubber ball up and down the hallway; she also cries, runs, and touches people with her unseen little hands. She has allegedly been stuck there since her parents jumped from the roof with her in their arms after being wiped out in the Depression. Her particular spirit is noisy, and Louis explains that even the resonance of her ball sounds different from that of current ones, because it would have been made from actual rubber and not the lighter, synthetic materials we use now. I am suddenly, viscerally haunted by the thought of it. As a slow, chubby child who was hit by a lot of dodgeballs, just conjuring the soft, slightly metallic ping a red playground ball makes as it bounces off flesh makes my stomach drop. There is no play tonight, but I still get an overwhelming feeling of sadness thinking of poor little Molly, perpetually trapped in these rooms as a lonely child in a growing, changing world that has passed her by.

It passes quickly, partially because Louis does such a great job of spinning the whole tale and its historical context. He looks young, but he's not new at this; he had also been a beloved guide at the Edgar Allan Poe House not far from the hotel. He later tells me it all comes down to keeping a sense of humanity in the ghost stories. "I've been complimented on how I describe them in a very empathetic way. My favorite compliment I've ever gotten was 'that was the most pleasant story about suicide I've ever heard.'"[11] As a writer, I get what he means. Back in the lobby bar, we rejoin Vince, and they graciously let me pepper them with a million questions about ghosts and ghost hunting. He's written four books on the paranormal and done a load of TV documentaries, so he doesn't mind sharing his thoughts.

Vince estimates he has been involved in ghost hunting for over twenty-five years, and he's seen both the hunters and the hunting change. Without being a gatekeeper, a lot of what he says reminds me of some of my own complaints about the mainstreaming of subcultures, which amounts to the internet has both democratized and diluted some esoteric things. Back in the day, he joked, "If you wanted to learn about the ghost hunting, or the paranormal… you had to actually buy a book." About fifteen or twenty years ago, things started to change. He explained that "it really exploded after [TV shows like *Ghost Hunters*] started to become more and more popular." These shows are cheap to produce and popular, and perhaps most importantly, they changed the image of paranormal researchers from nerds to bros. Many of these shows seem to follow the same general format: dudes in designer T-shirts running through old buildings, screaming at the spirits. Save for the occasional psychic lady or bar owner, it's an almost entirely male space, and they don't seem to care much for history, folktales, or the bereaved. They frighten me, not because of the paranormal phenomena but because the whole thing seems like a frat party hazing ritual for the afterlife, and I'm always convinced one of the living is going to fall down a flight of rickety stairs and break their necks. They also largely remove the idea of a female medium as a sensitive conduit between the living and the dead and make contacting the other side of the veil a loud, extreme sport. This is no sedate parlor séance for the grieving; it's hunting in the dudely, manosphere sense.

Like fishing or golf, ghost hunting is a pursuit that attracts dudes who love gear. An infinite number of websites offer a whole slew of electronic equipment that you can drag along into abandoned asylums and old saloons. These gadgets are usually black and have a Death Star's worth of blinking lights and impressive-sounding names like the Flux 2 Responsive Device, Ovilus 5 Ghost Box, or the Phasm Light.* Vince encourages visitors to bring them along on the tour but also points out that "there's a juxtaposition that doesn't work out with a lot of these ghost hunting shows and groups, [with] the melding of pseudoscientific ideas with dogmatic ideologies from organized religion" and worries how this can affect how people go about the business of exploration. Not that it should discourage curious visitors from enjoying these trips, he said, adding, "more people should do it. I encourage every-one to go out and do that. It's a blast."[12] But pretty much anyone who wants to can declare themselves an "expert," and that lack of serious study invites trouble.

---

* No clue what they actually do, but they will run you up to $600.

This combination of scientific and psychic methods is not a new thing; the mediumship of Spiritualism has already been weighed and measured in a quest to quantify the presence of spirits. The early, fruitless experiments of Sir William Crookes did little to deter others who wanted to subject the paranormal to the scientific method on both sides of the Atlantic. Again, at the time, there was a section of scientists who sincerely believed that experimentation could reveal the mysteries of this world and the next, which wasn't that strange an idea given the wild leaps and bounds into the previously invisible worlds of electricity, microbes, and more. Psychical research, as it came to be known, would be formalized in the United Kingdom in 1882 at Cambridge by a group of scholars and scientists and would come to include such luminaries as physicist and radio pioneer Sir Oliver Lodge and Sherlock Holmes writer Sir Arthur Conan Doyle. Not to be outdone, Harvard started its own version in 1884 in the form of the American Society of Psychical Research (ASPR), founded by psychologist William James,* who had previously been a member of the British branch. Their VIP members would include the escapist Houdini and inventor Alexander Graham Bell. Naturally, the combination of scientific inquiry and paranormal phenomena was a hard sell from the beginning since science and faith had long been declared mortal enemies.

One concerned British citizen on #teamscience feared that any inquiry into the supernatural would plunge us back into the

---

* Spirits were also something of a family business for the Jameses. His father, Henry James Sr., was a Swedenborgian theologian, and his brother, the novelist Henry James Jr., wrote some of America's most influential ghost stories.

Middle Ages, writing to one magazine that "We shall have the jargon of pure science and the vocabulary of pure reason mixed with beliefs acceptable to nothing but the blindest credulity. Already the processed is far advanced... Yesterday it was spiritualism. Today we have the divining rod and psychical research. By the end of the nineteenth century there is a fair chance that we shall arrive at downright witchcraft, managed, of course, not by aid of the devil but by subtle and obscure powers, psychic magnetism resident in old women and black cats."[13] That response was a bit hysterical perhaps, but because the prosperity of the age was tied into the boom in invention and discovery, there was arguably a lot on the line. Oddly enough, the suspicion of women with cats (and if they're satanic) continues to plague us even into the moment's political discourse.

This criticism presents the conundrum in which paranormal investigation has always operated. Because good science demands tangible, repeatable proof, anything dealing with the mystical was already suspect. Conversely, it must be remembered that science is also a field that's ever evolving. Over the years, some theories advance, and some fall by the wayside upon examination. Take, for example, the then popular and *serious* field of phrenology, which used careful study of the bumps and ridges of the skull to determine intelligence and temperament. To phrenologists, psychical research was folly when compared to the important work of skull fondling. Writing in their monthly magazine, one specialist wondered, "Why should so many of our scientific men look askance when the term spiritualism is mentioned, and treat any that may be asked concerning it with contempt? The very fact that a million people in this country believe more or less in spirit phenomena should compel some attention to them, and the grounds of belief should be investigated until conclusions are reached that shall settle our uncertainty as to whether there is a basis of the supernatural in the phenomena, or prove that trickery, imposture, human credulity, physical and mental conditions, hysteria, insanity, etc., have woven the fabric of an extended and powerful delusion."[14] In short, anyone dealing with Spiritualism as a serious line of inquiry needed their head examined in a very literal sense.

Oddly enough, while phrenology has been put on the same dusty shelf as electric belts and radium water,* psychical research would be attached to a field that would grow and endure— psychology. Championed by some of the first generation of doctors to explore the workings of the mind as an organic process, psychical research was not exactly a dead end (so to speak). As members of a fledgling branch of scientific inquiry, these men and women were observing human behavior in a new way. It was a shaky beginning for both disciplines, but it was a start. Initially, the ASPR would do a lot of debunking as the more obvious physical mediums were easily found and exposed, but their work would and does continue with some findings that pose more questions than answers.

Among those thousands of people and circumstances studied by the members of the ASPR, Leonora Piper is perhaps the most intriguing and (to them) enduring in the sphere of mediumship. James would often refer to her as a "white crow," meaning that if

---

* Absolutely real Victorian-era consumer items.

you make the claim "not all crows are black," you only have to produce one white one to make your case.

Born and married into a humble family, Piper had already established herself as *the* medium to Boston's elite when Lodge, James, and company set out to study her abilities. While she did commune with the dead, she hedged when it came to embracing the label of Spiritualist, preferring instead to indicate that her gifts came without that specific form of cultivation. For what it was worth, her gifts apparently confounded her too, as she told a reporter, "I have read the report of my trances and, even though they have continued for fifteen years almost daily, I am just as astonished now as when they began."[15] For their part, scientists were impressed with her from the beginning and would devote fifteen years, scores of sittings, and several different scientists to observing her. Part of what was so intriguing about her trance readings was the fact that she eschewed the showy and easily disproved "physical mediumship" and still often managed to convey accurate, specific information that couldn't be readily guessed at. James himself said that "Mrs. Piper's trance memory is no ordinary human memory, and we have to explain its singular perfection as the natural endowment of her solitary subliminal self, or as a collection of distinct memory systems each with a 'spirit' as its vehicle. The choice obviously cannot be made offhand. If I may be allowed a personal expression of opinion at the end of this notice, I would say that the Piper phenomena are some of the most baffling I know."[16]

At a certain point, all this observation and analysis may have begun to have an impact on Piper's skills, whatever they were. Whether the strength of her gift was weakening or she just wanted to be able to practice her craft without a bunch of Harvard nerds clocking her every move can't be said definitively, but on October 20, 1901, she announced in The *New York Herald* that "After having given so many years of my life to this pursuit, I now desire to become a free agent, and devote myself and my time to more congenial pursuits."[17] Further, she decided that she was not a Spiritualist but instead believed that her messages came as a result of telepathy. This was bad news for ASPR member and examiner Richard Hodgson, who was a great believer in her powers; perhaps a little too great as his need to observe her began to border on the obsessive. The fandom wasn't mutual, since in trying to keep from tainting her séances with his own information, he was practically silent with her, which she considered "brusque." Conversely, he was so enamored of her work that he declared himself a former skeptic turned Spiritualist and refused to even accept her resignation, figuring that it had come in a "moment of depression"[18] and that she would be back at the tables soon enough. She countered in the papers that no, she meant it, and "This time, however, my decision is final. I shall stand by it and die if necessary."[19] Turns out he was right, because just a few days later on October 29, 1901, she reconciled with the ASPR and its members, and as The *New York Times* noted, "Mrs. Piper will continue her sittings according to agreement, and the relations that had existed between her and the society will not be broken."[20]

The members of the ASPR were more correct than they could ever know. In fact, Piper and Hodgson's struggle for control of

Piper's readings would endure even in death. In 1905, Hodgson would succumb to a heart attack during a game of handball not long after he began to appear as one of her "imperators," or controlling spirits. "William James collated 69 of these sittings and analyzed them in a 120-page paper published in the SPR Proceedings of 1909.* The record shows an excited, brief and largely incoherent first appearance quickly becoming more articulate in later appearances, carrying a strong indication of Hodgson's mannerism and character. James notes that the robust 'animal spirits' that were characteristic of the living Hodgson—his love of argument, chaff, repartee, his frequent laughter, and his unusual habit of quoting poetry at every opportunity—were very much in evidence, although they became stereotyped as time passed."[21]

Whatever the scope of Piper's powers or what form they came to her in, the ASPR remains certain of her legitimacy over a hundred years later. When I recently interviewed Patrice Keane, the current executive director of the organization, about the ASPR's background and current mission, she explained that while the organization isn't attached to Spiritualism, "William James worked with a very famous medium, Mrs. Piper, whom he felt was not a fraud, and who seemed to have some sort of ability to get information across distances." The goal was, as she puts it, to "take ESP out of the séance room and into a laboratory. Of course, when you do that, you know, other things are sacrificed, because there is

---

* As they say in academia, "publish or perish." Impressively, Hodgson was the rare exception who somehow managed both and in the opposite order.

performance art; there is the whole mood of people working in a group together, like what happens when people get excited about anticipating something."[22] This makes sense, since daylight ghost tours are a lot less fun.

Still, the ASPR has persisted in its mission for over one hundred years, although it focuses less on mediumship now and more on things like defining consciousness, determining whether shamanistic healing actually brings about change or if it's all placebo effect, and examining other outwardly unexplainable experiences. The group is hardly mainstream now, but in some ways, science has caught up with it, as Keane explained that even what is considered an acceptable measurement has changed, saying

"The way science has changed around us is quite interesting too because this whole idea of repeatability is just not the trend anymore. We don't judge phenomena in the world as real or not real because of its repeatability."

Keane is particularly interested in the way quantum physics is adjusting its field to a less repeatable standard. "If you look at what's happening with these gravitational waves from space, the fact that they found them once, twice, over billions of dollars' worth of research and decades of observation, just because certain phenomena are unique and happen rarely, it no longer can be the scale for judging authenticity... Over time, will you see it once, will you see it twice, will you see it every day? Will you see it once in a lifetime or once in a thousand years? There are different things that we know that are extraordinary phenomena."

Adding that paranormal investigation might not be as incompatible with science as some have suggested, she said, "I like to look at it in a global context. If we're interested, as William James was, because he was a really big thinker, in the whole idea of what is the cutting edge of science. What is this, that? We're going to observe and understand different phenomena in whatever time we live in, and science should be the tool with which we observe the world, but we can't get into defining it in a way that is too lost in dogma, because our interpretation of the world around us is constantly changing, because we learn more about science." I will come back to this idea again and again as I balance my own thoughts on both tolerating a certain amount of the miraculous in our lives and the real need for vaccines, well-informed public policy, fact-based journalism, and so on. I can also be glad my interest in these unknowable things will not get me locked away or labeled as "hysterical" or "satanic."

The basic takeaway from that (and everything else I will come across in writing this book) is that learning is fun and grief is deep. Back in the "Bawlmore" hotel room that smells like a robot funeral with all its artificial flowers, I'll fall asleep watching *Forensic Files* and thinking about ghost shoes and whether there's going to be some sort of specter after-party in my room that night for every soul I missed on my earlier tour. I kind of hope not, because I have an early brunch with local friends and need to sleep. Sadly, on this trip, I won't have time for the 7-Eleven that's on the spot where the second Ouija board factory stood (and its "self-proclaimed creator" died) or Poe's grave or the giant Divine statue, because there are just not enough hours in the day. Also, a few months after I leave, John Kozik will open another Witch Board Museum in Fell's Point, but for now, I have to just promise myself that in the future, I'll come back for that and lessons in séance magic with Vince Wilson. I sometimes leave a place feeling that there's still so much to unpack, but I'm only here for one night and still have a lot of traveling to do.

HAIR APPARENT

—◦◦◦◦◦—

STRANDS OF THE PAST, TRENDS OF THE PRESENT

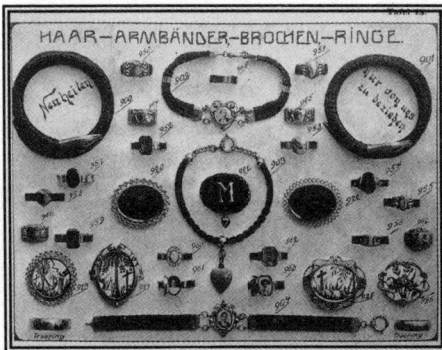

Advertisement for German mourning
jewelry circa 1900.

Recently, my mother had people over for Passover for the first time in ages. She's a great cook and maintains a number of friends, but understandably as a widow, she just doesn't feel like entertaining as much. My folks were a team in all things, and I think the thought of prepping, serving, amusing guests, and then cleaning up without my dad breaks her heart all over again. It was kind of their thing, and those kinds of activities and objects can open the little pockets in your mind where the deepest grief hides. I understand the feeling. While pulling out cloth napkins for the table, I came across a mismatched one with a couple of his hairs stuck in the folds. He must have ironed them and put them away without noticing. My heart just dropped at the recognition; hair is so primal, so personal. It is part of a person, then it's not.

As I took a moment to stare at the two cottony white strands, I had a vivid, tangible memory of petting his head. It was my usual greeting when I entered their apartment and found him working at the dining room table, where he would joke "arf" or "don't pet my bald spot." It was our thing. I wondered if I should do something with the hairs. They seemed really important for a second. They were so fragile, so ephemeral—how would I even save two human hairs for later use? It was too little to save, too precious to throw away, too much to think about when we had guests coming. I think I just put them in a drawer and went back to setting the table.

Hair has long been intertwined with death. Some Native

Americans cut it off as a sign of loss and a fresh start, some Orthodox Jewish men grow it long during the mourning period,* and the Victorians turned their loved ones' strands into a fashion statement. Hairwork has its roots† in the European tradition of memento mori, which means "remember that you too will die" in Latin. It predates Christianity, but the Catholic church would pick up on the decorative possibilities throughout the Middle Ages and encourage artisans to splash skulls, hourglasses, and wilting flowers across all manner of funerary goods and architecture. It was at first pointed but impersonal, not the grieving of a personal loss but an admonition that this life is fleeting and damnation or salvation is the real main attraction, so you better get ready for it. So much so that a common epitaph read "Remember me as you pass by/As you are now, so once was I/As I am now, so you must be/Prepare for death and follow me."

Sometime in the Georgian era, the English of the upper classes began to translate these notions into tasteful and expensive jewelry that featured skulls and coffins in diamonds, gold fittings, and black enamel. The Industrial Revolution of the nineteenth century would take these trinkets from couture to mass market in the same way it democratized a lot of other consumer goods, namely by finding ways to produce them somewhat faster and by advertising them as a celebrity must-have. Queen Victoria probably did more

---

* Jewish men in mourning are supposed to grow their hair until a friend reminds them to cut it three months later. No idea what you do if your friend forgets this little task.

† Not all hairwork was from the deceased. Lockets of hair were a popular keepsake in the days before (and after) photographs, and hair was also used for jewelry, framed pictures, family trees, and other objects given to loved ones and family members.

for a basic black wardrobe than any fashion house before or since when she entered forty years of deep mourning in 1861 with the death of her beloved Prince Albert. She also began to wear lockets and other accessories containing his hair and presented elaborate bracelets of her own hair to honored visitors. The practice would soon catch on with her subjects, who could afford similar objects more easily than any of the other crown jewels.

If you wanted your own hair bauble, you had a number of options: you could order one from a jeweler, send the hair you'd collected to a service that braided and mounted it for you, or buy an inexpensive premade locket and do it yourself. Additionally, because hair is both unique to each person and readily available, hairwork was an ideal do-it-yourself project for women, like knitting or scrapbooking. People today find it a little gross, but at a time when death was a little more domestic and far more frequent and mourning rituals fell largely under the label of women's work, crafters on both sides of the Atlantic really took to it. In fact, they went a little nuts with it, according to my friend, oddities dealer Evan Michaelson, who has spent years collecting and restoring various hair objects. In her research, she learned that an entire tea and coffee service decorated with hair and a hair-embroidered royal portrait were created for the Crystal Palace Exhibition of 1851. Creations like those are wild and collectible, but they're super rare, since people usually went for more everyday items like bracelets, rings, and watch chains. Though when I interviewed Evan years ago, she admitted there was something that felt subversive about collecting hairwork in the current era, saying, "I think part of the reason people are fascinated by it is that it does repulse on a certain level. It's powerfully charged, because hair really affects people on this visceral level."[1]

If this all seems a little morbid and over the top, it's important to remember that the act of mourning was a very formal, familiar process for Victorian-era Americans of the middle class and above. Women's grief was also regimented by obligation, status, and social isolation. Black-edged cards were to be sent to everyone who had sent condolences, the house had to be draped in black bunting, the clocks were stopped, and time was spent alone or with family at home. Widows were expected to do the most mourning, including spending anywhere from two years* to the rest of their lives in deep mourning, which was marked by wearing a dull,† all-black wardrobe in public with very little or no ornamentation. Once you completed that level, you could go on to ordinary or second mourning, where you could have different fabrics and a few black sparkles. Next up was half mourning, where you could add purple, gray, and black-and-white patterns to your wardrobe.

Additionally, where you went, how you behaved, and what you could do were carefully monitored. It was propriety, but it was also sort of a lifestyle. An 1893 article titled "The Fashion of Grief: Mourning Garb Is the Calm Retreat for Fashion's Slaves" snickered at the idea of women opting for all-black wardrobes as a way of saving on dresses and avoiding social obligations. "We have laughed appreciatively over her gruesome trick and concluded that

---

* The rules for men were completely different: they got three to six months for a wife and then could go back to business as usual.

† Literally without any shine to the fabric. Silks and satins were discouraged, and matte crepe or taffeta was thought more appropriate.

we would attend the funeral of some distant relatives of our own with diluted woe if we could save money by it, too."[2] Of course, once something becomes a trend (especially among women), social critics invariably cluck about conceit and emptiness. One British writer warned about dressing the part: "Respect for the memory of the dead is a holy and pure feeling, always to be encouraged; but a conventional mourning, that varies with every whim of fashion, is a weak and wicked vanity."[3]

Of course, women didn't see it that way. In corners of the press that were specifically aimed at women, writers defended both the right of those experiencing loss to be seen in black and the punishing nature of meeting the strict demands that were placed on them.

There is always something touching and exceedingly sorrowful in orphanhood; and mourning, if ever, is then an appropriate emblem. A widow finds in it the shelter, and accordance with her loneliness, which she naturally seeks. For near kindred, the heart often seeks this outward type of loss, and we quarrel with the fashion, not the custom of mourning; even though this has, until of late, been too arbitrary for those whose means would not allow the expense into making it at a time when money can least be spared... We quarrel with the fashion, which judges mourning by the depth of the fold...that modifies shades according to weeks or months, not softened feeling.[4]

Like running a household, raising children, and being a wife, how to grieve properly was one of those things that women were just expected to have covertly mastered sometime between birth and their wedding night. Except loss doesn't work like setting a table with the right forks or knowing when it's okay to wear white shoes. It's complicated and personal and does not follow a calendar.

This everyday familiarity with death and its rules was probably a boon to Spiritualism. If six months of mourning the loss of a beloved child were somehow not enough, where could you turn? Medicine was not up to the task, therapy wasn't a thing, and talking to others about your misery was considered rude and burdensome. You could appear in black in your rare public outings, so you were appropriately marked, but behind closed doors and even in the company of loved ones, you were very much alone in your pain. For all its foibles, Spiritualism's goal of creating a conduit between the living and the dead may have provided some much-needed relief for those who wanted it the most.

Whatever the form, mediumship and ritualized grieving have always been a way of making sense of the world that has stopped making sense. So where are these things now? My working theory was that we are in a place similar to the late nineteenth century in terms of societal change, mass death, and adapting to technology. Turns out they're both everywhere and nowhere. We're a less religious, less formal nation than ever before, so we've given up many of the visible trappings of mourning, and while I'm not advocating for a return to veils and social isolation, I think there need to be more options for wearing your grief on your sleeve (literally or figuratively), and science agrees. In discussing the "long tail" of COVID grief, Sarah Wagner, a social anthropologist at The George Washington University studying the rituals that people created in the void of the pandemic, explains that it's what we don't talk about that haunts us. "We're enveloped in this silence around pandemic death. I think there's a willingness to talk about the pandemic losses in other realms, the economic losses or the loss of social connection. Why is there this silence around 1.2 million deaths—the enormity of the tragedy?"[5]

This is, of course, on my mind a lot and central to this book. At the height of the pandemic, MSNBC ran a literal body count the way they used to run a stock ticker. At some point—without any fanfare—it just disappeared along with warnings about wearing masks, conversations about sourdough starter, and applauding nurses. I could have missed it, but no one seemed to be talking about it. As I've said, though, I have some goth tendencies and have always spent a lot of time contemplating these things. In the last few years, that has mainly consisted of relistening to a lot of early British death rock bands[*] and a tangential involvement in the Order of the Good Death. Founded by author and funeral director Caitlin Doughty and other death care professionals, its stated mission is "about making death a part of your life. That means committing to staring down your death fears— whether it be your own death, the death of those you love, the pain of dying, the afterlife (or lack thereof), grief, corpses, bodily decomposition, or all of the above. Accepting that death itself is natural, but the death anxiety and terror of modern culture are not."[6] These are great ideas, and I definitely think everyone should explore them, but they only go so far when we're waylaid by our own personal grief.

---

[*] It is my considered opinion that Siouxsie, Bauhaus, and The Damned still slap.

On the bright side, the organization has given me a great network of death professionals to draw on when I have big cultural discourse questions. There are, of course, professors who study how society handles dying, death, grief, and mourning, and they're struggling with these questions too. Part of it is just that we're demographically a very different society than we were in the Victorian era. We're more diverse and less religious, so the outward trappings and rituals that have traditionally marked a period of mourning have gone the way of the corset and the buggy whip. Professor Jillian Tullis adds that it's also political in a weird way, coming from the bizarre, conservative notion that Americans should practice "rugged individualism" in all things. As she explains it, "there's lots of people acting like it's their own individual right to not wear a mask, to not get vaccinated... How do we get those people to acknowledge somebody else's grief?"[7]

Another major change is how many layers stand between us and the realities of death and dying. Thanks to advances in medicine, people live longer, which is great, but they also tend to die in medical and elder care facilities rather than at home, which takes us away from some of the grimmer realities of decay and death and deprives us in some measure of the letting-go element of losing someone. COVID, with its enforced isolation, only expanded this, which allowed a lot of people to keep an "out of sight, out of mind" attitude toward the whole thing. Rather than being faced with death and finding a way to exorcise our reactions, we simply shelved it, largely because we could. Tullis agrees and was a little surprised at the reaction as well. She recalled, "I can remember somebody asking me when COVID was happening, somebody who knows what I study, asking me if I had noticed any changes—like if suddenly people were more death positive, and I said I haven't seen evidence of it. It would be one thing if lawyers said their phones are ringing off the hook, because people were putting their affairs in order, and notaries couldn't keep up signing powers of attorney, and I just am not seeing that kind of sea change, where people are like, 'oh, we got to, we got to get it together.'" She finds this "a bit mystifying, because I also heard, I also heard a statistic that for every death, there are at least ten grievers."

Professor John Troyer, who teaches at the Centre for Death and Society in Bath, England (one of if not the only programs of its kind in the world), has also observed this and adds a historical view. He believes that the ability to compartmentalize mass death is not a new phenomenon, particularly when it comes to loss due to disease. As he points out, there are almost no public memorials to the losses of the 1918 influenza pandemic. He said, "it's kind of an open question as to what kind of memorial will happen, [and] there's lots of different reasons. Partly, I think, is out of exhaustion, and I think there can also be a kind of survivor's guilt about it. 'Like, you know, I made it, and other people didn't.'"[8]

In my own lifetime, I've lived through a number of mass death events, including ones I had a direct connection to, like the AIDS crisis and 9/11. Those were handled very differently in terms of mourning as a collective activity. As Troyer sees it, "I think what has been lacking or what hasn't been as present as you might expect has been real activism around trying to create a memorial, [like] the memorializing of everyone who died of AIDS. You haven't seen that level of activism in part because it's different; different, different constituents, different groups, and it's…I think that's part of it. I think without any question, it just hasn't taken shape, because I think there hasn't been the will to get it going, which isn't a failure. I think it's just I see it as more kind of just sort of exhaustion."

Further, while we might have to exercise some patience when it comes to society-wide remembrance, personal rituals are already here. They just look different from the customs of the past. They may be smaller and more casual than heaps of black draping and rigid ceremony. According to Troyer, "I think we just do it different ways." Expanding on memorials we'd developed ourselves that involved eating, he mused, "I think going to like a favorite restaurant becomes one of those ways to do it. But also, because going to a restaurant can seem so common, it wouldn't necessarily stand out to anyone as being a kind of ritual. But I think now, a lot of the mourning rituals have become practices have become perhaps, [while] they're still public, but I think they've become a lot more private too." A lot of the way we express our sorrow, how publicly we go through unwinding the knots of our sadness and nostalgia, is a by-product of our age. As Tullis put it, "I think it's also very generational. It's layers upon layers and it's different for whatever your layers are. I also remember reading a *Time* magazine article that was like, Baby Boomers are going to change dying and death." And while she's a bit skeptical that that has happened, it seems plausible to her that younger generations, who are generally more open about their lives and familiar with the elements of mental health, might have some new ideas.

Troyer is particularly fascinated by memorial tattoos (and has several of his own)* and can often spot them on others. He noted, "I've actually gotten pretty good at spotting a memorial tattoo, even if it just looks like an innocuous tattoo. Sometimes I'll ask someone, sometimes I won't. It has to be physically visible, on their arm or something. Sometimes I'll ask, 'is that a tattoo for someone who died?' And they'll be like, 'yeah, how'd you know that?' And I'll say, 'it just looked like it might be something you'd spend some time to get done.'" This may not be such a radical thing now, since according to a 2023 Pew Research poll, 32 percent[9] of all Americans now have at least one tattoo. This trend has also come around to some of the same basic ideas that prompted the hair jewelry craze, namely that primal desire to keep a piece of a loved one with us forever. In tattooing, this keepsake takes form in the ink. Even a cursory Google search will turn up a number of companies that offer ink made from cremated remains, with names like Your Angel's Ink, Engrave Ink, and Cremation Ink.

If that feels too intense for you, other facets of the self-care industry are trying to include ritual and recognition in their service offerings. Perhaps not surprisingly, hairdressing is one of them. I spoke recently with several different beauty professionals about changes they're bringing to salons based on their own experiences as people and practitioners.

For Andi Scarbrough, whose company Crownworks's stated

---

* I've considered memorial tattoos myself but have always rejected them for religious reasons. I'm not that observant, but I did grow up around a lot of Holocaust survivors, and that puts a different frame on it. Also, being the untattooed lady in the sideshow world makes me something of a novelty these days.

goal is "bringing ceremony back into their beauty ritual," one of her first realizations was that hairdressers themselves have a high degree of professional burnout. This makes sense when you consider that their livelihood often requires them to possess both the necessary technical wizardry to care for hair and the warm patience of a therapist, confessor, and bartender all rolled into one body. So why not add medium or healer to that skill set? As a former high-end stylist herself, Scarbrough learned these lessons both "behind the chair but also working for manufacturers and education and product development and salon management…Overall, what I learned was that there's a whole lot more happening there than just a haircut and the interpersonal aspect of the work and what that role both historically and in the modern age has served. Communally it's really powerful, and so looking at where that [idea was] showing up for me and what I was observing in the classrooms."[10]

In modern times, it's become a strangely intimate relationship with a service professional and one that we tend not to have with the servers at our favorite restaurants or dry cleaners or others we see often and could know some touchy stuff about our lives. Perhaps it's the time, the setting, or the physical contact, but whatever the reason, hairdressers tend to get a lot of intimate information and help guide us through life changes, which, when you think about it, is not unlike the position that the medium once held. My own beloved hairdresser, Sue, has been with me through several hair colors, a friend breakup (I kept her in the split), the death of a parent, a bunch of career changes, a number of presidential elections, and the retirement of my mom's hairdresser, and she has smartly talked me out of bangs* on more than one occasion. As one article on the depth of the relationship explains it, "88 percent of women say it's important to have a personal rapport with their stylists, according to the Professional Beauty Association. Clients tend to expect—even demand—a relationship with their stylist that rivals one they might have with a significant other."[11]

As Austin, Texas–based energy healer and hairstylist Ashleah Walker of Becoming Ceremony puts it, hairdressing is one field that can't be replaced by a digital interface. We go there to keep up appearances, but it's also a very human interaction in a world where we can have fewer and fewer of those. She noted, "We have such a fast-paced digital age and people, then I'm making you sit your ass down in my chair for like an hour minimum, and that's maybe the first fucking time that you've had to sit still all day and like you cannot go anywhere else… So then all of a sudden, it's like a release."[12] From there, people feel easy about opening up. Plus, that moment when you're ready to walk out again is a moment of powerful transformation, which is part of the reason she's lasted in the business. Walker explained, "I actually really loved the way that a person would feel when they left my chair; they felt energetically lighter. They left brighter." So getting something like highlights and a chakra alignment at the same time may not be as weird an idea as it seems at first.

Like the earlier debate over women's mourning dress, Scarbrough also believes what seems like "wicked vanity" from the outside is

---

* For context, I have insanely thick hair. Not a brag; it's a lot of work for both of us. For example, Sue has swept up after a cut and looked down at the pile and said, "It looks like someone stepped on a Wookiee."

actually a part of the greater good for people as individuals. "It's so trite, right?" she said. "But it all begins with self-care. The space I hold for somebody else is only going to be as much as I hold for myself. So keeping myself in my own practices of inward reflection and accountability, energetic clearing, energetic hygiene, if you will, is first and foremost." Industry-wise, that can go into everything from the shampoo sinks to waiting area in salons, "setting up an environment that really has the resources, the spaciousness in timing, the atmosphere, the kinds of care that we take, and then over the years, finding what of those modalities work well inside the traditional salon experience, and elements of sound healing, tuning forks, and singing bowls play really well. Breath, of course, is a practice that integrates really well." Walker offers healings to both stylists who are beginning to burn out and clients who are seeking something beyond a change to their outside. She also views the salon as an open space, because "there is a lot of magic in that, so we're still growing pop-up events, more community events, like having tarot readers, astrologists, and sound bath healers. All sorts of stuff there to bring people together, because at the end of the day, we are tribal."

While this seems healthy and fun, of course, to my way of thinking, there's a dark flipside to this as well. As someone who's been on the inside of the beauty industry for years myself, I feel that while self-care is good and necessary for people of all ages and genders, it can also be a messenger of our obsession with youth. In the same way we're now grossed out by hair jewelry, we've become a society that has almost no place for the reality of dying. More than ever, we refuse to even age; we inject Botox, we eat "clean," we demand that our models and movie stars stop time. Moreover, since more Americans die in hospitals than at home, when that moment does come, we can whisk the body away to a funeral home where professionals make our loved ones look as "natural" as they can or to a crematorium where their remains are reduced to ash behind closed doors. How can we deal with grief if we don't quite believe we can die? Maybe it's time to revisit some of the things we don't want to handle, like hair. As Scarbrough pointed out, "I think the difference between Western culture and many other parts of the world is this orientation to a real aversion to acknowledging mortality and permanence in that way. So as a result, we want to quickly get our roots retouched and never see the gray hair. We want to quickly move on from this, and as soon as the cut toenails or cut hair or whatever it is is off our body, literally the second it becomes separate from us, there is repulsion and aversion and not wanting to look at this thing that is death and decay and the rest of the story, because we are so ourselves disconnected from the preciousness that that creates."

Maybe integrating some different practices will reopen our interest in hair as a totem. Industry consultant Colleen McCann, who refers to her role working with beauty professionals and individuals as "energy stylist," encourages people to create their own rituals out of the act of cutting their hair. She said, "I invite clients to take some cut hair pieces and we'll discuss some different kinds of offerings they can make with it, whether it's in their garden for the birds or just acknowledging that it carries energy."[13] While the industry and some of its clients may be more open to different possibilities, I wouldn't hold my breath for a Supercuts 'n' Spirit Messages combo anytime soon.

As Americans, we spend billions on our hair every year for any number of reasons, whether it's ambition, grooming, or "rugged individualism." It defines how we see ourselves and how we want the world to see us. Spiritualists understood this and the intrinsic power it held. In just one 1871 issue of the *Banner of Light* alongside ads for "Magnetic Paper" and the "Planchette Song," half a dozen or so mediums promised everything from "Soul Reading" to "the gift of healing" if interested parties would send one dollar and a lock of hair to the address below. With that cutting and two three-cent stamps, Mrs. A. B. Severance promised that "a lock of hair will give an accurate description of their leading traits of character and peculiarities of disposition."[14] Sitting with that tangible, fragile piece of a person, she and other mediums in cities across America tried to offer answers to the medical mysteries that had stumped the professionals, consolation for loss, or insights into the worries that kept people up at night—life's pains salved and its truths revealed across the miles, often for those still in the deepest pangs of mourning. In the current moment, it's unlikely that we'll ever return to a time when we make elaborate, even ostentatious displays of grief, but now is a good time to reexamine how—and if—we're dealing with it all. We and our loved ones are not going to live forever, and whether we ink that fact into our skins or create little, everyday rituals to reframe the things we've lost and gained over the years, maybe we need to reconnect with these facts in our own way and not just bluster bravely forward as a nation. As someone who's living with grief and fighting my grays, I might like a weird little return to my roots.

ALTERNATIVE CRACKS

MEDICINE, MAGNETIC HEALING, AND THE WAR FOR OUR HEALTH

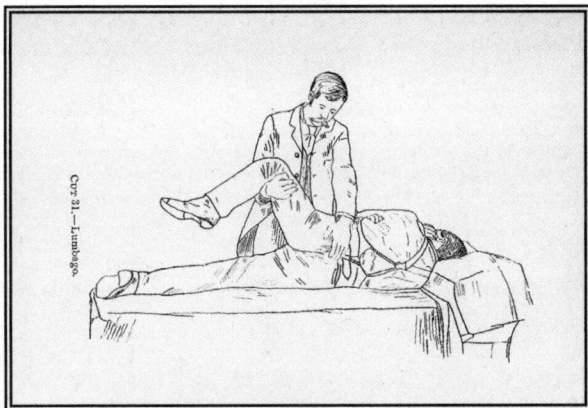

Osteopathic illustration of a spinal
adjustment circa 1898.

> "There's always a market
> for the occult."

JAMES STEWART,
IN *BELL, BOOK, AND CANDLE*

J ust before I started writing this book, I began a pretty steady yoga practice. I'm neither a sporty nor a woo-woo person, but I found that yoga is a perfect practice for me. It's good exercise, it stretches out the old joints, and it helps me unwind. I do sometimes worry for the peace of the yogis on the mats next to mine, since at this point in my life, my joints crack like a bag of potato chips being kicked down a flight of stairs. In addition to the muscle building, if my thoughts are still a little busy, the "mindful rest" of shavasana also gives me a moment to rest quietly and think about the many connections between the creaky noises a body makes and the long-term impact Spiritualism has had on American popular and material culture. Sure, we have the alleged magical feet of the Fox Sisters, but there's also the lasting modality of chiropractic.

In addition to mediumship, one of the main focuses of Spiritualism was and is physical healing. Often referred to as "magnetic healing," it's rooted in Franz Mesmer's earlier work in animal magnetism, in which practitioners manipulate rogue energy waves in the body to cure an afflicted person's ailments (according to his theory anyway). Later magnetic healers used trances, aura readings, Ouija boards, hair clippings, and a number of other methods to diagnose and treat every ailment known to humankind, with varying degrees of success. As I mentioned before, I had a psychic healing in Lily Dale with surprisingly potent, if temporary, results. So I'm fully willing to believe that these practices can provide a powerful dose of the placebo effect or create a needed space for our mental health, which is sometimes just the boost a person needs when a cure or an accurate diagnosis is not an immediate option, and that the mind-body connection has yet to be fully explored. And then there's chiropractic.

While I cut complementary treatments a pretty wide berth as part of a care program, I have nothing but side-eye for "spinal manipulation" as a treatment for the vast majority of human diseases and disorders.* As I mentioned, I'm the daughter of an orthopedist (and the sister of a physiatrist), which means that *chiropractor* was a dirty word in our household. It was dismissed as less than useless, possibly dangerous, and not a part of any legitimate treatment. Turns out this distaste is not just the AMA party line; it has a lot of bases in fact beyond just the oddity of chiropractors' Summerland origins. The practice of spinal manipulation did not begin in a hospital or a clinic or a laboratory or even with someone who had a solid background in medicine. It began with magnetic healer and former beekeeper Daniel David (or D. D.) Palmer.

According to his posthumously published 1914 memoirs, the details of the practice of chiropractic came to him via séance visits with the spirit of a deceased doctor. "The knowledge and philosophy given me by Dr. Jim Atkinson, an intelligent spiritual being,

---

* While Palmer didn't directly acknowledge it as an influence, osteopathy was already integrating spinal manipulation into its treatment practice. However, osteopaths also receive a comprehensive, classic medical education of gross anatomy, residency, etc., so it's "in addition to" rather than the central focus of their practice.

together with explanations of phenomena, principles resolved from causes, effects, powers, laws, and utility, appealed to my reason. The method by which I obtained an explanation of certain physical phenomena, from an intelligence in the spiritual world, is known in biblical language as inspiration."[1] To be clear, I'm not knocking divine inspiration. Great ideas come from all sorts of places. Heck, I do some of my best brain work in showers and during naps and corpse pose myself. The main issue here is that unlike theoretical physics or pop nonfiction, medicine is a "put up or shut up" field, and Palmer was basically proposing a form of faith with office hours. Further, he went on to state that when he says "religion," he doesn't exactly mean it in the same sense of a holy space with bingo and Christmas pageants. He also said, "Those who have a knowledge of, or a belief in, a future state of existence, regardless of church or creed, can become believers in and practitioners of, the religion OF chiropractors."[2] In some ways, I can't argue with this, because some of the central tenets of the practice have to be taken on faith alone rather than lab results.

I'm not saying traditional medicine is by any means perfect. The history of modern health care is littered with some flaming car wrecks of moral failure, indifferent practice, and cruel treatments, but the general guiding idea is that you learn and get better. Chiropractic was founded with a singular idea—manipulating the spine can fix everything—and it has basically stuck to that despite all evidence to the contrary. Furthermore, because vaccines upset his theories on the spine as central to disease, Palmer was an early vaccine denier, and he wasn't particularly keen on germ theory, and both were beginning to radically transform the life expectancy of Americans when he gave his first "adjustment" in 1895.* The pushback from the medical mainstream came not long after the practice began to catch on and expand. For example, in an editorial aimed at the medical trade in 1905, one doctor snippily compared Palmer's methods to that of osteopathy and not favorably, stating that since "they are both destined to be poured down the same sewer-hole, it is perhaps superfluous to raise an issue on this. Nevertheless, [Palmer] says in speaking of the bacilli, which are reputed in non-chiropractic to be the cause of diphtheria, that they are the result of dead matter, like 'the mold found on decaying cheese.'"[3] Despite that doctor's wishes, all three disciplines have proven non-flushable, with doctors of osteopathy[†] being recognized as a branch of traditional medicine that includes some spinal manipulation where it's appropriate and chiropractic continuing its outsider status.

The same year, the war between chiropractors and doctors would also end up in the hands of lawyers when practitioner Thomas H. Storey proved himself to be a menace to the lives and limbs of the citizens of Southern California. Storey was a big fish in the growing pond of chiropractic; he had been an early acolyte of Palmer's, had graduated from his mentor's school, and invented the bifid hole table, which is the examining table with an

---

* How this healing came about varies by the story's teller, but the basics are that in 1895, Palmer came across a janitor named Henry Lillard who had hearing loss or partial healing loss, manipulated his back or neck, and alleviated his deafness. Lillard's daughter says the adjustment actually came from Palmer slapping him on the back while telling a joke (assuming he had some hearing in this version of the story). Either way, resolving back injury can't cure deafness.

† Doctors of osteopathy are all in on germs and viruses these days.

opening for the patient's face.* He didn't exactly bring glory to his chosen field. He was arrested the first time after his patient James Reichsteiner† became paralyzed and died after what Storey said was "an examination."[4] Reichsteiner had a different recollection of events and testified from his deathbed that "he hit me hard in the back of my neck. Then I fell over senseless."[5] Ultimately, Storey escaped manslaughter charges because it couldn't be proven that Reichsteiner's injuries weren't a result of his initial accident that had brought him into Storey's office in the first place. He was, however, fined $500 for practicing medicine without a license and released on bail. In his defense, Storey claimed he not only had gone to medical school but also "is a graduate of McGill University and *twelve*‡ other medical colleges."[6] In the months that followed, Storey was somehow still treating patients, and you can pretty much guess what happens next.

The headlines described the situation as "Takes Mallet Cure, Dies within the Hour." This time, the patient was Domenick Premus, who came in with some kidney issues and left behind a wife. The press painted a pretty dramatic picture of Storey's treatment methods, in which Premus's "widow declares Storey tortured the sick man by inserting a heavy wooden drill between the vertebrae and pounding it with a heavy mallet; that doctor

---

* Before that innovation, spinal manipulation often ended in nosebleed.

† A note on their surnames: the contemporary papers list the chiropractor as both Storey and Story and the patient as Richsteiner and Reichsteiner. I went with the most frequently used versions.

‡ Emphasis mine, because these days, that constitutes at least forty-eight years of study not including residency.

placed his hands on the spine and jumped up and down."[7] With legal trouble on the horizon again and a warrant out for his arrest, Storey decided it would be a good time to visit Mexico, or as the headlines screamed, "Takes a Rest, Avoids Arrest."[8] He would eventually return to LA, and again, thanks to another stroke of luck for him (and a disaster for the Premus family), it turns out his patient had died of a hemorrhage that couldn't be conclusively linked to the chiropractor's ministrations. The legal result was the same, a $500 fine for practicing medicine without a license, which would eventually be overturned on appeal, thereby freeing up Storey to help found the California College of Chiropractic to train a new generation of manipulators.

So how did his chiropractic peers view Professor Hammer Time? In a private sense, probably with mixed emotions. In their public-facing statements, he was one of theirs, and they stood by him. At the time of his arrests, the industry as a whole was fighting to get the states and the nation to recognize chiropractic as a legitimate field of medicine, so rather than distancing themselves, they cast Storey as a martyr to the cause of luxations. However, they did make sure to let people know that the hardware technique was his innovation alone and not an everyday thing with them. According to an industry historian, "An article in *The Chiropractor* reiterated that the 'mallet and chisel that did the mischief and damage to the cause of Chiropractic, is not part of Chiropractic,'"[9] and that independent technique aside, he was more than welcome among their ranks. His impact is more than that of a single bad practitioner (and every field certainly has those) due largely to the fact that he was not alone—at the time, there were a number of chiropractors facing similar charges. In the big picture of American health, Storey stands as an early example of what would become a familiar pattern with chiropractors and a lot of other alternative treatments on offer: oversell the possibilities, deny the damage, and claim victimhood at the hands of mainstream medicine.

Toward that end, having avoided jail time, Storey would be welcomed back into the field for the remaining years of his life, where he would continue to practice and teach and would live just long enough to see California recognize chiropractic as a legitimate practice in 1922. His mentor, D. D. Palmer (who had faced similar legal troubles of his own), would not live to see that development. After entrusting his original school in Davenport, Iowa, to his son Bartlett Joseph (known as B.J.) Palmer and heading west, the senior Palmer died either from accidentally being struck by his son's car during a parade,[10] according to a contemporary Los Angeles newspaper, or typhoid, per his biography on the Palmer College of Chiropractic website, both of which, you have to admit, are kind of a bad look for his theories. Whether out of guilt, passion, or ambition, B.J. would continue to expand the field nationwide, introduce X-rays to the practice, and carry on his father's legacy in the most modern and familiar way yet—via the airwaves, celebrity endorsement, and an all-out charm offensive on all forms of media.

Like his father, B.J. was a colorful character, but beyond that, he was an absolute master of marketing. With taglines like "Be a Man of Backbone," his advertising promised money and health by mail via "a P. S. C. correspondence course"; by investing just "a little time each day or evening you will have presently mastered the ART, SCIENCE, and PHILOSOPHY of CHIROPRACTIC, which insures you immediate financial returns, also, a fixed future of social independence."[11] Not sure how one got literal hands-on practice in this scenario, but I imagine it made for some very awkward small talk with coworkers and neighbors. However his students fared, the system worked very well for B.J., since in the years following his father's death, he expanded his home (complete with a waterfall, the world's smallest chapel at eight square feet, and an umbrella stand made from an elephant's foot, among other treasures),* became a world traveler, and invested in radio stations, which he would use to spread the gospel of "drugless cures."

He'd also become a popular speaker, crisscrossing the country offering speeches about the finer points of "Selling Yourself."[12] In all fairness, he was in a good position to speak on the subject, since year after year, he would prove very adept at self-promotion, including as a pioneer in the field of the celebrity influencer. The showbiz magazine *Billboard* touted a program of "travelgrams" (i.e., cards that could be presented to practitioners the world over for free adjustments) for actors and other entertainers that "are endorsed by B.J. Palmer, one of the foremost chiropractics." The Atlantic City practitioner "Dr."† Feldman, who was spearheading the offer, explained the program as follows: "Actors and artists all

---

* It's located on the campus of the family's chiropractic college and is still open to the public if you find yourself looking for things to do in Davenport, Iowa.

† This doctor was another one of those self-declared things, since the state of New Jersey didn't start issuing licenses for "healers" until 1939, seventeen years after this article was written. Chiropractors could be board certified in the Garden State starting in 1953.

over the country have shown their gratitude for these travelgrams by boosting chiropractic wherever possible, for which we in turn, are grateful, as it helps educate and convince the public as to the merits of our profession."[13] Note that their appeal was to the sentiments of the public and not medical powers that be.

Around the same time that Thomas Storey was making headlines for his body count, doctors and chiropractors were drawing their battle lines, each one casting the other as the bad guy. Conventional medicine would continue to batter chiro as unproven and potentially dangerous, while chiropractors (along with others practicing alternative medicine) framed themselves as outsiders fighting the unfair grip of the medical monopoly. If it's not too late, long story short: the back-and-forth of arrests, trials, appeals, lobbying, and state and federal bills between the two parties would stretch out for decades, with each party digging its trenches deeper and deeper. Therein lies the trouble we still live (and can die) with.

From the beginning, much of the language chiropractors draped their cause in was designed to appeal to Americans' sense of patriotism and individuality and not necessarily rooted in ironclad results. In 1912, The *New York Times* ran an article titled "Fighting Healers Who Use Religion to Evade the Law," which focused on two practices with Spiritualist roots—Christian Science and chiropractic—that were in the crosshairs of state regulators. Making his case for the innocence of his client, Heinrich Dueringer, DC, attorney James W. Osborne declared to the court: "'He is one of and belongs to a body consisting of a large number of people throughout the United States, engaged in the practice of certain religious tenets for the restoration of health; and the acts performed, were within the meaning of the health laws, the practice of religious tenets of the church of Chiropractic religion, the essential features of which are described in a pamphlet by D. D. Palmer of Santa Barbara, California.' So, Dr. Dueringer is a religionist, and Chiropractic a religion—a faith."[14] Further, when their "religion" did triumph in the legal system, it was posited as a victory for life, liberty, and all the other things our nation holds so dear.

Besides freedom of religion, chiropractic would also portray itself as the scrappy underdog to medicine's unjust cartel. In an early alternative medicine publication, one editor declared that a 1907 court victory for chiropractors was a victory for all citizens while not advocating for spinal manipulation per se: "What we do stand for, however, is unflinching opposition to any man, or any set of men, who presume to dictate what type of medical treatment a man shall employ. A man has as much right to choose his physician as he has to select his tailor or shoemaker; and the methods employed by organized medicine to subvert that right can only recoil upon the heads of those that practice them."[15] Putting aside the chasmic difference between the services rendered by the person who hems your pants and the one who might take out your appendix, it might be a familiar argument to anyone who's opened a newspaper in recent years, because it's basically the same appeal made by citizens against vaccines, masking, and other public health measures. This demand for expertise equality may be one of the darker legacies of Spiritualism by putting personal belief on equal footing with proven hypothesis.

Labeled "conspirituality" by researchers, it's taken some of the legacy of Spiritualism in an angry, dangerous, and regressive direction. If Spiritualism was trying to reconcile a rapidly changing world with the timeless need for community and comfort, conspirituality is trying to turn back the clock to an imaginary time when it was every man for himself and we healed "naturally." The neologism comes from the toxic combination of conspiracy theories and spirituality. Like the search for proof of life after death of the Victorian era, it's something that has united some strange bedfellows, namely New Age "wellness practitioners," such as yoga teachers, and followers of the Trump-centered conspiracy network around QAnon. Having said all that, I kind of get it. Our medical system is a mess, and science needs better spokespeople at every level.

I'm a freelancer, but thanks to the Marketplace, I have some real bottom-of-the-barrel insurance. It's better than no insurance at all, but there are days when it really works my every nerve. I have to call my primary care doctor to authorize someone to update my glasses, it can take months to get someone to look at my skin (I'm a pale American; the sun is my enemy), and I better floss like the dickens, because unauthorized dental care is the new Chanel bag. Routine care is a soul-sucking drag; chronic or acute illness has to be a labyrinthine nightmare—and that's just getting to the appointment. Treatment is a whole other monster. I had a doctor huffily dismiss concerns about my care because she couldn't read my handwriting, and while it's not great, in my defense, I was only twenty-four hours out from "routine" surgery that had gone wrong and resulted in my needing a ventilator, twenty-three pints of blood, and a snootful of morphine. In my corner, I had come in with my own family team of two doctors and a PhD in immunology, and it helped, but in the hours when I was alone in a hospital bed, coming out of the twilight of opiates, and realizing my own mortality, I was confused, scared, and unheard.*

I had listened to a reputable doctor, and that's where it got me; after that, I could've easily sworn off them all for evermore. I haven't and I won't, but thinking back on it now, that would have been a prime time to get me to seriously consider aromatherapy or cleanses or whatever else was out there.

Like their Spiritualist and chiropractic forefathers, companies and practitioners providing services outside the medical norm are using the same toxic blend of language around freedom, individuality, faith, and lifestyle. While I'm empathetic to the reasons people seek out these things, I am also infuriated that this is where the current conversation lands. Our shared reality, our actual, literal life-and-death reality, has become something of a "Choose Your Own Adventure" debate, and I blame Gwyneth Paltrow. Okay, not entirely Gwyneth Paltrow, but she's not helping, and I'll totally own up to the fact that I don't like her for reasons that have nothing to do with the damage she's doing. We're about the same age, went to similar high schools, and I feel like I know her cool-girl type who would get away with bullying weirdos like me. I worked for her hairdresser when I was in college, and I met her exactly once for only a brief moment before she became big, and I wasn't impressed. So rightly or wrongly, I've dragged that annoyance with me since the midnineties. Mea culpa, I totally admit that. On the other hand, what she's doing with her

---

* Both literally because I was intubated and figuratively. That doctor wasn't interested in my complaints.

Goop platform is emblematic of a larger problem we have in this world, where we've made our opinions (no matter how they were formed) the sole measure of efficacy and goodness.

Let's look at her ongoing advocacy for supplements and cleanses. These are pretty much the modern equivalent of patent medicines—unregulated, made from lord knows what, and a way of keeping traditional medicine at bay. They're also at best probably useless, maybe more so than the ancestral elixirs they descend from, because those may have had a shot of alcohol or some opium to calm your frazzled nerves. Moreover, like the Spiritualist tonics of Lydia Pinkham, Paltrow has created a vocabulary and mythology around them that gives them a halo of health and expertise. For example, her "cleansing" line of products promises that "Our approach to formulation is a future-forward consciousness about our health." [16] These are all words, but do they mean anything?

Here is where my expertise comes in: While she went on to become a movie star and wellness impresario, I spent many years eking out a living as a beauty copywriter and sideshow performer. I didn't get to go to Cannes, but I do have an insider's view of how to promise a lot and deliver just enough. Youth and health have always been big sellers, and in the last couple decades, the supplement and cosmetics industries have learned to use scientific terms, such as *toxins* and *organics*, alongside their more nebulous promises, like radiance, glow, and skin that "appears* smoother."

---

* Trust me when I say this last phrase is a get-out-of-jail free card for copywriters. You can never promise surgical age-reversing results, but you can say something along the lines of "it might possibly have been visually perceptibly improved," but quicker, because ads and boxes are small.

Only that's not really how your skin or liver works, so we're basically back to a form of faith healing. Additionally, because of the fasting girls of sainthood and Spiritualism like Mollie Fancher, we also have a long association between self-denial and holiness that gives these methods the tantalizing shimmer of enlightenment (and thinness—do not ever underestimate our desires around low BMI). Combined with the fact that in the current moment, because we have a lot of environmental pollution, everyday stress, junk food, and frustration with doctors, the general notion of housekeeping our own bodies sounds really good. But thus far, there's no actual evidence that fasting, juicing, or sweating achieves that goal. Still, Goop has a waiting list for its "Superpowders." This is not to lay all the blame at the feet of Gwyneth;* she's just one high-profile entrepreneur in a largely unregulated multi-billion-dollar industry.

This faith in fasting and cleansing as a near-miraculous cure or ability may feel very "of the moment," but it's not—we've actually been going around in these circles for ages. In 1888, an article appeared in the *New York Courier-Advertiser* decrying what it called "Spiritualism, Fasting, and Lies." Sneering at "The well-known fasting man Succi" who was about to start a forty-day fast under medical supervision, the author weaves together the era's cynicism around the links between the miraculous, the profitable, and science.

Such feats have not been uncommon of late. In such cases, individuals have shown that they can subsist anywhere from

---

* Again, I was kidding about that; don't sue me.

one to forty days upon nothing but water, but such tests as a rule prove nothing more than the ability of certain individuals to accomplish things which to ordinary individuals seem impossible. Unfortunately, too many of these experiments, conducted as money-making things, have not been without suspicion or trickery.[17]

The author ties these stunts into the fortieth anniversary of the Fox Sisters' first rappings and the way Spiritualism had taken hold of the popular imagination. "So strenuous have been the supporters of spiritualism; how curious some of its manifestations, and so deeply interested in its beliefs have men whose opinions command respect, that many who are not spiritualists place spiritualism among the possibilities and are satisfied to await developments."[18]

If he was tired of the Fox Sisters' Spiritualist antics, he wasn't alone in that—so were Maggie and Kate Fox. That same year, they released their tell-all book, *The Death-Blow to Spiritualism*. The four decades between the "Hydesville rappings" and that book had been a real roller coaster for the three sisters. According to her account of the relationship[†] in her book *The Love-Life of Dr. Kane*, Maggie secretly married the dashing arctic explore Elisha Hunt Kane in 1856 and quit the mediumship business at his prompting. From the beginning, their relationship was marked by long

---

* Among the tricks the unnamed author was suggesting might be employed was the then unregulated supplement the "coca leaf," that is, the main ingredient in cocaine.

† His family, who didn't think she was worthy of their son from the beginning, disputed the legitimacy of their "secret" marriage and fought her over her claims to his estate.

absences for his travels, disputes about his family's disapproval of her mediumship, and bouts of ill health that followed his treacherous journeys. Death would ultimately part them in 1857 when Dr. Kane succumbed to his illnesses during a trip to Havana, Cuba. In the wake of his death, Maggie would convert to Catholicism and swear off mediumship for a number of years. Further, it was rumored she also began drinking heavily to cope with her losses.

During the years following their greatest fame, Kate would marry an English lawyer, have two sons, and be widowed herself in 1881. Upon her return to United States, Kate faced at least two major issues: supporting her sons and her alcoholism. Despite the latter, she had a strong reputation as a medium and continued to see clients. Her addiction finally caught up with her not long after losing her husband when she was arrested for drunkenness and lost custody of her boys for a time (the arrest was possibly due to Leah's machinations). She was eventually able to have them released into her care (maybe thanks to some legal hanky-panky from Maggie) and was able to flee with her children to England, where she and Maggie were reunited.

Both were miserable, exhausted, and broke—and both blamed Leah. Leah, on the other hand, was doing just fine. She had married a well-to-do man, Daniel Underhill, and while she retired from public séances, she continued to practice privately and became a leading light in the field when she published her missive and memoirs, *The Missing Link in Modern Spiritualism*, in 1885. In it, she notes that the population was lucky to live in such a golden era for communication with the Summerland: "One thing seems certain, namely, that at least in the present age or 'dispensation,' the

Spirits about us seem desirous of communicating with us, human Spirits still in the flesh, and glad of the opportunities afforded them through the mediums for doing so."[19]

Her sisters did not agree with her conclusions and decided now was the time to come clean about the whole affair and possibly earn some income while they were at it. Kate and Maggie signed off on a tell-all book, which detailed Leah's exploitation, their own role in the schemes, and their current sad state. Speaking to their ghost writer (ahem), Reuben Briggs Davenport, Maggie did not hold back her fury. "Spiritualism started from nothing. We were but innocent children. What did we know? Ah, we grew to know too much. Our sister used us in her exhibitions, and we made money for her. Now she turns on us because she's the wife of a rich man and opposes us wherever she can. Oh, I am after her! You can kill sometimes without using weapons, you know."[20] While no one was murdered telepathically or otherwise, there was no need. All Maggie and Kate's bombshell managed to do was create a brief flap in the media consisting of coverage of Maggie's toe-cracking demonstrations and her complaints. Some members of the press gloated: "The Fox women are now in this country, and it is said that Mrs. Maggie Fox Kane proposes to lecture here on 'The Curse of Spiritualism,' supported by her sister Mrs. Jencken, who charges her troubles in New York with respect to her children to the spiritualists led by her elder sister Leah. Mrs. [Kane] said in an interview had with her the other day that if her sister Kate were to lecture here, she would certainly join her; that spiritualism was 'the biggest humbug of the era.'"[21] In response, Spiritualists immediately closed ranks and made their own case to the media: "They, one and all, denounced the Fox sisters* and said that anyone who believed that any spirit manifestations were performed in such a flimsy manner or by any such legerdemain was a fool." Further, they tried to discredit these supposed insiders by letting it slip that "they are not women of the best character. One of them was picked up drunk in New York one day, and her children taken from her."[22]

Maggie's timing was awful, since by this time, Spiritualism was so much bigger than three naive sisters from the Burned-Over District and so entrenched in some everyday lives that one family skirmish barely made a dent in overall belief. After the short-lived hubbub in the press, people (and their mediums) moved on. Once again, Kate and Maggie would find themselves alone, unpopular, and in need of support. So much so that Maggie would eventually recant her rebuke of Spiritualism and try to rejoin the fold, tearfully telling reporters, "Would to God I could undo the injustice to the cause of spiritualism." She added that she had been vulnerable and duped by some nefarious forces, saying that at that time, "I was in great need of money and persons whom for the present I prefer not to name took advantage of my situation."[23] Sadly for her, it was too little too late, and neither side of the debate had any use for her any longer.

Unfortunately for the younger Fox Sisters, some people preferred their humbug. Kate would die impoverished and racked by drink just three years later in 1892. Maggie would meet the same fate a year later. Leah had crossed over in 1890, and even death could not soften hard feelings. Leah had herself buried in the family plot in Green-Wood

---

* Maggie and Kate; everyone was still cool with Leah.

Cemetery in the tony Park Slope section of Brooklyn, while Kate and Maggie rest about seven miles away in Cypress Hill Cemetery.* They may have marked the beginning of Spiritualism in America, but their squabbles and confessions were not even the beginning of its end. The moment had embraced Spiritualism, and no amount of toe-cracking demonstrations could turn back the clock.

In our own American era, COVID would prove to be a similar inflection point of belief versus demonstration. A large part of the problem is also how we have this conversation of alternative medicine versus traditional medicine, with each side trying to make their way the one true faith. This issue didn't start during the pandemic; the foundations were laid a long time ago. In 1931, B.J. Palmer was still suggesting that "Germs are very beneficial things and if you haven't got any you ought to go out and get yourself some."[24] It should go without saying, but the anecdotes he offers in support of his pet theory suggest he really didn't have a good working idea of how germs work, adding, "I have never known a case of a doctor who sincerely believed in germs." This would probably be news to most doctors, who'd been using measures like gloves, masks, antiseptics, handwashing, and autoclaves in their practices since the late nineteenth century. Still, it was an opinion, and it was granted the weight of an article in the daily paper without rebuttal.

---

* They're still in an interesting neighborhood, so to speak, interred near lifelong Spiritualist and movie star Mae West, gangster Monk Eastman, and painter Piet Mondrian. Leah's neighbors are a who's who of famous New Yorkers, including supporters such as editor Horace Greeley and pastor Henry Ward Beecher, in addition to composer Leonard Bernstein and the man who brought hot dogs to Coney Island, Charles Feltman.

Fast-forward ninety years and add the shine of celebrity, the machines of misinformation, and a moment of mass panic, and perfectly normal questions about medicine harden to form a kind of dogma. Sure, it's easy and fun to bag on people like Gwyneth Paltrow, various Kardashians, and Dr. Oz and their kale and ozone enemas* or whatever else they're touting at this moment, and we should definitely continue to do so, but we also have to find a way to bring people into the public health conversation that isn't just based on taking away the sense of control that diet and lifestyle give them. Conversely, we don't have to invite everyone with an Instagram following who is actively harming people (and profiting off that harm) to be part of the conversation.

Oddly enough, for solutions, I'm actually going back to chiropractic for a moment. Like "detoxing" or "cleansing,"† it's actually not easy to find quality, objective studies about chiropractic's effectiveness on various illnesses and any unintended side effects. In my research, there was one study I found interesting in this context with the catchy title of "Comparing the Satisfaction of Low Back Pain Patients Randomized to Receive Medical or Chiropractic Care: Results from UCLA Low Back Pain Study." While this one paper is by no means the definitive study, chiropractors actually win this round with higher scores for patient satisfaction. But as

---

* I kid about this imaginary product, but Gwyneth has touted "rectal ozone," at which point one doctor, Eric Burnett, MD, felt he had to tweet, "Thought this went without saying but: Friendly reminder to NOT put ozone up your rectum."

† The studies that are out there are not hopeful for the cause of these quick fixes, and the FDA has issued warnings about dozens of products for people and pets that not only don't work but also contain dangerous materials.

the authors point out, this may not mean chiropractic adjustment is better than medical treatments for lumbar trouble; it means patients felt listened to, and that goes a long way toward outcome. As they describe it, "In this randomized trial, chiropractic patients were more satisfied with their back care providers after 4 weeks of treatment than medical patients. Although, similar results have been reported by others, those examiners did not examine the role of other factors in explaining the satisfaction gap... By contrast, we found that receipt of self-care advice and explanation of treatment had strong estimated effects on patient satisfaction."[25] Put another way, the patients of the chiropractors didn't actually get more pain relief; they felt better about their interactions with their care providers because they felt heard and were given ongoing advice on how to take care of themselves.

Not being heard and understood is a totally legit complaint to have in a world of medicine that is more controlled by insurers than caregivers and is evolving faster than some people's ability to parse new information. Whether it was Lydia Pinkham or D. D. Palmer, Spiritualists often offered patients the comfort of feeling in control and understood, and in some ways, I understand—and even applaud—that support. Does aromatherapy seem to help your anxiety? Douse yourself in your favorite scent. Yoga for your bad joints? I do it. Namaste, babe. Want to bring a crystal to chemotherapy? Literally rock on. But these "modalities" should be complementary treatments that (1) do no harm, (2) are used in combination with proven medical methods, and (3) come from actual experts who've done the homework and not just smooth-talking salespeople. The media, politicians, and doctors really fell down on the job in communicating these things during the pandemic, and we buried a lot of Americans who might have otherwise survived. Approximately 1.2 million of our fellow citizens died, some of them to prove a horrible point, and we're facing future heartbreak if we don't find a way to break the cycle on something as settled as vaccine safety and efficacy. Otherwise, a whole new generation of mothers and fathers are going to have to change their pet research project from the best supplements to how to contact the other side of the veil. That's one legacy of Spiritualism I don't think needs a revival.

ENOUGH ROPE

MAGIC, MEDIUMSHIP, AND UNRAVELING THE MYSTERIES OF SPIRITUALISM

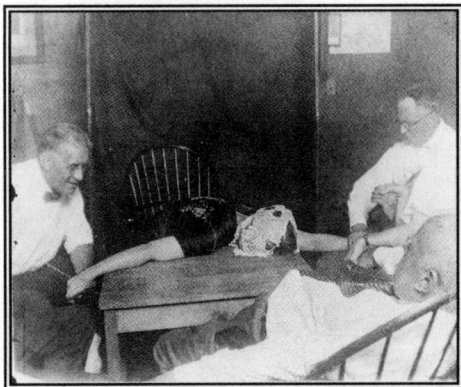

A medium producing ectoplasm.

DR. CRANDON, WOMAN MEDIUM LYING ON TABLE, WITH ECTOPLASM ON HER HEAD, SURROUNDED BY FOUR OTHER PEOPLE, DURING SÉANCE, PHOTOGRAPHIC PRINT, 1925, LIBRARY OF CONGRESS PRINTS AND PHOTOGRAPHS DIVISION WASHINGTON, D.C.

> "Anyone who believes
> in magic is a fool."

HARRY HOUDINI

A year after my initial visit to California, I'd find myself back on goth-cation with the same set of friends. Another great day: we'd eat fried stuff, wander the different worlds looking for shady places to sit, and debate which rides were the least traumatic.* I was, however, bummed to find out that the Haunted Mansion was closed for updates. I have no idea what those changes will bring, but I presume it will have a fresh set of cobwebs and maybe some high-tech new scares. Also thwarted on this trip: any chance of my getting into the Magic Castle, since all the magicians who offered to help me get into the Houdini Room have disappeared. Ta-da!

On returning to New York, I had hoped to make the trip to Wayne, New Jersey, to see a private museum of some Houdini artifacts, but that also never materialized. I briefly considered a trip to his house in Harlem (privately owned and there's not really anything of his there) and his grave in Queens, but it takes two subways and a bus to get there, and I don't know what I'd find near his final resting place. I'm certainly not going to contact him, because he'd hate that. I'm a Houdini fan, not an obsessive one like many in the variety arts, but I have a huge respect for him as another Jewish person who is trained to escape from a straitjacket, and I admire him as someone who really understood his era. In

---

* Not coincidentally, that's the day I learned that I'm fine with a little boat or a choo-choo but nothing that plunges toward the earth. Do not recommend Tower of Terror or whatever they call it now.

and of himself, he's a lesson in modernity, marketing, and what loss inspires in us. He also seems like he could be kind of a vindictive jerk, so my view is somewhat tempered by that.

Houdini was born Erik Weisz in Budapest, Hungary, in 1874 and moved to the United States as a small child. His father was nominally a rabbi but often had a hard time finding a permanent congregation, and their family struggled financially. He was famously close to his mother. Renamed Ehrich* Weiss for his new life in the United States, he would prove to be an ideal citizen for the new era of American life: smart, ambitious, and in love with technology. My personal favorite biographical factoid is that he worked in a tie factory for two years as a teenager, and his best friend and performing partner from those days was a man named Jack Hyman, which is also my beloved grandfather's name.†

Like Cher or Liberace, there's really no need to justify his one-name level of fame; suffice it to say he was a tremendous celebrity and in no small thanks to his understanding of how to play the press. He's remembered as a magician, but his celebrity was really built on his escapology and his persona as an expert on a number of things. He instinctively understood that slipping out of a straitjacket is fine, but to earn that ink and keep audiences coming back for more, you had to make it spectacular—add chains, jump into freezing rivers, and dangle upside down from cranes

---

* "Harry" may be derived from his family nickname, "Ehri."

† My *zaide* is a totally different Jewish guy who worked in the rag trade, but if anyone in my family had supernatural powers, it would be Jack. He was funny, kind, and unceasingly honest, and he told mystical stories about the small town in Poland where he was from.

in front of news cameras and mesmerized crowds. Additionally, Houdini wasn't just a showman, he was a media personality and a polymath—learning to fly a plane, making early silent films, developing new illusions, and studying a number of subjects with rabbinical intensity. When he turned his sights on Spiritualism, he would be a man possessed—or maybe not possessed, since he was steadfast in his disbelief. Perhaps "man on a mission" is a better way to put it.

Stepping back for a moment, Houdini was not the first (and certainly not the last) magician to draw a bright red line between the conjuring arts and the miraculous; that had always been there to some extent, but the introduction of Spiritualism to the mix of wonder and skill was positively combustible. Before Houdini entered the fray in earnest, there had been Maskelyne. The English-born John Nevil Maskelyne* was originally trained as a locksmith but described his profession on the frontispiece of his essays as an "Illusionist and Anti-Spiritualist." He was a writer, magician, and expert at card cheats, and he would be otherwise notable for a number of reasons, not the least of which is that he invented the lock that created the great UK institution—the pay toilet. Not surprisingly, perhaps, he was also an expert at various escape methods. Intent on exposing frauds away from the gaming table too, he would become entangled with another popular Spiritualist sibling act out of the Burned-Over District, the Davenport Brothers.

---

* Not to be confused with Nevil Maskelyne, who was a British astronomer and the first person to accurately calculate the Earth's mass.

Arriving on the scene just after the Rochester rappings, the Davenport Brothers, Ira Erastus and William Henry, would give Spiritualism a glitzy showbiz makeover and take it back and forth across the Atlantic, giving displays of the spirits' powers to enraptured audiences. Freed from the obligation to seem modest and ladylike that plagued the Fox Sisters, they were welcome to build a bigger, more ostentatious display of their skills that included instruments played by unseen hands, rope escapes, and a custom-built box that would be sealed in front of audiences with the trussed-up brothers inside to prove no one was hiding any devices that might help them make noises or escape from their ropes. Maskelyne recognized these tricks right away as basic escapology paired with some plain old misdirection that led audiences to believe the brothers had no hand in the ghostly sounds of bells and banjos that emanated from the box. Maskelyne and his costar, George Cooke, would recreate the same effects in their shows to skewer the Davenports' claims (and one-up them). As one contemporary magazine described it, "The tricks of modern Spiritualism have attracted so much attention and created so many proselytes, that Messrs. Maskelyne and Cooke are fully justified in showing them up for what they really are, the productions of pure legerdemain."[1]

Maskelyne was not the only conjuror to unravel the mysteries of their spirit box. There would be something of a pile-on of industry professionals, who sought to separate their hard-earned skills from the promises of Spiritualists. A number of magicians published pamphlets on how to do the brothers' rope escapes, make their luminous paint for props, and perform other literal tricks of the trade that made their spirit box seem otherworldly.

All this attention did not help the brothers' career. Their audiences dwindled, moving on to more entertaining magicians with bigger acts and smaller claims. After William died of consumption in 1877, Ira tried to revive the act with their former assistant to little fanfare, and he eventually faded from the scene into retirement. By the time Houdini reached the apex of his debunking skills in the new century, it was already something of a subgenre of magic. However, Houdini's quest to tear the curtain away from every last physical medium went further than your standard professional "anything you can do, I can do better," since there was likely a personal element to it. Poor Erik Weisz was working from an inexhaustible well of grief and anger at the permanent loss of his beloved mother, Cecelia, in 1913.

This fruitless search would reach its turning point as part of his relationship with Sherlock Holmes's author, Sir Arthur Conan Doyle, and his second wife, Jean, who believed deeply in Spiritualism and its possibilities. No easy mark, Doyle was a sophisticated man of letters, an MD, and a world traveler. He also wasn't averse to an audience or a headline and had toured the United States and Europe extensively, speaking on a number of topics, including his rationale for mediumship and other principles of Spiritualism. The men's initial relationship had a great measure of mutual admiration and understanding of the pressures on a man at the top of his field. The fervor of Doyle's own belief was also rooted in genuine loss; by the end of World War I, he had lost no less than eleven relatives including his son, Kingsley. Séances had provided the Doyles with some much-needed relief, and they were eager to pass that comfort on to Houdini who, eight years on, still mourned the loss of his mother. As Doyle would later describe it, "His love for his dead mother seemed to be the ruling passion of his life, which he expressed on all sorts of public occasions in a way which was, I am sure, sincere, but is strange to our colder Western blood."*[2]

Houdini recalled the fateful séance in Atlantic City in the spring of 1922 that broke their friendship:

> *I was willing to believe, even wanted to believe. It was weird to me and with a beating heart I waited, hoping that I might feel once more the presence of my beloved Mother. If there ever was a son who idolized and worshipped his Mother, whose every thought was for her happiness and comfort, that son was myself. My Mother meant my life, her happiness was synonymous with my peace of mind. For that reason, if no other, I wanted to give my very deepest attention to what was going on. It meant to me an easing of all pain that I had in my heart. I especially wanted to speak to my Mother, because that day, June 17, 1922, was her birthday. I was determined to embrace Spiritualism if there was any evidence strong enough to down the doubts that have crowded my brain for the past thirty years.*[3]

Lady Doyle, despite her delivery of an effusive message from Cecelia, would be unable to assuage those doubts.

---

* The suggestion that a Hungarian American is not "Western" refers to Houdini's Jewishness, which in Doyle's estimation makes him other.

While pleased with the results in the moment, Houdini would later doubt what he'd received, and rather than talking to his friend directly, he went to the press. Houdini publicly minimizing Jean's powers left Doyle feeling "sore" and insulted. In the volley of letters that followed, Houdini expounded on his doubts and countered, "I was heartily in accord and sympathy at that seance, but the letter was written entirely in English and my sainted Mother could not read, write, or speak the English language. I did not care to discuss it at the time because of my emotion in trying to sense the presence of my Mother, if there was such a thing possible, to keep me quiet until time passed, and I could give it the proper deduction."[4] Oy.

He wished the Doyles all the best and hoped they could agree to disagree on the matter, but the magician could not back down from his disbelief. Neither would the author give on his faith, and relations between the two of them would be strained from then on. Rather than bringing him consolation, that fleeting spark of possibility in connection with the deceased seemed to have redoubled Houdini's cynicism around mediumship and his desire to see mediums' work destroyed. His anger had made him a man on a mission and an evangelist for disbelief, and fate would soon put a dragon in front of him that he would become hell-bent on slaying.

Mina "Margery" Crandon was, in a number of senses, one of the most powerful mediums the movement would produce. Although not an early adherent, she was a formidable beginner, and from her debut, she dazzled witnesses on both sides. Born in Canada in 1888, Mina would move to Boston as a young woman, marry a modest grocer, and have a son. In 1916, she was admitted to a Dorchester Hospital for surgery where she would meet Dr. Le Roi

Crandon. Apparently, he had quite the bedside manner, because soon after becoming reacquainted two years later during his service in a military hospital and her volunteer work, she divorced her first husband and became the third Mrs. Crandon. No fool she, Dr. Crandon was a great catch—Harvard educated, socially prominent, and well-to-do. He was also wild about her, adopting her son John and encouraging her to live something of a flapper lifestyle, which shocked a number of their proper Boston neighbors—and that was before the wild séances started.

She had initially brushed off her husband's budding interest in Spiritualism until a fruitful meeting with a medium who contacted her brother and added that "Mina was being called to 'The Work.'"[5] Not long after that, their Lime Street home was hosting some wild nights with the spirits. When in a trance, Mina assumed the persona of Margery.[*] Margery's guiding spirit was Walter, Mina's brother, who had died in a train accident many years earlier. It was all very dramatic. It was also a hot ticket for the select circle of friends who were invited to nights in their parlor. From the beginning, her skills were sensational and her séances next level, with voluptuous displays of ectoplasm, disembodied hands touching guests, and Margery in little more than a silky kimono.

Word of her powers soon got out, and the sensation-hungry media covered it breathlessly—and initially anonymously. In 1924, the *New York Herald Tribune* declared "Surgeon's Wife Is 'Margery' in Psychic Contest" and detailed her unique powers as a

---

[*] From here on, I'm going to refer to her with the name she chose for herself and operated under in all things mediumship, Margery.

hostess when she "caused rose petals to flit across the cheeks of her guests at dinner."[6] Further, the paper excitedly detailed how she was about to gain a national profile thanks to her qualifying for a very unusual trial. In December 1922, no less an institution of reason than *Scientific American* magazine announced that it would offer $5,000* in prize money to anyone who could provide satisfactory proof of contact with the dead. This being science, the winner would, of course, have to perform this wonder under controlled, near-laboratory conditions. As the popular press described the challenge, "The jury to be convinced by these candidates for these prizes consists mainly of hard-headed practical men,"† including one "Harry Houdini, a thorough disbeliever, who has been a nemesis of fakers."[7]

This announcement would set the course for the ill-fated collision of Margery and Houdini. Margery was selected not just for the wonders she produced but for what she didn't do, namely command a fee for her séances. According to newspaper accounts, "Her powers are well known to her intimates, but Mrs. Crandon has refused to commercialize her talent. Even in the present tests she is paying all the expenses."[8] Her refusal to ask for money (and her high social position) may have made her work purer in the eyes of some skeptics, because it begged the question of why fake it if there was no fame or money to be had. Whatever her reason for doing it, it went pretty well for her in the beginning.

---

* Almost $100,000 in 2024 dollars.

† Other members of the board included the MIT scientist who invented Technicolor film and other high-profile paranormal investigators who had more mixed feelings about psychic phenomena than Houdini.

Not long after the testing began, headlines down the East Coast blared that Margery's powers "baffle scientists,"[9] with her literally outshining other contestants. "During six sittings the investigators were quite baffled by the brilliance of Walter's performance. A luminous disk or 'doughnut' was levitated about the room when all the controls seemed perfect, a bell box was rung, and Walter cooperated in weight and other experiments. At one time a light was flashed on by accident and nothing suspicious was noticed."[10] As dazzling as that was, some people would simply never be convinced. Those people were Houdini.

After a couple of sittings, he had seen enough. Margery and Walter could produce as many "teleplasmic hands"* as they wanted, but he would not be swayed. Houdini instead showed up with his own fetters, including a Margery-sized box specifically designed† to prevent her from executing any sleight of hand (or other parts). Under these conditions, she did manage to manifest Walter's voice but no rose petals, pigeons, doughnuts, or hands. "Ghosts shy around Houdini,"[11] snickered the *New York Herald Tribune*. The daily papers lapped it up. "In a big black box fashioned out of one-inch oak in the manner of an old-time pillory, the medium was said to have failed to invoke proof. In another box, somewhat similar but with more freedom, results were positive, bells being rung, and messages delivered, it was said."[12] Those setbacks aside, she could still win *Scientific American*'s prize if she received four out of five jury votes, but Houdini's passion would simply not let

---

* Disembodied hands that would "emerge" from Margery during séances. They were examined and thought to be made from very earthly paraffin.

† Only her head and hands were free from this version of the contraption.

that happen. He was going to prove her fraud, sway the jury, and end the public fascination with Spiritualism once and for all, if it was the last thing he ever did.

He started with exposure; her unstoppable force was about to meet his immovable objection. He began with a pamphlet revealing how she'd performed her tricks and the ingenious way he'd detected them, telling the papers, "Anticipating the sort of work I would have to do in detecting the movements of her foot I had rolled my right trouser leg up above my knee. All that day I had worn a silk rubber bandage around that leg above the knee. By night the part of the leg below the knee had become painfully swollen and painfully tender, thus giving me a keener sense of feeling and making it easier to notice the slightest sliding of Mrs. Crandon's ankle or flexing of her muscles. She wore silk stockings and during the séance had her skirts above her knees."[13] Which makes her seem not only deceptive but possibly seductive as well. True or untrue, these sorts of accusations would continue to swirl around Margery long after the tests ended. It looked bad for her: the more she was able to interact with the room around her, the more she could manifest, which seemed to suggest that she was not merely a passive conduit of Walter's vibes.

In the end, Margery did not carry enough of the contest's judges to win the prize or to be declared living proof of communication with the other side of the veil. This is not to say everyone dismissed her with the alacrity of Houdini; many were convinced that she held some sort of powers, just not the ones that would have clinched the $5,000. Separate from the *Scientific American* trials, the Institute of Psychical Research was incredibly impressed with Margery; a year later, it would declare her to be the real deal of some sort, believing that if she had not demonstrated medium-ship, she may have been exhibiting some kind of telepathy, and they found "no evidence of fraud."[14] That should have been the end of it, with Houdini returning to his successful stage career and Mrs. Crandon to her remarkable dinner parties, but the battle lines had been drawn, and both sides still felt they had something to prove. They would wage their war of words in the press, each side trying to leverage the weight of their own reputations against people's worst assumptions about the other.

In public, Dr. Crandon would defend his wife and "In showing a picture of the medium with Houdini, [he] hinted at 'fraud' by the investigator. Walter, the independent voice, asked Houdini how much he got for preventing phenomena, Dr. Crandon said, and explained that a pencil eraser was found holding the bell box so that it could not ring."[15] In private, the surgeon was not so genteel, questioning Houdini's right to even criticize his wife, writing the magician's former friend, Sir Arthur Conan Doyle, that "My deep regret is that this low-minded Jew has any claim on the word American."[16] Walter (via Margery, natch) apparently agreed and would compose poems containing various antisemitic slurs to describe him.

For his part, Houdini would continue to rail against Margery and all other mediums from the stage, in the press, and even in front of Congress. In 1926, the magician squared off against mediums and elected officials in a hearing designed to reveal if mediumship was a money-making scam and if President Calvin Coolidge had hosted séances in the White House. "At the outset of his testimony, Houdini said that he was not opposing any religion or the religion of spiritualism but said he was merely trying to expose fraudulent mediums."[17] As one might expect, the committee meetings were boisterous. "Houdini said that conditions in the national capitol as regards to fake fortune tellers are worse than any other city in the country, because mediums are not licensed here." The mediums present responded with cries of "Liar! Liar!" and the presiding senator struggled to keep order over the fray.

Unknown to him, of course, was the fact that his time left on this earth was short. On October 31 of that year, Houdini would succumb to peritonitis, which was due to injuries sustained from a punch and/or appendicitis. Even in death, both he and Margery would try to have the last word in their own ways. On Houdini's side, the fact that he lived that long may have been a supernatural act of spite, since according to friend and fellow magician Bernard M. L. Ernst, "in 1925, while engaged in the famous controversy with the spirit medium 'Margery,' who is Mrs. Le Roi Crandon, wife of a Boston physician, Houdini was told by the medium that he would die before December 21 of that year. In a speech at the Hippodrome on January 16, the magician laughed at the prophecy and said: 'Margery' has placed a curse on me—that I shall die before December 21. If I do it will be a coincidence. No one knows when I will die."[18]

From her side of the veil, she decided she wouldn't waste her powers on reaching his spirit, telling the press, "Mrs. L. R. G. Crandon, widely known as Margery, will make no attempt to receive a spirit message from the late Houdini, magician, who once claimed to have exposed her mediumship. She said today, commenting on Houdini's reported plan to communicate with relatives after death. 'We are not directly interested because we do not go in for that sort of thing.'"[19] This was probably for the best, since he would prove to be beyond reach even to those he loved. For years, Houdini never reached back when his beloved wife, Bess, reached out at annual Halloween séances. That said, you could hardly say death was the end of Houdini's influence. A century after his passing, his name is still synonymous with magic itself. Margery would go to the Summerland in 1941, but she would be less remembered—or remembered only as a footnote in Houdini's own story.

Without defending her unsavory beliefs and strange motives, maybe there's something to be learned from Margery. She was a medium for the modern era. If the Fox Sisters embodied the fragile modesty of their Victorian lives, Margery had no such burden and could operate in the self-determined, go-go-go ethos of that roaring era while still retaining all the shields of white, upper-class femininity when needed. She knew how to work the press, and she had an unshakable confidence in her ability to convince people of her skills. I like to imagine that in the current era (if she wasn't banned from social media and forced to hire an image management company for the whole antisemitism thing), she'd probably have some kind of TED Talk or long interview with Oprah about connecting with positive sensual vibrations to optimize your life or something. Like Victoria Woodhull, she's an interesting and complicated figure, but not necessarily one I want on a souvenir mug.

Still, her legacy deserves another look. Particularly when it's weighed against where on the arc of Spiritualist history she appears.

While Spiritualism—as defined by the American movement that kicked off on that dark night near Rochester in 1848—still exists, in 1924, its most powerful days were behind it. It had survived the Fox Sisters' squabbles, endless debunkings, and its own internal power struggles. It would live to see a new century and achieve some of its aims of abolition, suffrage, and temperance, but its national influence was winding down by the time Margery was making headlines. This is due to a lot of factors, but I don't think it's possible to underestimate just how important the whole notion of "modernity" was to us in the twenties. Ironically, some of the same factors that had moved people into the movement during the nineteenth century were pushing them away now, namely mass death and evolving technology. In the grim wake of World War I and the influenza epidemic of 1918, people may have thought that it was best to move on and live rather than dwell on what was lost. Spirituality would fall out of fashion the same way that widow's weeds and mourning jewelry would be tossed aside for bee-stung lips and cloche hats. Of course, people will always feel the lasting sting of loss, but now our eyes were on the bright horizon of the future that we saw in the movies and heard on the radio. We would live longer, move faster, climb higher, and adopt positivity as the ethos of American citizenship. We could shamelessly read our horoscope in the daily paper and only worry about witches around Halloween.* Spiritualism had left an indelible imprint on the nation and would survive in some ways, but it wouldn't make the front pages anymore.

---

* Mostly, although some segments really do love to kick up the occasional satanic panic now and again, generally around rock 'n' roll, but LGBTQ+ people and books remain popular, perpetual scapegoats.

Culturally, because of its positivity and the fact that people of the time really knew how to throw a party, the twenties are a fascinating moment in American history. In modern-day New York, where I live, I've found that we have a fierce nostalgia for the Jazz Age—so fierce, in fact, that many of the local magazines have published roundups of the twenty best "speakeasies" in town, which means there are more than enough bars with twenty-three-dollar artisanal cocktails hidden behind locksmiths and coffee shops in New York City to fill these lists. So much so that about ten years after doing two "Gatsby" themed events a week as a performer, I made a crack on my social media to the effect of "If you like this, you're going to love seeing the return of polio and the rise of fascism," and, ouch, that's one "it's funny because it's true" I could do without. But oddly enough, it's in one of these liminal spaces between past and present that Margery and Houdini will meet again.

Having had limited luck with the keepers of Houdini's actual things, I thought I might try to contact the creator of *The Spirits' Speakeasy*, which presented a facsimile of the Margery/Houdini rivalry several nights a week, to ask why she had chosen this story at this time. Luckily, the show's writer, Monica Hammond, was kind enough to talk to me. Funny enough, it turns out that this show started off being centered on a certain brand-name spirit board,[*] but when the owners of that particular intellectual property pulled out of the show, she was still fascinated by the Spiritualist movement and wanted to

---

[*] Rhymes with Feegee.

put together a show that captured its intrigue, which is when she found this story. This being showbiz, however, in the name of creating dramatic arc, she did have to take some liberties with the facts and timeline of Margery's character. "Obviously, there's like an amazing feminist angle to all of this. So we're actually kind of rewriting history with the show where she does sort of come out on top… The Margery that we're creating is self-empowered. She's competent. Ultimately, she is a magician and a mentalist, and the woman we've cast [to play] her is Krystyn Lambert and she's very well known in the magic community and her whole thing is doing séances."[20]

She also made the decision that they'll be cutting out any nude scenes and keeping it PG-13, so that while the Margery character "will be sensual, she's not going to be doing any of the crazy stuff, the naked rolling around, no hands up skirts or anything like that."

Aside from what sounds like a really fun evening, I asked her what she wants audiences to take away from the tango of Margery and Houdini. She paused for a moment and thought about it before offering some insight into what it's like to sit in on a séance: "It can be a very intense experience, and people often react to it as though you are offering them this connection, and that's an intense connection." Plus, she truly believes that it will resonate with current theatergoers. As she sees it, "In researching more about the Spiritualist movement in this time period, like I feel like it became so popular in the 1920s because people were dealing with death all around them. There was the war. There was the influenza pandemic, which I was like 'holy crap!' That's almost exactly a hundred years ago, so to me, we're definitely going to be pulling moments that echo." My timeline is different, but my feeling is the same. When I do get time to see the show, I have to agree, audiences still really want to be a part of the whole séance experience, even knowing on some level that they're LARPing a historical fiction novel of communication with the dead.

In researching the story of the *Scientific American* competition, I also found some interesting current parallels, specifically that people still blame the curse of Margery for Houdini's death and love a good press opportunity. In 2007, the authors of *The Secret Life of Houdini: The Making of America's First Superhero*, which, as The *Washington Post* put it, "purports to reveal new and astounding elements of the great magician's life and death—including the claim that he was murdered, a crime plotted by the husband of a spiritualist whom Houdini had debunked," held a press conference where they argued for the exhumation and autopsy of Harry Houdini. In fact, they were willing to disturb the eternal rest of the poor late, great magician to prove that the Crandons somehow had him poisoned. Soon thereafter, they held a press conference in Washington, DC, where they explained that they were seeking permission from "the last living relative"* of Houdini to dig up and reexamine the legendary escapist's remains for signs of foul play. According to the representative, if allowed to do this, science would finally triumph over the medium's subterfuge. "'We are here today at the beginning of a historical moment,' said attorney

---

* His grandnephew, George Hardeen, is definitely a relative; he's just not the only one.

Joseph Tacopina,* starting off the festivities and speaking before a few dozen reporters and photographers. 'Advances in forensic science have increased our desire as a society to disinter the distinguished in order to solve outstanding mysteries. This is one.'" Law and Order: Spectral Victims Unit!

It was a grand claim, but not one they had a shred of actual evidence for, as one of the authors admitted, "'Crandon had a lot of connections. Do we have a smoking gun that Crandon had a friend in Houdini's camp who could have put something in his soup? No.'" In the end, "It turns out this media spectacle was not orchestrated and paid for by the family of Houdini, as one might have inferred from Tacopina's opening remarks. It was organized and paid for by the authors, who hired the uber-crafty PR firm Dan Klores Communications to put it together. The idea, perhaps, was to goose sales of *The Secret Life*."[21] Which is a remarkable display of what Cecelia may have referred to as chutzpah.

Whatever Margery's powers were, they likely did not include curses or murder. Still, we'll always be willing to save a little room for belief of the idea that powerful women are capable of being dangerous sirens. Also, men who are singularly committed to their ideas are strong and passionate, whereas women are vengeful and crazy. Or not. Both Houdini and Margery are complex characters who still have the power to entrance us with their mysteries decades after the death of the physical selves. As magician and curator David London puts it, "To me the most interesting thing

---

* If his name seems familiar, it's because he unsuccessfully defended President Donald Trump in a civil suit over his sexual assault of writer E. Jean Carroll, thereby cementing his legacy as a *Law & Order: Special Victims Unit*–type bad-guy lawyer, but in real life.

about Houdini is that he has managed to stay undead for this long. You ask people to name a magician and you will still get Houdini in the top three and he's been dead for one hundred years. That is amazing."[22]

A few years ago, London organized an exhibit about Houdini's Jewishness and his involvement in Spiritualism at the Baltimore Jewish Museum called *Inescapable: The Life and Legacy of Harry Houdini*. This was not an easy task since Houdini was both very cagey about his beliefs in public (perhaps as a way of deflecting antisemitism) and pretty quiet about them in private too, never really displaying much by way of formal practice outside of saying the mourner's prayer for his parents on the prescribed dates. It's yet another enigma he left. If he spoke with God in those moments he dangled upside down from a crane over Times Square or in the darkest hours of his grief, or if he felt alone in the universe, only the Creator knows (if they exist). Sometimes there is just no way to slip the bonds of our doubts. Next to straitjacket escape, this may be his most relatable facet to me since I've come to understand how our minds can hold both skepticism and sorrow at the same time. Just because we don't expect miracles doesn't mean we don't want them.

For Houdini, that disappointment meant turning away from all possibility of the inexplicable. As for myself, in this moment, I'm not quite done yet with wondering. I will soon meet my "mostly companion" and learn that I am willing to suspend disbelief a few moments longer, and even when I can't do that, I can hold those two thoughts simultaneously.

14

MEETING MY MOSTLY COMPANION

---◦◦◦◦◦◦---

THE JANET SESSIONS

"You shall no longer take things at
second or third hand, nor look through
the eyes of the dead, nor feed
on the spectres in books."

WALT WHITMAN,
"SONG OF MYSELF"

When I first started thinking about writing this book, I started to imagine the conversations I would have if I could reach my father on the other side. The first thought that popped into my head was him responding to a medium, "Can this wait? Because Cole Porter and I are going for sushi," because that would be Marty's idea of heaven (in my mind anyway). I continue to imagine him as I knew him in life, but maybe more so an honored guest at an eternal sort of Algonquin Round Table with friends and notables. Absent any real belief in a "clouds and angels" sort of afterlife, I had to improvise, because that's one of the ways I comforted myself. I put aside the idea of his eternal kibbitzing for a while when I was in the process of putting together the proposal and finding a publisher for this book. It would come rushing back to me again the day I realized that in all the writing, researching, interviewing, and traveling I'd done for this work, I had neglected to go to an actual séance. There was no way I could speak with any actual authority on the subject unless I spoke with the dead myself.

I just felt like I needed to see it. I didn't have a big plan about what I was hoping to accomplish. I didn't expect to be awestruck with belief or to be a party crasher like our friend Harry Houdini, who would dramatically throw off his disguise at the right moment during a reading and declare to a stunned medium, "I am Houdini, and you are a fraud!" But it struck me as too clinical and academic to just read up on how it used to be and then render my judgment and analysis without having seen the process for myself. Luckily for me, I live in New York, and we have a little bit of everything, so a quick Google search revealed that there are in fact monthly Spiritualist services in the small annex of an esoteric bookstore on Fifty-Third Street near Third Avenue.* It would be easy enough to drag myself out there one rainy night. I email them beforehand to let them know what I'm writing and that I'm coming, so I don't feel like I'm being exploitive about it, and they email back and say that's fine. So on a damp April night, I take the bus a few stops and step through their door.

The room where they meet is not exactly uplifting and lacks the Victorian charm of Lily Dale. Everything seems a little grimy and worn, and the place could use a fresh coat of paint and some new flooring. This being Manhattan, you have to let these things slide because space is at a premium and straight-up Spiritualism is not exactly packing in audiences these days in the same way that artisanal cocktail speakeasies are (there's also one of those on the block). Still, everyone is welcoming, and I take a folding chair and wait to see what happens. Truth be told, outside of a few weddings, I haven't spent a lot of time in church services, so I never know what to compare them to. This observance seems pretty open; there's a brief homily, some prayers, and a short message service not unlike the ones I witnessed in Lily Dale.

The homily is delivered by an elegant older woman, Janet, who looks like she understood the assignment in a black dress

---

* I'm a Ramones fan, so basically anything operating on that street reminds me of the warbling lyrics to their song "53rd and Third."

and cardigan with lacy sleeves. She tells the story of her life as a medium and being raised by two aunts who were traveling healers and Spiritualist lecturers. She exudes calm and kindness; I'm immediately intrigued by her. I make a mental note to email to arrange an interview with her and the other woman, Matisse, running the services.

When the conventional services are over, they shuffle the chairs into a circle, dim the lights, and put out rechargeable candles for the message service. A small part of me is expecting something akin to Hollywood theatrics—with flickering lights, claps of thunder, and a chilling wind blowing through to snuff out the flames—but I'm clearly not going to get that with LED candles in a midtown meeting room. Just the same, I'm here to observe and learn. I let myself go along with the program. When they ask me to say my name into the middle of the circle to invite the spirits in, I do that. I feel weird about it, but I do it. The mediums in the room go around the circle and read the other visitors. Their messages are kind but vague. They connect with motherly energies and Scorpio men. It's not a huge group, but I go unmentioned, and I wonder for a second if I'll be forgotten when a male medium turns to me and says he has a message for me from someone who crossed over with pain in their leg and they saw me on an elaborate spiral staircase and that I should get off it.

Yeah… Sure… Okay… But then it dawns on me that my mother had just removed a spiral staircase from her home. She had a flood, and the designer recommended it in the remodel of the damaged kitchen. She was hesitant because it had been there for fifty years, but my brother and I had talked her into it.

"Does that make sense to you?" he asks.

"I have to think about it," I answer, and I will. I will think about it a lot. At home later, I'll go down a rabbit hole researching the name of the phenomenon that causes our brains to make meaningful patterns out of unrelated things. The word is *apophenia*. Still, I tell my mom about the message, hoping she'll feel better about her design choices. When I wake up the next day, I have decided the person sending the message was Mimi, a friend of the family who had been a patient of my father's whom he'd treated for a broken leg that she'd eventually lose to a rare skin disease. I get that this is probably a side effect of my personal apophenia, but I'm kind of okay with that. She passed away not long after my dad, and I miss her too; she had a presence in life that was like a hug.

Again, I haven't had an epiphany, but my nosy journalist sense of intrigue is tingling. At this point, I've been in the reading room at the New York Public Library so often that the security guard greets me with "welcome back." I don't even get that at my chosen dive bars* anymore, and I decide I need to spend more time immersing myself in Spiritualism and its current practices as a way of understanding its long-term impact. That's what I tell myself anyway. Truthfully, I sometimes pitch things just so I can go into hidden rooms. In my professional life as a writer, I have covered cat fashion shows, meetings of professional hat makers, and conventions of women who dress like Japanese baby dolls, just because it empowered me to ask "why?" and really listen to the answers.

---

* Except maybe the Freak Bar at Coney Island USA, but that's professional courtesy and bless them for that.

Entering that rented space on Fifty-Third Street has led me into one of these rooms and will lead me into others.

I email the Spiritualist Church and ask if they can put me in contact with Janet and Matisse, and they kindly oblige. I contact Matisse, and she quickly agrees to meet with me in a West Side coffee shop to discuss Spiritualism and how she came to be a medium in upper Manhattan. Blond, bright-eyed, and friendly, Matisse Frazier has a sunny disposition that just says West Coast cool to a naturally frazzled New Yorker like me.

I ask if her family has any background in Spiritualism, and she's surprisingly forthcoming. Raised as an American Sikh, she and her family would eventually come to realize "that it very much was a cult" and move away from that practice but carried with them the teachings of "love and light." As she explains it, she moved away from that religion knowing "that spirituality was so a part of who I was that at some point in time, it was going to be a big part of my life."[1] Even with that instinct, her life took a pretty conventional path: finishing college in three years, starting a successful career in marketing, and moving to San Francisco. Until she hit the age of twenty-eight. Then everything changed.

"Most people feel a dramatic shift at that time," she says, "and it hit me like a ton of bricks. I woke up one day in my beautiful apartment in Pacific Heights, the nicest neighborhood in San Francisco, with my BMW and my title and all these things and I was living the high life and woke up and I was like, 'none of this means anything; it's all just stuff.' So I quit my job, I sold everything I owned, I packed a backpack, I bought a one-way ticket to Mexico City, and I traveled the world for a year." Her journey turned out to be more than just cool Instagram snaps; everywhere she went, she found herself talking to healers, monks, and other spiritual people.

After feeling drawn to rethink her own life, she began her education as a medium, which landed her here in the city. I ask her what it's like practicing in New York, which is so crowded with humanity and all that entails. As she explains it, "You know, you go home grumpy when you had a decent day, but you just picked up all these other people's crap and it's sticking to you and you're not aware of it. So it's almost like that. But when I walked into New York, I asked my mind to expand even further and my heart was really further and it was really intense." She also says she's able to tune things out, so she can ride the subway and do other New York activities without going nuts picking up on other people's energies. This is a real thing: ask anyone who takes mass transit on a regular basis, and they'll tell you this splattering of bad vibes is an everyday phenomenon even if you don't have extrasensory powers. It's basically emotional BO in cramped subway cars and buses. It can cling to a person.

In New York, she moved in with Janet for a while, who helped her hone her skills and get started in building her practice. I mention that I'm already dead set (so to speak) on talking to Janet for the book, since she seems to have the long view of Spiritualism, and Matisse agrees to put in a good word for me. We have a long looping conversation about life, loss, and changing careers. At the end, I thank her for her time and head back to my writing exile to finish up the rest of my chapters on chiropractors and magicians and their surprisingly huge impact on American popular and material culture. After that, it'll take me a couple of days to call Janet. For someone who interviews for a living, I have a big dumb phobia* of talking on the phone, and it always takes me a while to get myself psyched up for big, important calls.

I finally make the call, and it takes her a couple of weeks to answer. When we do finally link up, she explains that there was something going on astrologically that didn't work out until now. She soon invites me over to her apartment, and we begin a series of conversations that will haul my chapter plans sideways and cause me to do what I consider actual soul searching. By the time I get to her apartment, it's a slight shock. I have spent so much time in the last few months reading about Victorian parlors and music halls that I have a definite idea of what her place will look like...and her place is not that at all. It's kind of like being invited to a forest witch's home, but instead of a gingerbread house, you find yourself in the bright living room of a midtown high-rise surrounded by a great deal of modern sculpture and a spectacular view of the Empire State Building.

Janet herself is a gracious hostess, always ready with coffee, and she encourages me to put my feet on the coffee table. She tells me her life story and how she came to be a professional medium. Born in Detroit during the Depression, she was sent to live with two aunts to make things easier on her cash-strapped parents. It was through observing and learning from them that she learned she had the gift and that it could be very powerful. "My aunt, who

---

* I also don't like snakes or clowns, and I've managed a career around them. Sometimes you just have to push yourself.

was a minister, was known as a very inspirational speaker, and her older sister was an incredible healer. When I was living with them, I was age eight. See, in the 1940s, people didn't go to healers unless the medical establishment had given up on them, and I was there, peering through the doorway watching my aunt, because she was a healer. A family had brought a man in a wheelchair, because the doctor said he'd never walk again. I saw her eyes going all over him. I realize now that she was reading his aura for his health and she said he'd walk again, and she got him walking again."

During summers, they'd drive from their home in Pontiac, Michigan, up through Canada and down to Lily Dale, where the sisters would preach and meet with people seeking their healing and mediumship services, and from there they'd drive out to California and back home again. Growing up in this environment nurtured her confidence and her skill. "[My aunt] sat on the edge of my bed that first night and it was dark, and she said, 'Do you see all the lights sparkling?'" Janet replied yes, and her aunt said, "Well, that's the spirits and they're here to protect you and look after you and don't make it scary at all." That eased Janet's mind and allowed her to adjust to her gift, explaining: "It's very calming and so I relaxed with it and [my aunt] said, 'You may see them or you may hear them.' I said, 'Oh, I hear them already.'"

Which is not to say that life was all sparkling lights. Like any person, she's had her ups and downs—she's been married three times, lost her beloved husband Leon, had the usual uphill battle as a woman in a man's world in her careers as a teacher and liturgical singer, is recovering from a stroke, and so on. Still, she's one of those people with a twinkle in her eye and a quick laugh, and she's just incredibly easy to talk to. She's not pumping me for information, she's not needling, we just fall to talking. This might be her greatest skill as a medium or just as a person—she's just warmly engaged and nonjudgmental. I can see why people come to her with their troubles and questions. That's just my initial instinct, which, of course, I start to pick apart with all sorts of cynical questions. Over the course of conversations, she will encourage me to trust my intuition—and not just because it's a good life lesson. During our first talk, she says to me, "You are highly intuitive, obviously." She means in the mediumship sense, not in my usual wanting to read some complete strangers for filth way.

"You're a receiver," she tells me. "Yes, you, if you had training, you could be. Come on. Let me take a look at you for that too." She takes me in for a moment. "Yeah. It's the same stuff there. Just like Matisse, you have the makings of a first-class medium if you were to pursue it, but it would require pursuing it. Yeah, I don't see you doing that, but that's why you're picking up so much stuff." This is where I will hit the borders of my own beliefs. At the same time, I'm weirdly flattered and intrigued.

We discuss it and I decide I can explore my newly diagnosed powers a little bit. She gives me a couple of meditation exercises to do and invites me back in a few days. "I would give you a trance session where you could meet your guide and just experience what it's like." I have weirdly mixed feelings about this but say yes. I spend my next week driving my friends insane about it. My best friend, Christine, is both levelheaded and curious about any dark elements, which is basically what makes her my bestie to begin with. She tells me to just take it in—and to text her immediately if some kind of hell gate opens. She doesn't need to remind me; she's one of those friends you think of first. Going down the list of my life's advisory board: Eddie, Meirav, Mitch, Emma, and Christina are about the same in terms of advice. They're bemused and match Christine's cool demeanor. Emma reminds me of the time she saw a medium in Lily Dale who had to stop in the middle of a consultation, because Em's spirit guides were making fun of her outfit and she couldn't concentrate on the messages.

I hope my spirit guides aren't insulting to Janet, because she's been so lovely, but it also makes sense to me that any soul that might attach itself to me might be snarky. I also have a hard time coming up with questions for my guides and meditating quietly for more than a few seconds at a time. I'm under a deadline, and I have a lot on my mind. I bring her a copy of my first book as a present for her time when I show up and confess over coffee that I had a hard time doing my homework. She barely blinks and assures me that I'll get to it when I'm ready.

That off my mind, she lays out the parameters of how her trance sessions work. She has been meditating faithfully for fifty years, regularly doing up to two hours a day. And in that process, she has "raised her vibration" enough that her spirit guide, Enterra, was able to lower his vibration to come through to her. She says she has no idea what his earthly form was like, but he's very old and very wise, and when she goes into trance, it's his spirit that comes through. There are a couple physical things she tells me about sharing a body. First she can tell that he's near because she gets postnasal drip, and as he leaves, she gasps for air, since he doesn't have the need to breathe. With those warnings, she settles

quietly into her chair and closes her eyes and relaxes to begin our
session. In a few moments, she sits up straight, opens her eyes, and
addresses me in a different voice. This one is deeper, gruffer. Her
overall attitude is more formal, more regal. This is Enterra, or she
is Enterra—it's hard to know how to describe it accurately. I'm
willing to take her word on it, and I try to push away my skepticism and just be a part of the experience in her sunlit living room
on a high floor off Third Avenue.

Enterra asks me to call my guides forward and checks to see
if they're around and will make themselves known to us. Luckily,
they are. The first one is Mish, which he tells me is pronounced
"meesh," derived from the Yiddish word *michegas*, meaning
nonsense. "I am pleased to meet you," he says, adding, "I have
been your guide. Not your whole life. You have always had a guide
from birth, usually five or six." So far, so good. I can handle this.
We're a little bit into our introductions when he says something
that will cause my heart to stop and free-fall for a moment like the
Disney ride that scared the pants off me.

"Anyway, my dear, I'm very pleased to meet you. You are
comfortable with me now, knowing me? Yes, okay good, because I
can become your 'mostly companion' as Eloise used to say. Yes, she
used to call someone her 'mostly companion,' I think." *Eloise* by
Kay Thompson was my favorite book growing up. It was the one
that I made my father read over and over again. I just loved it and
related to her chaotic "city child" energy. In my twenties, I mulled
over getting a tattoo of her joyously rampaging through the Plaza
Hotel. I never did it, but she's one of my favorite characters of all
time, and I was just looking at an Eloise shower curtain for my

bathroom at my mother's house in my fifties. It's such a random, seemingly personal thing to pick. I'll spend days thinking about this moment and keep coming back to it when I'm shaving my legs or making coffee or waiting for a subway. *My mostly companion...*

I'll also learn during this session that I have a specific spirit guide for writing. Her name is Felice. Felice is a little more subtle than Mish and doesn't come out with any of my other favorite books or writers, but I'll develop a practice of talking to Felice now and again when I can use a creative boost. Like when I'm facing a blank page or a tricky storytelling pivot or grasping for the right adjective. I can't say that I have literal interactions with her in the sense that she's talking back to me or that I see anything that could be a considered a sign, but I figure it can't hurt to say something like, "Morning, Felice, is there any way we could write a little faster today?" She's not exactly my editor or my muse, but I'm happy to let her live in the part of my brain that causes me to read my tarot card every day and carry a Marie Laveau charm on my key chain. Call it creative visualization or meditation or a good luck charm; instead of getting worked up about being rational or logical about it, I'm just going to coexist lightly with Felice for now.

When in trance, Janet, the person I know and like, disappears. Suddenly, she *is* Enterra. And when Enterra is at the controls, he refers to Janet simply as "the medium." If you wish to talk to Janet again or if Enterra has decided it's time to go, he will politely sign off with something along the lines of "Goodbye" or "Nice to meet you," and Janet will start to reappear in her face and mannerisms. Janet's body will slump slightly in the chair and then take a deep, gasping breath. She explained the reason for this earlier: "Spirit doesn't need any air. He's Spirit. But I need air." In later sessions, I'll learn from Janet to gently remind Spirit to take a deep breath when he leaves his host so she doesn't end up clamoring to fill her lungs. I like talking to Enterra. It's a fascinating experience, but I honestly like talking to Janet more. She's just very interesting and kind. We talk about my resistance to doing the assigned exercise, and she nods knowingly and says, "You're just at the beginning." We'll also talk about politics, losing her husband and my father, our friends and our jobs, and a number of things that make up conversation with a new friend and mentor.

She reads the book I gave her over the course of a day and comes back to me the next time with praise and questions, which is the quickest way to the nervous writer's heart. For this session, I will ask the spirits about the usual things that worry a person—my finances, my career choices, if people will buy this book, if there's a husband in my future—and the word is pretty positive on all of it. I don't rush out and buy a lottery ticket, but I'll take it and (metaphorically) put it in my pocket with a lucky penny I found on the sidewalk. On my way out, Janet (and only Janet) hugs me and says, "Thank you for being you," with a sincerity that just makes my heart happy. It was a welcome kindness in a moment when I needed it. In our future meetings, I will spend a lot of time reassuring her (but myself, really) that I won't be exploitive or cruel in my writing, and she says she knows, and I again feel absolved. I will always leave her presence feeling lighter and more joyous, and maybe that's more miraculous to me than the Spirit or anything else that could be pulled out during a séance. In all our conversations, I never ask to talk to my dad. I don't know if I'd believe it, but I also don't need it at this point, but I understand those who did enter these rooms looking for a line to the other side.

Thinking about it now, that need reminds me of another transitional moment in my life. When I first started performing, I had terrible stage fright, so I created my stage persona, The Lady Aye, and I would give her accessories that helped me feel brave behind the mike in front of a roomful of strangers. I called it my "magic feather" based on the movie *Dumbo*, which I always loved (except the racist parts but, y'know, that pretty much describes almost all Walt-era productions). My particular magic feather could be fake lashes or cute high heels or vodka soda. The former were just a way of stepping into the character, and the latter, while not a method I at all recommend, didn't become a destructive habit. For me, that's a good way to look at the magical thinking we let into our lives—is it a little magical feather boost or is it a delusional crutch? If it's the feather, then why not leave a little room for that, particularly in times of grief when we really need a light in our darkness. On the other hand, when we look for signs and wonders or place faith above concrete things like medicine or the welfare of other people, that's where we get into trouble.

What I've learned from my travels, my talks, and my research is that Spiritualism has covered the entirety of that spectrum: It offered comfort to those who needed it, gave a platform to women's voices, and sought to make America live up to its promise of a "more perfect union" in its own weird way. But like any large-scale human endeavor, it also gave harbor to some ruthless people who preyed on people at their worst and empowered some who would stick to their own dangerous gut feelings above any evidence to the contrary—which basically puts it directly on the arc of most American movements.

Put another, more modern way, it's possible to look at Spiritualism the same way cultural critics are now looking at the disco era. Bear with me here. Disco was a cultural movement that initially empowered its marginalized fans—LGBTQ+ community, people of color, powerful divas, etc. Its growth would match the cultural mood and its adaptations to new technology, and then as it caught on with larger audiences, it went mainstream in a great whoosh of power, money, and excess. In its next phase, it became bloated with novelty hits and bad actors* to the point where there was a cultural backlash and it became a punch line. Now, with the perspective of time, it's possible to step back and see its fingerprints everywhere in our popular culture from fashion to dance hits. Now make the underlying occasion a wake instead of a party, and we have a framework for viewing the invisible crater that Spiritualism left behind. Obviously, Spiritualism has fewer sequins and dance hits, but the point remains, it's something that deserves a second look.

I have now traveled thousands of miles, been through piles of books and articles, and interviewed dozens of people, and I can safely say I haven't seen a ghost. I remain convinced, however, that America is well and truly haunted. Not in the literal sense of entities roaming our dark halls in their death shrouds but by some collective specter of our past—of who we were and who we wanted to be. Spiritualism may be the most literal expression of this haunting. As America was coming into its own power as a force in the

---

* Literally and figuratively if you count the Village People movie.

world, as we were hurtling toward a new era of science and modernity, when some citizens were more equal than others in a so-called land of liberty, Spiritualism grew out of a need for the miraculous in the face of some very real troubles. Its aesthetics and ideas haunt us, even as its literal physical form fades from view. Because some of the factors that allowed it to blossom are paralleled in our current era—the massive losses we've faced, women clamoring for their right to agency, and new technology that threatens to dwarf our sense of humanity—it might be a good time to conjure its lessons and see if there's anything we can take from it. As for myself, I'm still someone who's haunted by her losses and trying to make sense of what she's been left with.

ACKNOWLEDGMENTS

As a writer, I feel like when people entrust you with their stories, that's a sacred privilege and you have to be as careful as you can with that gift, particularly when it comes from a vulnerable place. So I would like to thank those who gave me their time, energy, and perspective for the creation of this book. In Lily Dale: Shannon Taggart, the Lily Dale Board, Rev. Celeste Elliot, and Dr. Lauren Thibodeau for their warm welcome. In New York City: Rev. Janet Hariton and Matisse Frazier for their great care and conversation. Far and wide: all the scholars, healers, hairdressers, magicians, tour guides, Disney cast members, and librarians (the NYPL rules!) who graciously supplied my endless need for answers. Additionally, a great thanks to my agent, Alice Spielberg, for ensuring that they were heard in the first place and answering my wobbly writer emails. For Erin McClary and Kate Roddy at Sourcebooks for giving it a home.

Also, with much love to my circles that support me when I think I'm out of words. To my family circle: my mom, my brother, sister-in-law, nephew, niece-in-law (?), and cousins, and our circle of family friends. To my personal circle of somewhat morbid weirdo friends: Xtine, Emma, Meirav, Eddie, Meetch, Christina, and more. To my circle of mentors and peers in sideshow and other occult endeavors: James Taylor (the sideshow historian, not the singer), Jo Weldon, the good folks at Coney Island USA, Morbid Anatomy, Sob Siters, and the Sideshow Hootenanny. To JR Pepper for her ongoing photographic help. And to those whose absence both inspires and haunts me: Dad, Uncle Dan, Cousin Judy, Mimi, Bella, Rachel, Aye Jaye, Sue, and Kenwyn, who was a good witch.

NOTES

---◆❧◆❧◆---

Preface

1   Timothy Worrad, "The 'Channelling' of George Floyd and Spiritualism's Racist History," The Conversation, July 29, 2020, https://theconversation.com/.

2   Michael Haines, "Fertility and Mortality in the United States," Economic History Association, accessed June 4, 2025. https://eh.net/encyclopedia/fertility-and-mortality-in-the-united-states/.

Chapter 1: It's Mourning in America

1   Claude Lévi-Strauss, *Structural Anthropology*, trans. Claire Jacobson and Brooke Grundfest Schoepf (Penguin, 1972), 21N.

2   Jeffrey M. Jones, "In U.S., 47% Identify as Religious, 33% as Spiritual," Gallup, September 22, 2023, https://news.gallup.com/poll/511133/identify-religious-spiritual.aspx.

3   Anna P. Kambhampaty, "Many Americans Say They Believe in Ghosts. Do You?," *New York Times*, October 28, 2021, https://www.nytimes.com/.

4   Roxy Amirazizi, "America's Top Fears 2020/2021," Chapman University, 2022,, https://www.chapman.edu/wilkinson/research-centers/babbie-center/_files/Babbie%20center%20fear2021/blogpost-americas-top-fears-2020_-21-final.pdf.

5   Amirazizi , "America's Top Fears."

6   Amirazizi, "America's Top Fears."

7   Mary Shelley, *On Ghosts*, 1825, https://gutenberg.net.au/ebooks06/0602881h.html.

Chapter 2: Smells Like Teen Spirits

1   Charles J. Finney, *Charles J. Finney: An Autobiography*, 1908, 80, http://www.ntslibrary.com/PDF%20Books/Charles%20Finney.pdf.

2   Horace Greeley, "The Rochester Rappings," *Christian Inquirer*, August 17, 1850, 3.

3   W.C.T., "The 'Knockings/Rappings'," *Cincinnati Enquirer*, December 1, 1850, 2.

Chapter 3: Radiant Matter

1   "X-rays," Nobel Prize, 2022, https://educationalgames.nobelprize.org/educational/physics/x-rays/history.php.

2   F. R. S. Crookes, *Researches in the Phenomena of Spiritualism* (William J. Burns, London, 1874), 47.

3   Crookes, *Researches*, 109.

4   Crookes, *Researches*, 113.

5   *Declaration of Sentiments and Constitution of the American Anti-slavery Society*, 1861, American Anti-Slavery Society, YA Pamphlet Collection, Library of Congress, https://www.loc.gov/item/11007599/.

6   "Literary Notices," *Knickerbocker; or New York Monthly Magazine*, April 1848, 348.

7   Edgar Allan Poe , "First page of "Mesmeric Revelation"," *Exhibits: The Sheridan Libraries and Museums*, accessed June 24, 2025, https://exhibits.library.jhu.edu/items/show/668.

8   Nancy Rubin Stuart, *The Reluctant Spiritualist: A Life of Maggie Fox* (Harcourt, 2005), 83.

9   Mary Irving, "The 'Spirits' of the Age," *National Era*, June 6, 1850, 89.

Chapter 4: What I Did on My Summerland Vacation

1   "Lily Dale," Lily Dale Assembly, accessed June 30, 2025, https://www.lilydaleassembly.org/.

2   "Camp of Spiritualists: Believers in Mediums Camping Out in the Woods," *St. Louis Post–Dispatch*, July 29, 1894.

3   "Camp of Spiritualists."

4   "Camp of Spiritualists."

5   "A Visit to Lily Dale, the Land of Spiritism: All Sorts and Conditions Circus Behind the Curtain," *Globe*, September 14, 1895, 12.

6   Celeste Elliot, personal interview with the author.

7   Emma Hardinge, *Modern American Spiritualism: A Twenty Years' Record of Communication of the Communion Between Earth and the World of the Spirits*, 1870, 493.

8   Drew Gilpin Faust, "Death and Dying," National Park Service, https://www.nps.gov/articles/death-and-dying.htm.

Chapter 5: Give My Regards to Broad Street

1   "Abolition, Free Love, Infidel, and Women's Rights Convention," *Daily Dispatch*, September 20, 1859, 3.

2 David Quinn, *Interior Causes of the War: The Nation Demonized, and Its President a Spirit-Rapper by a Citizen of Ohio* (M. Doolady, 1863), 7.

3 J. H. Conant, *Biography of Mrs. J. H. Conant: The World's Medium of the Nineteenth Century* (William White, 1873), 121.

4 Maynard, *Was Abraham Lincoln a Spiritualist?*, Nettie Colburn Maynard, Was Abraham Lincoln a Spiritualist? (Rufus C. Hartranft, 1891), 72–73.

5 Demosthenes, *Speeches*, 18.198.

6 Victoria Woodhull, *The Victoria Woodhull Reader* (M&S Press, 1974), 16.

7 "The Queens of Finance," *Cincinnati Daily Enquirer*, January 25, 1870, 2.

8 Barbara Goldsmith, *Other Powers: The Age of Suffrage, Spiritualism, and the Scandalous Victoria Woodhull* (Alfred A. Knopf, 1999), 159.

9 "Personal," *Harper's Bazaar*, February 19, 1870, 115.

10 "A Lamp Without Oil," *New York Times*, February 22, 1872, 4.

11 "Presidential Candidates," *Philadelphia Inquirer*, March 4, 1872, 4.

12 "The Trance-Medium Party," *New York Evangelist*.

13 "The Exhibit," Bring Your Own Chair, accessed June 30, 2025, https://www.bringyourownchair.org/the-exhibit/.

14 "AmRev360: Well-Behaved Women Seldom Make History with Laurel Thatcher Ulrich," Museum of the American Revolution, March 30, 20222, https://www.amrevmuseum.org/amrev360-well-behaved-women-seldom-make-history-with-laurel-thatcher-ulrich.

Chapter 6: Salem

1 Kristina Garcia, "Possessed: The Salem Witch Trials," *Penn Today*, March 11, 2022, https://penntoday.upenn.edu/.

2 "Notes," *Albany Law Journal; A Weekly Record of the Law and the Lawyers*, May 18, 1878, 396.

3 "That Conspiracy: Further Details of the Story to Murder a 'Christian Scientist,'" *Boston Daily Globe*, October 30, 1878, 1.

4 "The Planchette: A Curious and Inexplainable Little Instrument," *San Francisco Chronicle*, June 18, 1885, 2.

5 "Planchette: New Wonders of the 'Irrepressible Agency,'" *New York Times*, August 30, 1869, 4.

6 "The Planchette."

7 "Planchette," *Daily Morning Chronicle (San Francisco, CA)*, November 18, 1868, 2.

8 "Helen Peters Nostworthy," Talking Board Historical Society, accessed June 4, 2025, https://www.tbhs.org/copy-of-event-oujizilla.

9 "The 'Ouija,'" *Atlanta Constitution*, April 26, 1891, 13.

10 "Helen Peters Nosworthy."

11 John Kozik, personal interview with the author.

12 Antony Clements-Thrower, "Hysteria at School as 36 Students Hospitalised after 'Playing with Ouija Board,'" *Mirror*, July 8, 2023, https://www.mirror.co.uk/.

13 Percival Bailey, "Hysteria: The History of a Disease," *Archives of General Psychiatry* 14, no. 3 (March 1966): 332–33, https://doi.org/10.1001/archpsyc.1966.01730090108024..

14 Walter Johnson, *The Morbid Emotions of Women: Their Origin, Tendencies, and Treatment* (Simpkin, Marshall, 1850), 235.

15 Lucien Calvin Warner, *A Popular Treatise on the Functions and Diseases of Woman* (Manhattan Publishing, 1875), 85.

16 Robert Collier Washburn, *The Life and Times of Lydia E. Pinkham* (Knickerbocker Press, 1931), 49.

17 Melinda Wenner Moyer, "Women Are Calling Out 'Medical Gaslighting,'" *New York Times*, June 22, 2022, https://www.nytimes.com/.

18 Ann Braude, *Radical Spirits: Spiritualism and Women's Rights in Nineteenth-Century America* (Indiana University Press, 2001), 145.

19 Robert McCrum, "Great Scott! Fitzgerald is Enjoying a Third Act," *Guardian*, February 4, 2012, https://www.theguardian.com/books/2012/feb/05/scott-fitzgerald-gatsby-mccrum.

20 Meirav Devash, "13 Witch-Inspired Beauty Products to Celebrate the Halloween Season," *Allure*, October 11, 2015, https://www.allure.com/.

Chapter 7: Woke from a Trance

1 William Wells Brown, "Copperhead Spiritualists," *Liberator*, February 26, 1864, 35.

2 Brown, "Copperhead Spiritualists."

3 "Is Spiritualism Good for Anything but to Talk About?," *Liberator*, August 6, 1858, 126.

4 E. W. Twing, "Spiritualism and Abolitionism," *Liberator*, January 1, 1858.

5 Leonard Twyning, "Achsa W. Sprague (1827–1862)," *Proceedings of the Vermont Historical Society*, December 1941, 271.

6 S. E. Porter, "The Complicated—Yet Inspiring!—History of Spiritualism in America," Literary Hub, February 16, 2024, https://lithub.com/the-complicated-yet-inspiring-history-of-spiritualism-in-america/.

7 *The Diary of Achsa Sprague*, June 11, 1857, https://catalogue.swanngalleries.com/Lots/auction-lot/(SPIRITUALISM)-Achsa-W-Sprague-Diary-of-a-renowned-touring-s?saleno=2646&lotNo=262&refNo=810546.

8 "Free Convention: To the Friends of Human Progress," *Liberator*, June 11, 1858, 95.

9 "Radicals in Council: The Rutland Convention—A Curious Gathering," *New York Times*, June 29, 1858, 1.

10 "The Rutland Reformers: Personnel of the Convention," *New York Times*, June 30, 1858, 2.

11 "The Reformers' Free Convention," *New York Daily Tribune*, June 25, 1858, http://iapsop .com/spirithistory/1858_new_york_tribune.html.

12 Twyning, "Achsa W. Sprague," 278.

13 Achsa Sprague, *The Poet, and Other Poems* (W. White, 1864), 198, https://quod.lib.umich .edu/m/moa/aan6800.0001.001/224?rgn=full+text;view=image;q1=emancipation.

14 William H. Mantz, "The Harmonial Philosophy," *Spiritual Telegraph, Vol. II* (Partridge & Britta, 1853), 248–49.

15 "Conference at 14 Bromfield Street," *Banner of Light*, November 6, 1858, 5.

16 "Pizarro, a Native of Genoa," *Banner of Light*, May 21, 1857, 7.

17 "Sam, a Slave from Richmond," *Banner of Light*, November 7, 1857, 7.

18 "Tole an Alabama Slave," Banner of Light, Boston, MA, May 21, 1857, 7.

19 "Indian Chief Scio to John Prince of Boston," *Banner of Light*, May 21, 1857, 7.

20 "Meetings in Cambridgeport," *Banner of Light*, May 25, 1867, 4.

21 Harriet E. Wilson, *Our Nig: or, Sketches from the Life of a Free Black* (Trent Editions, 1998), 54.

22 Dick Ellis, personal interview with the author.

23 Dick Ellis, personal interview.

24 Melissa Nobles, Chad Womack, Ambroise Wonkan, and Elizabeth Wathuti, "Science Must Overcome Its Racist Legacy: Nature's Guest Editors Speak," *Nature* 606, no. 7913 (June 8, 2022): 225–27, https://doi.org/10.1038/d41586-022-01527-z.

25 Christine Ferguson, *Determined Spirits: Eugenics, Heredity, and Racial Regeneration in Anglo-American Spiritualist Writing, 1848–1930* (Edinburgh University Press, 2012), 113.

Chapter 8: Not Haunted

1 Michelle Y. Gordon, "Midnight Scenes and Orgies: Public Narratives of Voodoo in New Orleans and Nineteenth-Century Discourses of White Supremacy," *American Quarterly* 64, no. 4 (December 2012): 76786, https://doi.org/10.1353/aq.2012.0060.

2 "Death of Marie Laveau: A Woman with a Wonderful History Almost a Century Old, Carried to the Tomb Yesterday Evening," *Daily Picayune*, June 18, 1881.

3 "A Sainted Woman," *New Orleans Democrat*, June 18, 1881.

4 Zora Neale Hurston, "Hoodoo in America," *Journal of American Folklore* 44, no. 174 (October–December 1931): 317–417, https://doi.org/10.2307/535394.

5 Hurston, "Hoodoo in America."

6 Herbert Asbury, *The French Quarter: An Informal History of the New Orleans Underworld* (Alfred A. Knopf, 1936), 237.

7 Charles Nethaway, "Voodoo," *State Journal* (Lansing, MI), December 22, 1947.

8 Richard A. Webster, "Tomb of Marie Laveau, Voodoo Queen of New Orleans, Refurbished in Time for Halloween," *Times-Picayune*, October 30, 2014, https://www.nola.com/.

9 Webster, "Tomb of Marie Laveau."

10 "'Haunted' Real Estate Signs in New Orleans Are Grabbers", *USA Today*, February 18, 2014, https://www.usatoday.com/story/news/nation/2014/02/18/new-orleans-haunted-real -estate/5572685/.

11 Colin Dickey, *Ghostland: An American History in Haunted Places* (Viking, 2016), 2.

12 "Spiritualism," *Daily Picayune*, January 28, 1853, 2.

13 "The Pope and Professor Mahan on Spiritualism," *Daily Picayune*, March 1, 1857, 9.

14 Melissa Daggett, *Spiritualism in Nineteenth Century New Orleans: The Life and Times of Henry Louis Rey* (University Press of Mississippi, 2017), 37.

15 "Civil War Casualties: The Cost of War: Killed, Wounded, Captured, and Missing," American Battlefield Trust, November 16, 2012, updated January 26, 2023, https://www .battlefields.org/learn/articles/civil-war-casualties.

16 Drew Gilpin Faust, *This Republic of Suffering: Death and the American Civil War* (Knopf Doubleday, 2009), 185.

Chapter 9: Mediums and the Media

1 Ellyn Briggs, "Gen Zers Still Really Want to Be Influencers," *Morning Consult Pro*, October 4, 2023, https://pro.morningconsult.com/analysis/gen-z-interest-influencer-marketing.

2 Theodore Tilton, *The Downfall of Henry Ward Beecher* (Norman L. Munro, 1874), 11.

3 Tilton, *Downfall of Henry Ward Beecher*, 6.

4 Robert Shaplen, "The Beecher-Tilton Affair," *New Yorker*, June 4, 1954, https://www .newyorker.com/.

5 Theodore Tilton, *Victoria C. Woodhull, A Biographical Sketch* (Golden Age Tracts, 1871), 26.

6 Shaplen, "Beecher-Tilton Affair."

7 Victoria Woodhull, "The Beecher-Tilton Scandal Case," *Woodhull & Claflin's Weekly*, November 2, 1872, 9.

8 Woodhull, "Beecher-Tilton Scandal Case," 10.

9 Shaplen, "Beecher-Tilton Affair."

10 "Photographs of Ghosts," *Scientific American*, November 30, 1861, 340.

11 Richard Leisenring, "Requiescat in Pace: Memorial Photographs of the Civil War," *Military Images* 37, no. 2(Spring 2019): 42, https://www.jstor.org/stable/26590753.

12 "Spirit Photographs—More Details from Boston," *Liberator*, November 21, 1863, 188.

13 "Spirit Photographs: The Mayor's Marshal after Two Photographers," *Courier-Journal* (Louisville, KY), April 16, 1869, 1.

14 Louis Kaplan, *The Strange Case of William Mumler, Spirit Photographer* (University of Minnesota Press, 2008), 60–61.

15 "Article 3," *Photographic Times and American Photographer*, June 1, 1884, 304.

Chapter 10: A Haunting We Will Go

1   "Separation of Mrs. Hatch and Husband," *Baltimore Sun*, September 16, 1858, 1.

2   "The Hatches," *New York Observer and Chronicle*, September 30, 1858, 309.

3   "The Spiritual Divorce Case: Mrs. Hatch," *New York Herald*, January 6, 1859, 2.

4   "Domestic Difficulties Amongst the Spiritualists—Hatch vs. Hatch," *New York Herald*, February 11, 1859. 2.

5   B. F. Hatch, *Spiritualists' Iniquities Unmasked, and the Hatch Divorce Case*, 1859, 6, https://www.loc.gov/item/16009628/.

6   Hatch, *Spiritualists' Iniquities Unmasked*, 47.

7   "Editor's Table: Seventh Annual Report of the Superintendent of Hamilton County Lunatic Asylum to the Board of Commissioners, for the Year Ending June 5, 1859, Annual Report of the Commissioners, Superintendent and Treasurer of the Indiana Hospital for the Insane, for the Year Ending October 31, 1858," *Cincinnati Lancet & Observer*, October 1, 1859, 629.

8   Lauren McCarthy, "Being a Woman in Magic May Be the Hardest Trick of All," *New York Times*, December 2, 2023; https://www.nytimes.com/.

9   McCarthy, "Being a Woman in Magic."

10 Florence Hartley, *Ladies' Book of Etiquette, and Manual of Politeness*, 1860, 41.

11 Louis Vittorio, personal interview with the author.

12 Vince Wilson, personal interview with the author.

13 Gilbert Venables, "The Danger of Psychical Research," *Spectator*, October 28, 1882, 1378.

14 "The Investigation of Psychical Phenomena," *Phrenological Journal and Science of Health* (September 1886): 162.

15 Lavina Hart, "The Savants Marvel at Her: Mrs. Piper, Boston's Remarkable Psychic," *St. Louis Post-Dispatch*, June 18, 1899, 11.

16 "Untruth of Spiritualism: Startling Confession of Mrs. Piper," *Cincinnati Enquirer*, October 20, 1901, B1.

17 "Untruth of Spiritualism."

18 "Topics of the Times," *New York Times*, October 29, 1901, 8.

19 "Her Decision Is Final," *Boston Daily Globe*, October 25, 1901, 5.

20 "Mrs. Piper Reconciled: Boston Spiritualist Lenders Settle Their Differences," *New York Times*, October 29, 1901, 7, https://www.nytimes.com/1901/10/29/archives/mrs-piper-reconciled-boston-spiritualist-lenders-settle-their.html.

21   Michael Tymn, "Leonora Piper," *Psi Encyclopedia*, February 14, 2022, https://psi
     -encyclopedia.spr.ac.uk/articles/leonora-piper.

22   Patrice Keane, personal interview with the author.

Chapter 11: Hair Apparent

1   Ilise S. Carter, "The Women Who Collect Jewelry Made from Dead People's Hair," Racked,
     January 6, 2015, https://www.racked.com/.

2   "The Fashion of Grief: Mourning Garb Is the Calm Retreat for Fashion's Slaves," *Daily
     American*, February 27, 1893, 5.

3   "Mourning as a Fashion," *London Reader of Literature, Science, Art and General Information*,
     February 17, 1877, 376.

4   "Centre-Table Gossip: The Fashion of Mourning," *Godey's Lady's Book and Magazine*,
     March 1857, 286.

5   Aimee Cunningham, "Four Years on, the COVID-19 Pandemic Has a Long Tail of Grief,"
     Science News, March 11, 2024; https://www.sciencenews.org/.

6   "Our Story," The Order of the Good Death, accessed June 30, 2025, https://www.order
     ofthegooddeath.com/our-story/.

7   Jillian Tullis, personal interview with the author.

8   John Troyer, personal interview with the author.

9   Katherine Schaeffer and Shradha Dinesh, "32% of Americans Have a Tattoo, Including
     22% Who Have More Than One," Pew Research Center, August 15, 2023, https://www
     .pewresearch.org/short-reads/2023/08/15/32-of-americans-have-a-tattoo-including-22
     -who-have-more-than-one.

10   Andi Scarbrough, personal interview with the author.

11   Melissa Cassutt, "The Roots Run Deep in Client-Hairstylist Relationships," *Seattle Times*,
     February 8, 2008, https://www.seattletimes.com/.

12   Ashleah Walker, personal interview with the author.

13   Colleen McCann, personal interview with the author.

14   "Classifieds," *Banner of Light*, July 6, 1872, 6–7.

Chapter 12: Alternative Cracks

1   D. D. Palmer, *The Chiropractor* (Beacon Light Printing, 1914), 14.

2   Palmer, *Chiropractor*, 9.

3   "Hand-Fixing," Editorial Notes and Comments, *Atlanta Journal—Record of Medicine*, April
     1, 1905, 32.

4   "Chiropractic Doctor Guilty: Convicted by Jury and Let out on Bail," *Los Angeles Times*,
     August 26, 1905, II2.

5 "Hot after Doctor: The County Medical Association to Prosecute," *Los Angeles Times*, July 19, 1905, II1.

6 "Hot after Doctor."

7 "Takes 'Mallet Cure,' Dies Within an Hour," *Los Angeles Times*, October 2, 1907, II1.

8 "Takes a Rest, Avoids Arrest," *Los Angeles Times*, October 4, 1907, II1.

9 Brian A. Smith, "Chiropractic History: Just How Controversial Was Dr. Storey's 'Apparatus'?," *Archives and Journal of the Association for the History of Chiropractic* 19, no. 2 (December 1999): 76, https://ia904605.us.archive.org/26/items/ThomasHStoreyDCCH192/Thomas%20H%20Storey%20DC%20CH%2019%282%29.pdf.

10 "Dead from Blow of Son's Auto: Founder of 'Chiropractic' Passes in This City," *Los Angeles Times*, October 21, 1913, II2.

11 "Advertisement 31," *Health*, March 1911, 64.

12 "Dr. B. J. Palmer Will Be Heard at WGM Tonight," *Atlanta Constitution*, May 20, 1923, B8.

13 "Actors Receive Free Chiropractic Treatment," The Billboard 34, no. 22, June 3, 1922, https://archive.org/details/sim_billboard_1922-06-03_34_22/page/8/mode/2up?q=treatment.

14 "Fighting Healers Who Use Religion to Evade the Law," *New York Times*, September 1, 1912, SM7.

15 "Medical Liberty Vindicated," *Health*, February 1907, 86.

16 "goop Beauty," Goop, accessed July 3, 2025, https://goop.com/goop-beauty/c/.

17 "Fasting, Spiritualism and Lies," *Louisville Courier-Journal*, March 23, 1888, 2.

18 "Fasting, Spiritualism and Lies."

19 A. Leah Underhill, *The Missing Link in Modern Spiritualism* (Thomas A. Knox, 1885), 404, https://www.gutenberg.org/files/40485/40485-h/40485-h.htm#Page_404.

20 Reuben Briggs Davenport, *The Death-blow to Spiritualism: Being the True Story of the Fox Sisters, as Revealed by Authority of Margaret Fox Kane and Catherine Fox Jencken* (G. W. Dillingham, 1888), 36.

21 "The Spiritualists in a Flutter," *Baltimore Sun*, October 12, 1888, 5.

22 "Spiritualists: Object to the New York Expose," *Cincinnati Enquirer*, October 23, 1888, 8.

23 "Done for Coin: Maggie Fox Recants Her Confession Affirming Her Faith," *San Francisco Chronicle*, November 20, 1889, 1.

24 "Germs Benign, Palmer Tells Chiropractors," *New York Herald Tribune*, February 22, 1931, 12.

25 R. P. Hertzman-Miller et al., "Comparing the Satisfaction of Low Back Pain Patients Randomized to Receive Medical or Chiropractic Care: Results from UCLA Low Back Pain Study," *American Journal of Public Health* 92, no. 10 (October 2002): 1631, https://doi.org/10.2105/ajph.92.10.1628.

Chapter 13: Enough Rope

1 "Messrs. Maskelyne and Cooke's Entertainment," *Illustrated Review: A Fortnightly Journal of Literature, Science and Art* (April 1874): 268.

2 Arthur Conan Doyle, "Houdini: The Enigma," *Strand*, August 1927, 135.

3 Harry Houdini, *A Magician Among the Spirits* (Harper Brothers, 1924), https://www.gutenberg.org/cache/epub/66451/pg66451-images.html#toclink_138.

4 Houdini, *Magician Among the Spirits*.

5 David Jaher, *The Witch of Lime Street: Séance, Seduction, and Houdini in the Spirit World* (Crown, 2015), 85.

6 "Surgeon's Wife Is 'Margery' in Psychic Contest," *New York Herald Tribune*, August 11, 1924, 6.

7 "Methods of Psychics to Be Studied," *Los Angeles Times*, February 12, 1923, 14.

8 "Surgeon's Wife Is 'Margery.'"

9 "'Psychic' Powers of Woman Baffle Experts 5 Months," *Washington Post*, August 10, 1924, 3.

10 "Medium Puzzles Harvard Investigators," *New York Times*, March 14, 1926, XX4.

11 "Margery Fails in Test Talks with Spirits," *New York Herald Tribune*, August 28, 1924, 1.

12 "Houdini Cabinet Baffles Psychist," *Hartford Courant*, August 29, 1924, 4.

13 "Houdini Report Calls Margery's 'Spooks' Bogus," *New York Herald Tribune*, October 17, 1924, 5.

14 "Margery's' Feats Not 'Supernatural': Harvard Investigators Suggest," *New York Times*, October 21, 1925, 25.

15 "Dr. Crandon Hints 'Fraud' By Houdini," *Boston Daily Globe*, July 22, 1926, 14.

16 Jaher, *Witch of Lime Street*, 226.

17 "Clairvoyants and Mediums Clash with Harry Houdini: Noisy Hearings Held by Congress Bodies," *Atlanta Constitution*, February 27, 1926, 12.

18 "Lived Nearly Year after Death Forecast," *Boston Daily Globe*, November 2, 1926, 25.

19 "Houdini Spirit Gets 'Line Busy,'" *New York Daily News*, November 24, 1926, 10.

20 Monica Hammond, personal interview with the author.

21 David Segal, "Why Not Just Hold a Séance?," *Washington Post*, March 24, 2007, https://www.washingtonpost.com/.22 David London, personal interview with the author.

Chapter 14: Meeting My Mostly Companion

1 Matisse Fraizer, personal interview with the author.

About the Author

—·⚬⟨⚬⟩⚬·—

Ilise S. Carter is a freelance writer and performer based in New York City. Her first book, *The Red Menace: How Lipstick Changed the Face of American History*, from Prometheus Books has been called "one of the most fascinating fashion histories I've ever read" by *Harper's Bazaar*. As her award-winning stage persona, The Lady Aye, she has worked as a sideshow performer with acts ranging from Rob Zombie to Cirque du Soleil and has appeared on *Gossip Girl*, *Oddities*, *The President Show*, *Mysteries at the Museum*, and *Dickinson*.